HAVEN OR HELL?

MIGRATION, MINORITIES AND CITIZENSHIP SERIES

Series Editors: Zig Layton-Henry, *Professor of Politics and Head of the Centre for Research in Ethnic Relations, University of Warwick*; and Danièle Joly, *Lecturer in Politics, Centre for Research in Ethnic Relations, University of Warwick*

This series has been developed to promote books on a wide range of topics concerned with migration and settlement, immigration policy, refugees, the integration and engagement of minorities, dimensions of social exclusion, racism and xenophobia, ethnic mobilisation, ethnicity and nationalism. The focus of the series is multidisciplinary and international. The series will publish both theoretical and empirical works based on original research. Priority will be given to single authored books but edited books of high quality will be considered.

Titles include:

Naomi Carmon (*editor*)
IMMIGRATION AND INTEGRATION IN POST-INDUSTRIAL
SOCIETIES
Theoretical Analysis and Policy-Related Research

Danièle Joly
HAVEN OR HELL?
Asylum Policies and Refugees in Europe

John Rex
ETHNIC MINORITIES IN THE MODERN NATION STATE
Working Papers in the Theory of Multiculturalism and Political
Integration

Haven or Hell?

Asylum Policies and Refugees in Europe

Danièle Joly
Centre for Research in Ethnic Relations
University of Warwick

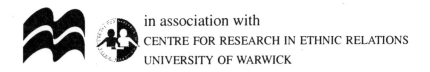

in association with
CENTRE FOR RESEARCH IN ETHNIC RELATIONS
UNIVERSITY OF WARWICK

First published in Great Britain 1996 by
MACMILLAN PRESS LTD
Houndmills, Basingstoke, Hampshire RG21 6XS
and London
Companies and representatives
throughout the world

A catalogue record for this book is available
from the British Library.

ISBN 0–333–64304–6 hardcover
ISBN 0–333–68692–6 paperback

First published in the United States of America 1996 by
ST. MARTIN'S PRESS, INC.,
Scholarly and Reference Division,
175 Fifth Avenue,
New York, N.Y. 10010

ISBN 0–312–16095–X

Library of Congress Cataloging-in-Publication Data
Joly, Danièle.
Haven or hell? : asylum policies and refugees in Europe / Danièle
Joly.
p. cm. — (Migration, minorities and citizenship)
Includes bibliographical references and index.
ISBN 0–312–16095–X
1. Refugees—Government policy—Europe. 2. Asylum, Right of–
–Europe. 3. Refugees—Services for—Europe. 4. Refugees—Europe.
I. Title. II. Series.
HV640.4.E8J626   1996
362.87'8'094—dc20   96–5582
                                                                CIP

10   9   8   7   6   5   4   3   2   1
05   04   03   02   01   00   99   98   97   96

Printed and bound in Great Britain by
Antony Rowe Ltd, Chippenham, Wiltshire

For Gustavo

Contents

Abbreviations   viii

Introduction   x

1 Definitions and Conventions: Asylum
   Dilemmas in Europe   1

2 The Political Construction of Asylum   17

3 Cracks in the Wall: European Harmonization
   on Asylum in the Nineties   44

4 Reception and Settlement Policies:
   A Comparative Study   86

5 Local Authority Policy on Refugees: The British
   Case   120

6 Towards a Study of Refugees in the Country of
   Exile   141

7 Refugee Associations: Between Society of
   Origin and Society of Exile   161

Conclusions   187

Bibliography   194

Index   210

Abbreviations

ADSS	Association of Directors of Social Services
AMA	Association of Metropolitan Authorities
ANPE	Agence Nationale pour l'Emploi
ASEAN	Association of South East Asian Nations
BCAR	British Council for Aid to Refugees
CIA	Central Intelligence Agency
CIREA	Centre d'Information de Réflexion et d'Echange en Matière d'Asile
COJASOR	Comité Juif d'Aide Sociale et de Réconstruction
CPR	Centres provisoires d'hébergement
CSCE	Conference on Security and Cooperation in Europe
EC	European Community
ECRE	European Council on Refugees and Exiles
EFTA	European Free Trade Association
ESL	English as a Second Language
EU	European Union
EVW	European Volunteer Workers (Britain)
EXCOM	Executive Committee
FAS	Fonds d'Action Sociale
FILOR	Fonds d'Installation Locale des Réfugiés
FTDA	France Terre d'Asile
GRISEA	Groupe de Recherche sur l'Immigration du Sud-Est Asiatique
HLM	Habitation à loyer modéré
JCVN	Joint Committee for Refugees from Vietnam
JWGCh	Joint Working Group for Refugees from Chile
LEA	Local Education Authority
MSC	Manpower Services Commission
NATO	North Atlantic Treaty Organization
NGO	Non-governmental organization
OAU	Organization of African Unity
ODIHR	Office for Democratic Institutions and Human Rights
ODM	Overseas Development Ministry

OFPRA	Office Français de Protection pour les Réfugiés et Apatrides
OSCE	Organisation for Security and Cooperation in Europe (formerly CSCE)
SCF	Save the Children Fund
SCLRAE	Standing Conference of Local and Regional Authorities of Europe
SCOR	Standing Conference on Refugees
SSAE	Service Social d'Aide aux Emigrants
UKIAS	United Kingdom Immigrants Advisory Service
UNHCR	United Nations High Commission for Refugees
WUS	World University Service
YTS	Youth Training Scheme

Introduction

The topicality of the themes developed in this volume does not need to be demonstrated; indeed asylum and refugees issues persist and grow on the European agenda. The 1970s ushered in non-European refugees, often from remote lands, and their numbers increased dramatically in the eighties, while in the nineties these figures were outstripped by the movement of three million European refugees from former Yugoslavia most of whom, however, remained within that territory. The relatively benevolent disposition towards asylum and refugees has in the meantime been reversed in most of the industrial world and particularly in Europe. The questions involved have sharpened and their seriousness undoubtedly warrants the attention of social scientists.

This book explores three discrete areas of interest pertaining to refugees in Europe: asylum policies, reception and settlement policies, and last but not least, the refugees themselves. This approach presents problems, since the subject could warrant the writing of three separate books. Moreover, these would probably be written within different disciplines and by different categories of authors. For instance, asylum policies have been studied principally by political scientists and legal experts and there exists good literature in this field serviced by a special journal, the *International Journal of Refugee Law*. Reception policies have been examined by practitioners and some social scientists dealing in social policy but studies are mostly limited to individual countries. As for the refugees themselves, they have aroused some interest amongst sociologists, which is recent but growing; however, only a few, such as Gold (1992) have adopted a comparative approach which looks at two refugee groups in one country. One of the main points of the present work, and one of its original features, is that it attempts to bring together in one single volume domains which are usually separated by social sciences although they are unhesitatingly interconnected by social reality. Another important property of this work is its comparative European dimension in each of the three areas considered.

The first section of the book deals with a theme which ranks high on the agenda of European governments and has provoked intense activity in intergovernmental fora, that is, the question of asylum. The first chapter looks at the conventions and definitions which govern the international and regional treatment of asylum, particularly in Europe. It follows the evolution of asylum instruments throughout the twentieth century in connection with the historical events which led to their formulation: in Europe these have moved from group determination to individual determination. This chapter points to the historical relativity of refugee definitions and international conventions as they have generally reflected the social reality of refugees and the events which provoked refugee flows, albeit with some delay. The second chapter, on the political construction of asylum, does not focus on conventions or laws but studies the societal factors that underlie policies regarding asylum and refugees. This includes political, economic and ideological considerations which influence the three areas considered here: domestic policy, foreign policy and ethical factors. The more complex question to be examined is how these three sets of factors interact and what respective weight they lend to the construction of an asylum policy, especially with regard to ethical concerns. The third chapter closes this section with a detailed study of European policies on asylum and their trajectory since the seventies. While in the seventies this issue aroused little Europe-wide interest on the part of governments it has become one of the most intense areas of activity in the late eighties and in the nineties. European Community intergovernmental agreements have taken the lead in the formulation of the agenda and developed an array of conventions and resolutions to implement it. The European Community (EC), now European Union (EU), has created a pole of influence which attracted surrounding states and engineered a trend towards enhanced restrictionism.

It seems logical that states, having admitted refugees, should face the responsibility for making some sort of space for them on their territory and in their society. This led me to undertake a study of reception and settlement policies in this second section. Chapter 4 presents a comparative analysis of four reception programmes: the Chilean and the Vietnamese programmes in France and in Britain, which were mostly carried out by NGOs with varying degrees of central government funding and involvement. A detailed study is undertaken of the various areas of policy pertaining to reception and settlement: reception centres, health, language, education, housing, employment and post-settlement. It also draws lessons and make recommendations which go beyond the scope of these programmes. Chapter 5 turns to local policy on refugees and consists of a survey of British local authorities and their treatment of all refugees. It was felt that mainstream institutions and statutory services had to be brought under scrutiny. As soon as refugees are housed within a locality they fall under the responsibility of the relevant local authority at a time when their process of installation is only beginning. This is why it is crucial to evaluate policies and their implementation as they will have a determining impact on the populations concerned.

If the book ended at this point, it would leave out the main protagonists who are at the receiving end of the policy-making examined above. This accounts for the last section, which is devoted to the refugees themselves. Chapter 6 develops a theoretical framework for the study of refugees as a social group. It establishes the parameters which can guide such a study and posits possible social categories of refugees and their main characteristics. Chapter 7 presents the results of a comparative research project on refugee associations. These associations were deemed an appropriate vehicle for accessing the refugees' viewpoint and evaluating their modes of settlement in the country of exile. Two national groups were selected in two European countries: refugees from Chile and Vietnam in France and Britain, which parallels the comparative chapter on reception policies.

It is noticeable that a certain discrepancy exists between the first section of the book and the two following sections. The section on asylum policies is Europe-wide and extends into the nineties; this was dictated by historical developments which brought about a process of European harmonization with an increased impetus in the late eighties and early nineties. However, the study of reception/settlement policies and of refugee communities required greater depth and focus to obtain meaningful data and results; it also needed to take place over a longer period of time. This is why these chapters concentrate on a limited number of countries and refugee groups. The choice of groups who have been established for a number of years also made it possible to gain a long-term perspective. The research was carried out between 1989 and 1994 but also drew on knowledge acquired since the mid-eighties through an earlier research project on refugees. The methods used combine a variety of approaches: they comprise quantitative and qualitative surveys, postal questionnaires, in-depth semi-structured interviews, participant-observation, the study of archives and of diverse documentary material including even ephemeral documents.

In the work on refugee associations I was assisted by Sandra Macedo, Cosme Morgado and by the Groupe de Recherche sur l'Immigration du Sud-Est Asiatique (GRISEA). In the survey of local authorities I collaborated with Sean Risdale from the Refugee Council. I am also indebted to ECRE, France Terre d'Asile, Documentation Réfugiés, the Refugee Council and the Association of Metropolitan Authorities. I would like to thank Rose Goodwin for her masterly preparation of this manuscript for publication. My thanks also go to policy-makers and staff of NGOs who provided valuable data and most of all, to the refugees themselves who enabled me to gain some insight into such perennial issues of humanity.

Finally my warmest thanks go to my husband Gustavo Jara Martínez who died three weeks after the completion of this book. Despite a long illness of which we knew the certain outcome, his courage, his love, his unremitting commitment to social justice and his immense knowledge made it possible for me to write this book.

1 Definitions and Conventions: Asylum Dilemmas in Europe

INTRODUCTION

The crises and wars in former Yugoslavia have brought to the fore tensions concerning the definition of refugee status and the legal instruments used in Europe today. Since the doors to immigration were closed in the mid-seventies, people have been allowed entry only in exceptional cases: two major channels are still available, namely family reunion and asylum. Moreover, Western European states do not have a completely free hand in deciding whom to admit with regard to refugees as they are signatory to Conventions to which they are bound. The decision to grant refugee status will therefore be guided by the terms of the definition as to who constitutes a refugee. So far European countries have implemented the 1951 Geneva Convention and taken its definition of refugee as a guideline. As a consequence the population of incomers was divided into two broad categories: (a) refugees (as defined by the Geneva Convention), and (b) immigrants, i.e. economic migrants. But as labour migration was no longer permitted, it meant that only Convention refugees would be allowed to stay. There did not seem to be a place for any other category so that inevitably an asylum-seeker who did not fit the Convention definition would be deemed an economic migrant and thus 'fraudulent'. The war in former Yugoslavia and the three million strong movement of people displaced as a result exploded the myth that asylum-seekers who did not meet the 1951 Convention criteria were necessarily economic migrants. The discrepancy between legality and reality has become evident.

The 1951 Convention and its definition of refugees expressed a particular historical reality and were the culmination of a process which began after the First World War. We shall examine first how the 1951 Convention was arrived at and then discuss the limits of this Convention within the context of contemporary realities in Europe and in the world. Finally, we will look at other international instruments regulating asylum and refugees.

The definition from the 1951 Geneva Convention stems from a period of history when the memories of fascist persecution were still raw and vivid and when a large proportion of Europe had come under communist rule. It deals with the contemporaneous refugee problem in Europe, the large numbers displaced by the war and e' nts leading up to it, but it also tackles situations resulting from changes of regimes in Eastern Europe and from the end of the Cold War. However, the definition and the Convention are not a creation *ex nihilo*. Several aspects can be found in previous international instruments and it is possible to trace the various steps that led to it arising from the needs revealed through successive refugee situations.

LOSS OF *DE JURE* STATE PROTECTION

The 1951 Convention finds its origins in international instruments developed in the wake of the First World War. This war caused vast movements of population which were compounded by the October revolution in Russia; over a million fled across the Soviet borders between 1917 and 1921 (Hope-Simpson, 1939). Destitute and unable to earn a living, displaced people and refugees not only found themselves in desperate situations, but also discovered that they could not move on to improve their lot because they had lost the protection of their state of origin. As a consequence they were unable to obtain the necessary travel documents to cross national borders. Whereas in the nineteenth century it had been possible to cross borders without being subjected to a great deal of control, the consolidation of national states in Europe and the formation of new states created a difficult situation for refugees (Hope-Simpson, 1939; Marrus, 1985). Their plight was noted by NGOs and on their behalf the International Committee of the Red Cross asked the League of Nations to take action (Jaeger, 1991).

In 1921 Fridtjof Nansen was appointed by the League of Nations as 'High Commissioner' on behalf of the League in connection with the problem of Russian refugees in Europe to look after legal status, repatriation and the coordination of externally funded assistance. The League did not concern itself with the resourcing of relief, which was left to NGOs. The essential feature of international action for the benefit of refugees was the 'Arrangement for the Issue of Certificates of Identity' first awarded to Russian refugees (5 July 1922) as a result of a conference convened by the League in Geneva. This is what has been called the 'juridical perspective' in so far as it was designed to correct a 'malfunction', an anomaly in the international legal system (Hathaway, 1984). These travel documents were granted to Russians (1922) and thereafter to Armenians from the Ottoman Empire (1924) defined as refugees if they had lost the *de jure* protection of their state of origin, respectively the Government of the Union of Soviet Republics and the Government of the Turkish Republic, as long as they had not acquired a new nationality (Hathaway, 1984). The certificate arrangements were recognized by a good number of nations (Holborn, 1975). However, the refugees had to be outside their state of origin to benefit from such a measure. When the granting of travel documents was instituted for other groups, Assyrians, Assyro-Chaldeans, Syrians, Kurds and Turks (all in 1928), not all of those who had been considered were accepted. An additional condition was introduced with a view to limiting numbers: their situation had to be related to the First World War; those whose unprotected status did not result from events directly connected with the First World War and those who could not be considered as the most urgent cases were not accepted (Hathaway, 1984).

The juridical approach described above introduced one of the bases of the 1951 Convention and constitutes an important clause of it, expressed in Articles 27 and 28:

> The Contracting States shall issue identity papers to any refugee lawfully staying in their territory who does not possess a valid travel document,
> 1. The Contracting States shall issue to refugees lawfully staying in their territory travel documents for the purpose of travel outside their territory...

What underpins these obligations is, as in the twenties, the stipulation that the beneficiary is 'outside the country of his nationality and is unable to avail himself of the protection of that country'. Likewise he must not have acquired another nationality. The 1951 Convention has, also in common with the arrangements of the twenties, the notion that refugees resulting from particular historical events only should be recognized; it also introduced a time limit. These obligations and arrangements were drawn up as a result of events which took place before 1951, but as we shall see below, these conditions are not sufficient in themselves to justify the status of refugee and the attribution of travel documents at the present time.

NATIONAL GROUP DETERMINATION: HUMANITARIAN REFUGEES

The next step in the development of legal instruments dealing with refugees took on board territorial and national criteria. These have been eliminated from the 1951 Convention but they are worth mentioning as the spirit which guided their adoption might help in understanding Europe's present situation and throw light on the dilemmas it faces. Although national and ethnic groups are mentioned in the early international instruments, social group determination assumed its full implications in the thirties. According to the 1936 Arrangement and the 1938 Convention on refugees from Germany, refugee status is merited not only by those having lost the *de jure* protection of their state of origin but also its *de facto* protection even though they may formally enjoy this protection.

Subsequent instruments dealing with refugees from the Third Reich (from Austria and the Sudeten area of Czechoslovakia in 1939) confirm this trend, taking into account the common cause to their situation as refugee, namely the violence and upheavals caused by Nazism. The refugees were thus granted recognition on the basis of group characteristics linked to their national origin and the political events which caused their flight. They did not have to demonstrate individual characteristics. This is a major point of divergence with the 1951 Convention. They were subsequently called 'humanitarian refugees' to differentiate them from the 1951 Convention 'human rights refugees' (Melander, 1987). However, it is worth noting that exclusion criteria specified in the 1938 Convention are very much alive today in the implementation of the 1951 Geneva Convention in Europe. Those are persons 'leaving Germany for reasons of purely personal convenience', 'for economic reasons but without being compelled to do so, or [...] gone abroad in order to evade taxation' (quoted in Hathaway, 1984, p.365). A similar distinction between refugee and economic migrants is established and explained in detail in the UNHCR Handbook on procedures and criteria for determining refugee status (1979):

> 62. A migrant is a person who, for reasons other than those contained in the definition, voluntarily leaves his country in order to take up residence elsewhere. He may be moved by the desire for change and adventure, or by family or other reasons of a personal nature. If he is moved exclusively by economic considerations, he is an economic migrant and not a refugee.

It was also in the thirties that the prohibition of *refoulement* was established by the 1933 Convention (Article 3) and the 1938 Convention (Article 5) (Bettati, 1985). This is one the cardinal points of the 1951 Convention.

INDIVIDUAL DETERMINATION

The basis for the current definition of a refugee as expressed in the 1951 Convention can be traced back to the end of the thirties. Throughout the thirties and during the Second World War, more and more victims and refugees were being generated by the whirlwind of Nazism and fascism. It was felt that those threatened by the Nazis should be helped to leave Germany. Altogether (according to one estimate) 60 million civilians were forced to move from their homes during that period (Proudfoot, 1957). Moreover, the plight of those who were unable to move could not be ignored. The Intergovernmental Committee on Refugees, established in 1938, demonstrated concern not only for refugees outside their country of origin but also for those who had not yet left. This was a departure from preceding agreements and from the 1951 Convention which exclude from their remit people still in their country of origin.

A specific set of criteria described those who would be entitled to assistance. In the first place, the country of origin was referred to by name, i.e. Germany, including Austria and later the Sudetenland. Secondly the reasons for their flight (whether accomplished or imminent) had to be their political opinions, religious beliefs or racial origins which in fact exposed them to persecutions at the hand of the Nazi state (Hathaway, 1984). In 1943 the definition was broadened in so far as no country of origin was mentioned, the only limitation being that their flight was caused by events in Europe, i.e. 'as a result of events in Europe'; it was further broadened when 'country of residence' was substituted for country of nationality. The definition thus endeavoured to ensure that no group would be left out. The International Committee on Refugees included within its mandate

> those persons wherever they may be who, as a result of events in Europe, have had to leave, or may have to leave, their country of residence because of the danger to their lives or liberties on account of their race, religion or political beliefs. (Quoted in Hathaway, 1984, p.371)

The definition was further refined with the Constitution of the International Refugee Organisation in 1946 and included as its core persons who had been persecuted or feared persecution on reasonable grounds because of race, religion, nationality or political opinion (Holborn, 1975). By then there were still one million refugees in Europe (Gallagher, 1989a).

There is a clear shift from a determination guided by national/territorial criteria to an individual determination based on the notion of persecution for specific reasons. The reasons outlined above covered all the main categories likely to need protection at the time. They continued to do so in 1951 since refugees at that time had the same origin. One additional group was to be included by Western powers after the war, i.e. persons fleeing from or not wanting to return to communist states, but they could come under the 'political opinion' criterion and they were thus covered despite disagreements and controversies which led Eastern European countries to noncooperation with the Geneva Convention. One has to keep in mind that by 1951 the war was well over and European countries had stabilized so that people who had been displaced by the ravages of the war rather than by targeted persecution could in principle return to their place of origin. Those who were considered to have valid reasons not to do so were supposed to be catered for in the 1946 and 1951 definitions. People who had obtained refugee status under previous instruments were able to keep it.

THE 1951 GENEVA CONVENTION

The 1951 Convention was not designed to cater for all refugees after 1951 and the USA was particularly keen to limit its scope (Holborn, 1975). The life-span of the United Nations Office of the High Commissioner for Refugees (who took office on 1 January 1951) came under discussion and it was established with a three-year mandate only. However, the continued need for the UNHCR mandate has led to its uninterrupted existence for over forty years and there is no indication that it is becoming redundant; quite the contrary. The 1951 Convention became the main international instrument to deal with refugees signed by countries to date and the geographical and historical limitations were removed to make it universal. A majority of countries extended their obligations to accept refugees not only resulting from 'events occurring in Europe' (B1a) but from 'events occurring in Europe or elsewhere' (B1b). The 1967 Protocol removed the historical limitation and has now been signed by more than one hundred countries. This Protocol was introduced in response to the changing pattern of refugee movements which by then largely came from non-European countries and were caused by events taking place after 1951 outside Europe.

The definition of refugee couched in the 1951 Convention is therefore a universal definition in so far as it is not tied to time or place:

> ...owing to a well-founded fear of being persecuted for reasons of race, religion, nationality, membership of a particular social group or political opinion...

However, it is not comprehensive. It is confined very clearly to persons in fear of persecution; moreover this persecution must relate to race, religion, nationality, membership of a

social group or political opinion. A number of sociological categories of refugees are included but not necessarily all the categories (Suhrke, 1993). People suffering persecution on other
grounds, victims of an indiscriminate persecution which is not
targeted at specific groups and people fleeing for other
reasons than persecution are excluded from the definition
(this is examined in greater detail below). In addition the
refugee must individually justify fear of persecution. The criteria are thus both subjective and objective.

The 1951 Convention has exclusion clauses which comprise
inter alia persons who can be seriously considered to have committed 'a crime against peace, a war crime, or a crime against
humanity', 'a serious non-political crime outside the country
of refuge before being admitted as refugee, and guilty of acts
contrary to the purposes and principles of the United
Nations'. It also provides for cessation clauses. One of the
most significant provisions of the 1951 Convention is that it
categorically prohibits the refugee's *refoulement* 'in any manner
whatsoever to the frontiers of territories where his life or
freedom would be threatened on account of his race, religion,
nationality, membership of a particular social group or political opinion'. This has become one of the most quoted clauses
of the 1951 Convention and now virtually constitutes a principle of customary international law in its own right (Goodwin-
Gill, 1986).

The actual determination of refugee status is incumbent
upon the state to which the refugee applies for asylum. The
granting of asylum itself is solely the prerogative of the state.
There exists a 1967 Declaration on Territorial Asylum but it is
not binding and the international community failed to agree
on a convention on territorial asylum debated in 1977
(Goodwin-Gill, 1983). In Europe recognition of status has
come to mean also the granting of asylum. But states have a
heavier responsibility than the mere determination of status
as the 1951 Convention has a much wider brief than that of
defining refugees. It also deals with the position of refugees in
the country of exile. It states the obligation of refugees to
conform to laws and regulations in their country of residence.
It specifies the obligations of states towards refugees on their
territory, requesting that refugees should at least benefit from
the most favourable treatment given to other aliens. These

obligations pertain to a vast range of domains with a view to making life possible and dignified in the country of exile. The juridical status of the refugee is dealt with in connection with personal status, artistic rights and industrial property, right of association and access to courts. Non-discrimination and a minimum standard of religious freedom are to be observed. Where gainful employment and welfare are concerned, the Convention requires that refugees should be granted a treatment at least no less favourable than other foreigners in similar circumstances and equal to that of nationals with regard to rationing, elementary education, public relief and assistance, labour legislation and social security. On the issue of wage-earning employment it stipulates the limits to restrictive measures imposed on aliens and the exemptions applying to refugees. The state which granted residence to refugees must also deliver appropriate identity documents (see above). The Convention indicates safeguards to be observed if an expulsion of a refugee is envisaged and it recommends that naturalization be facilitated. Finally it refers disputes to the International Court of Justice.

What this catalogue of clauses demonstrates is that granting refugee status and residence is not just a statement of principle and cannot be entered into lightly by states signatory to the 1951 Convention. Indeed it entails wide-ranging obligations towards the refugees in question. It undoubtedly involves a commitment and possibly a social cost all the more tangible as most European countries have awarded favourable conditions of settlement to the refugees granted residence on their territory. For instance, several Conventions ensure for refugees in Europe the same treatment as for nationals in matters of social security and medical care (Weis, 1982). This is certainly one factor which may influence decisions to grant status and asylum, especially where cases are not absolutely clear cut.

Over the years since its creation the Convention has remained the main instrument used in Europe despite the limitations of its definition, evidenced as the nature of refugee movements changed world-wide. It has become clear that a number of asylum-seekers do not meet the 1951 criteria who none the less need protection. Among those who have reached Europe, victims of generalized violence and wars are one major category; there are also victims of indiscriminate human rights violations, women, deserters and war resisters. So far these cases have been treated in a variety of ways.

While the economic situation in Western Europe was growing strongly in the 1960s it proved relatively easy to handle these cases. Many refugees did not even apply for asylum but entered as labour migrants (Blaschke 1989). During that period the 1951 definition was generally interpreted liberally so that many asylum-seekers who were not labour migrants were accommodated under the 1951 Convention. For instance, in some countries women were given Convention status under the 'social group' category. The Executive Committee of the UNHCR programme indicated in 1985 that states were free to grant refugee status to women who were persecuted as a 'particular social group'. The UNHCR handbook on procedures and criteria gives an indication of how this kind of flexibility can be adopted for special cases (Chapter 5) such as war refugees, deserters and persons avoiding military service. Even in situations of mass exodus such as the 200 000 Hungarians in 1956 and the Czechs in 1968, in practice the individual examination of applications was waived and a *prima facie* approach was implemented to award refugee status.

A number of countries also created *ad hoc* solutions allowing asylum-seekers to stay under another status: 'B' status in Scandinavian countries, 'exceptional leave' to remain in the UK, *Duldung* in Germany. For instance, in Germany the Länder may decide to allow asylum-seekers to stay although they have been refused status; in 1966, for example, the Interior Ministers of Länder formally agreed not to return any alien from a Warsaw Pact nation; other unilateral decisions on Afghans, Lebanese, and Christian Turks were taken (Aleinikoff, 1984). A number of international or regional instruments were used to justify permission to stay. The 1984 Convention against Torture and Other Cruel Inhuman or Degrading Treatment or Punishment prevents states from returning someone to a situation where he or she could be tortured (Article 3). The European Convention on Human Rights and Fundamental Freedoms has been used also and in particular its Article 3 prohibiting inhuman and degrading treatment, Article 8 protecting the family and the right to live with one's family, and Article 13 granting the right to appeal in administrative cases. Under this Convention the European Commission for Human Rights recognized a limited right of asylum (Scott Nance, 1982).

In reality in most of these cases the applicant was allowed to stay by default, because of a prohibition on sending him back. In this way the Convention clause against *refoulement* has been utilized widely, more frequently than the Convention itself. Yet this procedure took care of the permission to stay without offering guidelines on the status accorded and the rights associated with it. However, an alternative status to Convention status generally does not award the same quality of rights and conditions of settlement. These statuses are also very disparate throughout Europe and display vast discrepancies from one country to another. Of course such *de facto* refugees can benefit from international human rights instruments (Young, 1982) but those remain far more elusive than what is stipulated in the Geneva Convention. It has been argued by NGOs that governments had deliberately pushed refugees into an alternative status in order to avoid the commitments involved in the Convention status.

Tensions have not ceased to increase where asylum in Europe is concerned since the mid-seventies. This is due to a combination of circumstances. The main problem has been the economic recession followed by high rates of unemployment. At the same time the number of asylum-seekers increased dramatically, because the door to immigration was closed but also because cheap air travel combined with satellite communication media to render Europe far more accessible to non-European refugees both mentally and physically at a time when crises causing refugee flows took place on the borders of Europe. In the meantime crises, dictatorships and wars were rife throughout the world. In other words, more asylum-seekers were arriving at a time when few were welcome, and a growing number of these did not meet the criteria of the 1951 Convention.

One major trend developed among European governments: to restrict numbers by all the means available (this is examined in the following chapter). They were still partly constrained by the 1951 Convention to which they were signatory, however. In effect this has meant that the strictest interpretation of the Convention definition would be applied. The interpretation of what constitutes 'persecution' is also less liberally defined; as expressed by Grahl-Madsen (1989, p.423) 'there appears to be a tendency for authorities to contend that people ought to endure more in the way of hardships – political as well as economic – before they give up their homes and seek refugee status abroad'. According to some even the spirit of the definition was betrayed (Tiberghien quoted in *Le Monde*, 19.4.88). It had a grave impact on the fate of asylum-seekers in two ways. People who did not meet the exact criteria of the definition risked being returned sometimes to their death or to persecution; this has indeed happened (Joly with Nettleton and Poulton, 1992). A new perception of asylum-seekers developed through the discourse of policy-makers and the media. As only a small percentage of asylum-seekers obtained Convention status all the others were deemed 'bogus', 'fraudulent' or 'economic refugees' tantamount to illegal immigrants trying to circumvent immigration regulations. A backlash against asylum-seekers and refugees soon occurred on the part of the indigenous population. While some asylum-seekers may have been in reality economic migrants this is not true of all of those who were refused Convention status. The percentage of people granted alternative status seems to vindicate this view (see Figures 6 and 7 in Joly, with Nettleton and Poulton, 1992). The confusion stems from the insufficiencies of the Convention definition and discrepancies between this definition and the reality it is supposed to regulate.

This has been brought to the fore by present wars in former Yugoslavia. As long as refugees originated in distant lands, it was easy to assume that they were labour migrants and the accusation of 'bogus' could hold some credibility since the situations they came from were quite unknown in Europe. It was not feasible with regard to the former Yugoslavia. It cannot possibly be argued seriously that asylum-seekers from former Yugoslavia are 'economic refugees' i.e. labour migrants; and yet many are deemed not to meet the 1951 Convention criteria. There is a legal lacuna in Europe to handle the question of refugees. This lacuna is well demonstrated by the disarray of European states facing the flows of refugees from former Yugoslavia and the absence of a coherent instrument to deal with it. Austria, Germany and Switzerland imposed visas in July

1992. Italy and the Netherlands implemented new administrative regulations. Norway and Belgium decided not to process asylum application from former Yugoslavia but not to deport the applicants. Sweden, with an established community of Yugoslav origin, granted family visitors visas (Suhrke, 1993). A variety of arrangements broadly amounting to 'temporary protection' developed in Europe, which leave much to be desired in the way of procedures and social rights.

OTHER INTERNATIONAL INSTRUMENTS

The situation pertaining in former Yugoslavia was a new phenomenon in Europe but not in the rest of the world. It is worth examining definitions from other conventions and declarations which may help to clarify the issues. The truth is that Europe has lost the primacy it held in 1951 on the question of refugees. More 'advanced' instruments have been set up in other areas of the world to respond to the changing nature of refugee movements.

The Organisation of African Unity Convention Governing the Specific Aspects of Refugee Problems in Africa was adopted in 1969. It broadened the definition of refugee by augmenting the categories already included in the 1951 definition. It is extremely liberal and comprehensive:

2. The term 'refugee' shall also apply to every person who, owing to external aggression, occupation, foreign domination or events seriously disturbing public order in either part or the whole of his country of origin or nationality, is compelled to leave his place of habitual residence in order to seek refuge in another place outside his country of origin or nationality.

This part of the definition does not include an individual criterion of eligibility and proposes a collective determination. It stresses serious disturbance occurring at the hand of an external agent but also makes a space for internal upheaval. The prohibition of *refoulement* is also strongly stated, including rejection at the border. Asylum is supposed to be temporary as it was assumed that refugees caused by liberation struggles would return home after independence. By the eighties this was no longer so valid (Weis, 1970). This convention was drafted in specific circumstances of great turmoil arising in the wake of decolonization and liberation struggles causing mass exoduses. The genuineness of the refugees' need did not arouse any doubt. Moreover, as pointed out by Suhrke (1993), all states could see the benefit of such a comprehensive instrument as they were all potential senders and receivers of refugees.

In Latin America a refugee regime had been established through such instruments as the 1928 Havana Convention on Asylum, the 1933 Montevideo Convention on Political Asylum and the 1954 Caracas Conventions on Territorial Asylum and Diplomatic Asylum. However it could not cope with the situation which developed in the seventies and eighties with more than one million refugees fleeing from El Salvador, Guatemala and Nicaragua (Gallagher, 1989b). This is what prompted the adoption of the 1984 Cartagena Declaration by the Organization of American States (1985). Its definition of refugees is broader than the 1951 Convention and includes

> Persons who have fled their country because their lives, safety or freedom have been threatened by generalised violence, foreign aggression, internal conflicts, massive violation of human rights or other circumstances which have seriously disturbed the public order.

This definition expresses the situation obtaining in Central America where wars, civil wars and bloody dictatorships prevailed; some Central American states such as Guatemala and El Salvador have provided examples of the worst human rights violations in the world. However, the Cartagena Declaration does not have the same binding character as the Havana and Caracas conventions mentioned above.

In Asia, where a new definition was not coined, the Manila Declaration on the Internal Protection of Refugees and Displaced Persons in Asia stresses the fundamental importance of the observance of the principle of non-*refoulement* (Jaeger, 1981).

The UNHCR itself has also taken on board changes in the character of the refugee situation and its mandate was extended to include larger categories (Bettati, 1985) in particular outside Europe. As early as 1959 it was authorized by the General

Assembly to use its Good Offices for the benefit of refugees who do not come within the competence of the United Nations (Zarjevski, 1988)). In the sixties, when the number of African refugees increased dramatically (to more than one million in 1972) several resolutions of the General Assembly enabled the UNHCR to raise funds in order to assist them although they did not meet the criteria of the 1951 Convention (Gallagher, 1989b). From 1961 the General Assembly had accepted that the UNHCR was working for Convention refugees and Good Offices refugees. Later on additional resolutions mention UNHCR action in favour of refugees and displaced persons (Res 34/55 XXX) and of victims of man-made disasters in need of urgent humanitarian assistance (Res 31/35, 30 November 1976). At its thirty-second Session in 1981 the Conclusion made by the Executive Committee of the UNHCR Programme dealt with situations of large-scale influx. In 1985 it was stated that the High Commissioner's competence includes 'persons who have fled their home country due to armed conflicts, internal turmoil and situations involving gross and systematic violations of human rights' (Goodwin-Gill, 1986, p.899 note 7). In 1988 in Comments on the Preliminary Draft Proposal for a Council Directive to Approximate National Rules on the Grant of Asylum and Refugee Status (1988), the UNHCR reminds European states that they had agreed that refugees leaving their counties of origin in order to escape from severe internal upheavals or armed conflicts should be treated humanely and, in particular, should not be returned to areas where they might be exposed to danger. It is now well established that the UNHCR has already extended its protection and assistance to large numbers of people who did not come under the 1951 Convention through the system of 'Good Offices'. This came to include even internally displaced persons and victims of natural disasters. A notion of ecological refugees is being forged.

CONCLUSION

It has been shown above that there is a great variety of international/regional instruments and declarations to handle a great variety of refugee situations over and above the 1951 Geneva Convention. There are 30 international instru-

ments and 20 regional instruments addressing some aspect of
the refugee issue (Gallagher, 1989) in addition to UNHCR's
numerous resolutions. Moreover, new conventions and instruments keep developing in response to new situations. As
for Europe itself, it possesses a number of strategies to face
the current events. The European Parliament made a
Recommendation (773/1976) on the situation of *de facto*
refugees defined as those who are unable to return to their
country of origin for any 'other valid reason'. The Council of
Europe (1975) and the European Commission have also elaborated declarations and recommendations on refugees which
deserve attention. Even NGOs which until recently were
strongly opposed to the reformulation of the refugee
definition in Europe are now stressing the need for a 'supplementary refugee definition' (ECRE, 1993).

In the meantime European countries have tackled the
refugee crisis in former Yugoslavia in a very haphazard
manner. Some Western European countries rather seemed to
adopt the well-known strategy of the ostrich. Other states are
reacting with a variety of temporary *ad hoc* arrangements. This
was formalized in the European Union through two resolutions on persons from former Yugoslavia (see Chapter 3) but it
remained vague and failed to cater for the possibility of a
longer-term situation. The obvious fact is the lack and need of
a European instrument which defines refugees and lays down
provisions for their treatment, status and rights.

2 The Political Construction of Asylum

INTRODUCTION

This chapter looks at the broader issue of the factors that underlie policies regarding asylum and refugees. It focuses on European and other industrialized countries mostly in the period following the Second World War.

In general refugees also have to be considered within the general philosophy and policy on admitting all foreigners and immigrants. What is at stake is nothing less than a question of sovereignty as there seems to be universal agreement on states' exclusive authority on who can be admitted into the country and into the community of citizens (Weiner, 1985). For instance, the disputes preceding the American independence from Britain shows that one of the charges against the British Crown was its control over laws governing the admission and naturalization of foreigners (Weiner, 1985). Goodwin-Gill (1989) quotes judicial decisions confirming the State's competence to exclude foreign nationals at the turn of the century. In an analysis of the *City of New York* v. *Miln* (Zolberg, 1987), the author concludes that the court went out of its way to specify that the power of any state to regulate entry was a concomitant of sovereignty, originating in the law of nations. In some cases the 'sending' by a country of masses of refugees can be deemed a *casus belli*; for instance, during the Pakistani civil war of 1971 India justified its military intervention by the 'threat to her economy and general stability posed by the humanitarian flood from Pakistan' (United Nations, Commission on Human Rights, in Teitelbaum, 1984, p.434). There is further evidence supporting the assumption that the admission of foreigners is widely considered as the sole prerogative of the state. In a Statement on Refugee Policy and Mechanisms presented to the Australian Parliament by the Minister for Immigration and Ethnic Affairs in May 1977 one of the four principles outlined was that 'the decision as to who

17

will be accepted is the prerogative of the government alone'
(Cox, 1979, p.8). One convincing interpretation of the 1986
Simpson-Rodino bill on immigration in the USA is based on
the premise that sovereignty gives the nation absolute control
over its borders (Gibney, 1988). In Britain the ultimate decision is left to the discretion of the Home Secretary (or his
Under-Secretary) on the basis that he acts on behalf of the
Queen who 'allows whom she wants to come in her Realm'
(quoted in Joly, 1987, p.95).

Where immigrants are concerned, another assumption is
made regarding their admission: it must serve the national interest (Gibney, 1988) and this often applies to refugees. This
view is disputed by some political scientists who argue that it is
incompatible with the most basic tenet of 'liberalism' which
assumes the 'equal moral worth of individuals' and is thus eth-
ically unacceptable (Whelan, 1988; Ackerman quoted in
Zolberg, 1987, p.268). Indeed, in practice the rules and their
implementation indicate that decisions to admit foreigners are
mitigated by a number of factors other than mere 'national interest'. Moreover, the notion of national interest itself is
subject to a variety of interpretations and components, including the two areas of domestic and foreign policy. National interest figures prominently, albeit not exclusively, where policy
on refugees is concerned.

Where refugees themselves are concerned, while individuals
have the right to seek asylum as stipulated by the Universal
Declaration on Human Rights, it is nowhere stated that they
are guaranteed a right to obtain it. It is the State that holds the
right to grant asylum.

However, while it has been shown that deciding who shall be
admitted pertains to sovereignty it is no longer the case that
the State and sovereignty are one and the same thing in
Western democracies. '*L'Etat, c'est moi*' belongs to absolute
monarchy and not to the modern conception of the State.
The State is supposed to be merely a depository of sovereignty
on behalf of a collective which can be defined as, for example,
the 'nation' as in France since the Revolution, or the 'people'
as in the USA. The State in Western democracies will thus be
subject to different influences emanating from the national
community and classes or groups within it, on behalf of which
it is meant to act. This is the case whatever one's interpreta-

tion of the State, whether as the representative of the majority of citizens, an arbiter above classes or an instrument of domination by one class over another. Since in the countries considered here the use of naked arbitrary force is frowned upon, a measure of consensus is sought by the State, which is under pressure to take into account the differing views of distinct groups. As a consequence the structure of power and the configuration of classes and interest groups with their relative political clout and agenda help to explain the variations and complexities of asylum policies over space and time.

Moreover, sovereignty itself encounters boundaries. Despite claims to the contrary national communities do not enjoy an absolute right to make rules above and beyond the inalienable human rights of the individual. These are moral rights today enshrined in the Universal Declaration of Human Rights.

Article 2: Everyone is entitled to all the rights and freedoms set forth in this Declaration, without distinction of any kind, such as race, colour, property, birth or other status.

Furthermore, no distinction shall be made on the basis of the political, jurisdictional or international status of the country or territory to which a person belongs, whether it be independent, trust, non-self-governing or under any other limitation of sovereignty.

The nature of these human rights has changed through history (Bettati, 1985) and they are not an unassailable *acquis*. Yet while many states and individuals often flout them, there exists an international consensus over them. These rights can even be posited against governments and are 'inherent limits to the powers of governments' (Goodwin-Gill, 1989, p.532). These rights transcend the laws of the State and they constitute an ultimate guarantee even if a particular national community and its government decides to deny them in fact and in law. As expressed by a well-known human rights lawyer: 'Not only do the people need to be protected against their rulers, but also against the transient impressions into which they themselves might be led.' (Goodwin-Gill, 1989, pp.528–9)

The rights of refugees figure among these, which is a main reason why ethical factors play a part in asylum policies. The rights of refugees are not only couched in international instruments but are sometimes fundamentally grounded in the national constitution as in the preamble of the French Constitution (until 1994). On the whole throughout the twentieth century and until recently, the moral rights of refugees have attracted a growing international recognition which is expressed through a variety of instruments. States are bound by the international conventions and treaties to which they are signatory and which curtail national sovereignty.

This is one aspect to which states have recently become sensitive, namely the perceived loss of control over their borders, as the moral worth of the refugee's claim according to the relevant convention is the only criterion which is supposed to determine recognition, ruling out almost entirely other considerations. Naturally recognition of the status of refugee does not compel a state to grant permission to stay but this has so far been the custom and practice in Western European countries. Moreover, it has generally led to permanent or at least long-term settlement. As a consequence Western European states have taken an increased number of measures to restrict asylum (see Chapter 3).

Most of the examples cited in this chapter are drawn from industrialized countries, either as countries of first asylum or as countries of resettlement, with the purpose of clarifying what factors may guide decisions on asylum in Europe.

The period which interests us here is the second half of the twentieth century. In the immediate aftermath of the Second World War most refugees were European, being forced to flee from Nazism, from the war itself or as a result of the Cold War. In addition some refugees came from Franco's Spain, from Salazar's Portugal or from Greece after the colonels' *coup d'état*. They obtained asylum or entered as immigrants in Europe, North America and Latin America. In the sixties non-European refugees had become more numerous and they began to arrive in industrialized countries. Their numbers continued to increase, particularly in the eighties. In the nineties the numbers of European refugees rose dramatically as a consequence of the dismantlement of communist regimes and conflict or wars that ensued, in particular in the former Yugoslavia.

This chapter examines the factors that underpin policies regarding asylum and refugees. It evaluates the respective role played by domestic and foreign policy considerations and also ethical factors, what weight all those may lend to more or less favourable policies towards refugees and what conjuncture enables ethical concerns to be taken into consideration.

DOMESTIC POLICY

Generally speaking, naked 'national interest' seems to govern decisions and policies on asylum in the arena of domestic policy. However, such a situation is fraught with contradictions and entails a whole range of possible variations according to the understanding of what best promotes national interest and the correlation of forces supporting divergent interpretations of the term. Most frequently the predominant determination of what constitutes national interest is that of the government and ruling elites. But governmental elites can themselves be divided; moreover, different sectors of society may also differ with the views of the government and amongst themselves. The respective political power of the groups and actors supporting specific views and policies will thus determine the outcome. The interests of the economy, social costs and ideological and cultural issues, all of which may display a consensus or divergent points of view have a bearing on asylum policies.

The state of the economy

The fluctuation of asylum policy shows that economic conditions strongly influence both the attitudes of the State and the general population towards the acceptance of refugees and other immigrants (Schierup, 1990). In times of economic boom policies are generally more generous and relaxed than in times of recession; they appear to meet the interests of employers in an expanding economy and are generally not perceived as competitors threatening the jobs of autochthonous people. As refugees constitute an extra intake of population, identified needs for such additional people may entail positive policies by the state towards the entry of immigrants and refugees (Rystad, 1990). Labour requirements are an obvious instance whereby immigrants and refugees are accepted or even invited. The British European Volunteer Workers (EVW) programme is a case in point, making it possible for some

80 000 men and women to be recruited from displaced persons' camps in Austria and Germany between October 1946 and December 1949. They were contracted to work in essential industries such as the mines and textiles, in hospitals and on the land (Kay and Miles, 1992). The need for specific skills may lead to selecting particular groups of refugees. This would explain Canada's decision to grant entrance visas to educated Ugandan Asians expelled by Idi Amin in 1972. The Australian government has been frequently criticized for 'selecting the cream of a refugee population' (Cox, 1979, p.8) and was charged with exploiting the refugee situation for population building and workforce purposes (Price, 1979). Current debates among international fora such as the Intergovernmental Consultations propose that policies be reformulated taking into account *inter alia* the needs for skilled labour in industrialized countries (Joly with Nettleton and Poulton, 1992). Alternatively, the rise of unemployment, often interpreted as the result of excess labour, may provoke attitudes and policies hostile to the reception of refugees, as seems to be the situation in Europe today. However, the issue is not so simple and there is rarely a consensus among all sectors of society and within the ranks of the State itself. For instance, British trade unions opposed the EVWs programme, as they feared an erosion of their bargaining power and a depreciation of salaries, even at a time of economic expansion. Because of their privileged relationship with the Labour government of the time, their views carried weight and the government had to make a number of concessions to coax the trade unions into acceptance. In Italy on the other hand, the discussions leading to the passing of the 1990 law on asylum revealed that pressure groups emanating from Fiat promoted a generous asylum law, presumably on account of Fiat's requirements for labour (confidential source).

The fact that asylum-seekers continued to be allowed in Europe even after immigration had been stopped could be read as the replacement of one lot of foreign workers by another (Schierup, 1990). And it has been argued that tolerating numerous asylum-seekers in European countries while refusing to grant them status and residence ensures the supply of illegal or semi-legal cheap labour needed for some industries (Teitelbaum, 1984, Interview with UNHCR delegate

1988, confidential). Demographic elements may also play a part in determining asylum policy as in France between the two world wars (Joly with Nettleton and Poulton, 1992), in a country where the demographic deficit had been an issue of concern almost since the Napoleonic wars. In Australia a basic territorial issue is being raised in the shape of an ecological debate: while sectors promoting a generous asylum policy put forward the view that there are vast expanses of unused land, others ask to what extent increased numbers of people would damage the environment and the ecological balance in such a unique ecological environment (Glezer, 1979).

Social costs

Economic factors clearly go beyond a simple arithmetic of jobs and population numbers or square metres. Economic and social costs include a wide variety of other aspects, particularly in the area of welfare provisions (Teitelbaum, 1980). Housing, medical attention, social services, education and other services have to be provided for the newcomers (Joly with Nettleton, 1990). The lack of such provisions has sometimes been stated as a reason for not accepting any more refugees, as in Britain when a quota of Chilean refugees was granted visas (Joly, 1987b). The interest expressed by non-governmental welfare agencies and their readiness to share in this task may on the other hand provide an incentive for opening the door wider (Cox, 1979). Moreover, governments are always sensitive to the possibility of a backlash on the part of the autochthonous population which is putting forward its own demands for improved provisions (Teitelbaum, 1980). These factors lie behind the general guideline stipulated in Australia as the country's 'capacity to accept and absorb refugees' (Cox, 1979 p.16). On a more philosophical plane, states are promoting their rights to protect members of the community *vis-à-vis* outsiders (Suhrke, 1993).

Culture and ideology

Domestic factors also include a more intangible set of issues pertaining to ideology. The question of national cohesion and identity, of widely shared values and of the integrity of domestic political structures all contribute to immigrant and refugee policy (Weiner, 1985). But the nature of these notions changes over time. For instance, until the 1965 Immigration and Nationality Act, the USA had quotas for groups of particular national origin with the supposed aim of maintaining the ethnic balance; these quota laws were designed to give preference to Nordic Europeans as against Southern Europeans and then to exclude 'oriental' immigrants altogether with the purpose of preserving a certain 'racial' cohesion (Zolberg, 1987). Similarly, under its 'White Australia' policy the Australian government restricted immigration to individuals of Anglo-Saxon descent until 1971 (Price, 1979 and Carens, 1988). These views were not only those of the government but were supported by large sectors of society. Even though such provisions have been removed from law books in most countries they often persist implicitly in North America and in Europe under the guise of cultural incompatibility (Naess, 1989). Such criteria are nowadays expressed in a different form. Australia, for instance, uses as a determining criterion 'the individual's ability to integrate' (Cox, 1979, p.10). Britain offered as a criterion for selection the existence of a link with Britain (Joly, 1987b); but for some refugees this was relaxed and circumvented through the 'adoption' of asylum applicants by trade unions, churches or other groups. France gives preference to French speakers. Germany automatically admits and grants citizenship to people of German descent however distant the link may be (*Aussiedler*). And almost all the criteria for selection in the USA emphasize some sort of tie with the USA (Shacknove, 1988). Being related to a citizen of the state or to a permanent resident constitutes an advantage in obtaining admission in most industrialized countries (as for example in France and the United States).

It has also been argued that one should accept refugees who have affinities with the government and the economic and political system of the receiving country (Gibney, 1988). Early on in American history Jefferson warned about the political risk involved in accepting emigrants from absolute monarchies (Zolberg, 1987). The 1957 US Refugee-Escapee Act defined a refugee as a victim of political, religious or racial persecution fleeing from communist or communist-occupied or -dominated country or a Middle East country (Rystad, 1990). And although the anti-communist bias of the law was removed in

1980, practice continues to show that potential 'communist trouble-makers' were kept out (Loescher and Scanlan, 1985, p.31). Generally the notion of security is of great concern to the state. In Britain Chilean refugees were refused entry by Conservative governments (1973 and 1979) and received by the Labour government (1974–79) but every individual applicant was submitted to a security check. As it happens, Britain's lack of information about Chile led to the use of CIA files for this purpose (Joly, 1987b). The current conventions and agreements in Europe concerning asylum demonstrate this overriding concern (Joly with Nettleton, 1990; Joly, 1989). Most countries also specify negative criteria defining politically or socially unacceptable people (Scanlan and Kent, 1988). Many of these criteria are the ones which are supposed to run counter to the national interest. In this domain the term is ordinarily used to refer to the security of the State, to the physical security of the nation's population and territory, its economic well-being and the preservation of institutions and values (Shacknove, 1988). National interest is most often defined by the state and can have a wide appeal but frequently fails to secure unanimity. Within the ruling class itself there may be divergent opinions on how best to serve 'national interest' (Teitelbaum, 1980). In addition, a variety of pressure groups may influence policy. The presence of a substantial ethnic group with political allies and power is not negligible (Loescher and Scanlan, 1985). This is the case for the Lebanese in France where they have benefited from preferential treatment. Fraternal political parties or churches which are counterparts of those existing in the country of origin can also have an impact on government policy in favour of or against a particular group of refugees. In Britain the NUM was active in lobbying the Labour party in favour of Chilean refugees and was the first trade union to send representatives to Chile who brought back a damning report on the Pinochet dictatorship.

Those who can influence or control the media will also have an impact on policy decisions. The media are able to generate wide public sympathy for particular groups, such as the boat people from Vietnam, thus lending pressure for a generous policy because governments are sensitive to public opinion. They may equally instigate an anti-refugee mood, perhaps to justify tough governmental action by portraying asylum-

seekers as terrorists, illegal immigrants and drug-traffickers
(Joly with Nettleton and Poulton, 1992).

FOREIGN POLICY COMPONENTS AND STRATEGIC
OBJECTIVES

Global parameters

By definition, foreign policy considerations and their impact on
asylum policy have to be understood within a framework which
goes beyond pure national profiles. It is therefore necessary to
look at global parameters for policies on refugees. In the post-
war era and up to the end of the eighties, the framework for
refugee and asylum policy was determined by the Cold War.
After 1947 the world was divided into two blocs: Warsaw Pact
and NATO countries; 'Western' countries were poised against
'Eastern' ones and were led or dominated by the United States.
A sub-agenda was added to this simplistic division: the decolonization process of former European empires (mostly French
and British but also Belgian, Dutch and later Portuguese) was
completed through liberation wars and negotiations. These
states' attempts towards a non-aligned position were considered
by the USA as hostile but eventually created a small space for a
third camp. However, both the Cold War and the formation of
new decolonized states exacerbated the potential for producing
refugees. Within this context the complex fabric of international relations and specific national foreign policy interests are
brought to bear on refugee policy. It is useful here to quote
Chomsky delineating four separate aspects of US foreign policy
which need be taken into account at each point in time:

> One is the relations that are being constructed, either in
> fact or ideology, with the superpower enemy, i.e. with the
> Soviet Union and its bloc. Second, there is the set of rela-
> tions that are being established with the so-called allies, the
> First World of the industrialist capitalist countries. Third
> there are the relations with the usual victims – the Third
> World countries. And fourth, there is another class of
> victims – the domestic population of the USA. (Chomsky
> et al., 1984, p.24)

If one is dealing with other Western industrial powers one needs to add the relationship to the USA, as their specific and regional interests are to be carried out within a global framework managed by the United States. The world was redrawn by the United States at the end of the Second World War to secure the prosperity and domination of the American economy; this entailed that large areas of the world had to be open, 'open to investment, the repatriation of profits, access to resources and so on – and dominated by the United States' (Chomsky et al., 1984, p.25). The Cold War was thus both an end and a means. It blocked the intrusion of any other power in the US sphere of influence, and according to Chomsky it mobilized the support of the American population for an aggressive foreign policy. During this Cold War era variations in emphasis were introduced. For instance, from the mid-sixties Third World countries assumed more importance as some attempted to challenge US or other hegemonies. In Latin America social unrest and demands for better social programmes led the United States to launch the Alliance for Progress. The OPEC countries successfully organized for better control of and higher returns for their oil reserves using a strategy which threatened industrialized countries supplies (Gittings, 1984). In the meantime Europe had created the EEC, which was to become an economic rival to the USA. The detente of the seventies ushered in a lull in the Cold War which came back with renewed strength in the eighties. In Britain a bipartisan policy supported Britain's 'special relationship' with the United States which meant sharing their 'world policeman' role and 'defending the free world against the threat of communism' (Lapping, 1970, p.83). The French situation is somewhat different in that respect. It had neither the historical nor the cultural and ideological links which Britain had nurtured with the USA. Both the Right and the Left in France agreed on this point: for the communist Left then commanding a large audience, the USA represented the epitome of capitalist and imperialist hegemony and for de Gaulle and most of the French Right 'Atlanticism' was a situation and an ideology to be resisted (Howarth and Chilton, 1984). By 1966 France had asked for the withdrawal of NATO headquarters and bases from French territory and announced that it was withdrawing French troops from NATO. At the same time de Gaulle was making overtures to the Soviet Union and China and was denouncing American policy in Indo-China. France's opposition to the USA mellowed in the seventies but was not completely eliminated. At the same time both France and Britain had their own interests at stake in their ex-colonies.

By the end of the eighties a reorganization of the world order and alliances began to take place with the collapse of communist regimes. The removal of the strait-jacket of the Cold War is having a profound impact on international relations and its concrete consequences are still in the making and remain difficult to document.

Hostile relations with the country of origin

Within the general framework described above, the relationship to the country of origin is the main area of foreign policy which influences the receiving countries' policy on refugees. Until the nineties this had to be situated within the parameters of the Cold War. In Western states it broadly meant that any applicants coming from a communist regime would automatically be accepted. This doctrine was launched by Truman as part of the ideological war against communism and became enshrined in the US legislation on refugees (Rystad, 1990). Public and publicized welcome of 'dissidents' has been used to discredit opposing regimes and as an indictment of the country of origin. Eastern Europeans were received with open arms. Vietnamese were also given generous space, particularly in the United States where their flight in large numbers served to vindicate the Vietnam war retrospectively (Suhrke, 1983); this was much needed as it had finally raised so much controversy and opposition. Geopolitics and ideology were clearly expressed in the US attitudes towards Cuban applicants (Scanlan and Loescher, 1983). The first wave of Cubans was received with applause as they opposed Castro's Cuba, only a few miles away from the Florida cost. They were armed, trained and financed as 'freedom fighters' who would soon overthrow Fidel Castro's regime, perceived and portrayed as an enemy of the United States (1959–61). After the defeat of the Bay of Pigs the second wave of Cuban exiles was seen to be voting with their feet and to demonstrate the economic bankruptcy of communism; they were also used to destabilize Cuban economics as most of them were professionals and business people (1961–73). However, the third wave of Cubans, the 'Marielitos' (1974–80) was received much more reluctantly in the USA, partly because the US–USSR detente had been initiated but also because of US internal factors. There are many more examples of attempts to destabilize opponent regimes through the recognition and arming of refugees, such as Nicaraguan *contras* after the Sandinistas overthrew Somoza (1979), or Afghans in Pakistan (after 1978–9). In a more discrete way a similar attitude can be observed among ex-colonial powers not only where communist regimes are concerned but where countries are involved which led a liberation war or opposed that country's imperialism. For these reasons France was quick to receive Algerian and Vietnamese refugees, and Portugal Angolans and Mozambicans.

Friendly countries of origin

Alternatively, if relations are good between the country of origin and the country of reception it is likely to prove difficult for refugees to obtain admission and recognition as this could undermine relations by constituting public criticism of the regime. The most glaring example illustrating this point is the United States' attitude to Haitians, Salvadorans and Guatemalans. Despite damning reports on human rights violations in Guatemala and El Salvador, both by Amnesty International and the Inter-American Commission on Human Rights, 98 per cent of asylum-seekers from these countries have been refused asylum in the United States (Loescher, 1987). This is because Salvador and Guatemala were seen as allies of the USA against Cuba, Nicaragua and communism in general (Loescher and Scanlan, 1985); in El Salvador Duarte's government was considered as an alternative to the previous dictatorship and well-equipped to put down the Farabundo Marti Liberation Front. In Haiti, in the eighties, the Duvalier regime kept the backing of the United States for the same ideological and geopolitical reasons and Haitians could not obtain asylum on the official grounds that they were presumed to be economic migrants. Decisions were taken not on the basis of examining individual applications as stipulated by the Geneva Convention and the 1980 Refugee Act but Haitians were considered and refused asylum as a group (Naomi Flink Zucker, 1983) while Vietnamese were presumed to be refugees, as a group at the same period (1981–2). Boats transporting Haitians were not even allowed to land and an interdiction order made them be turned back. This situation continued even though the fallacy that a progressive improvement of the human rights record was taking place as a justification not to recognize Haitian applicants was exposed in 1979 (Loescher and Scanlan, 1985). The same rationale underlay US policy towards Chilean refugees as the Pinochet dictatorship had overthrown the previous government with the active support of the CIA.

In Britain policies towards Chilean refugees were also determined by the relationship with the Pinochet dictatorship, but varied according to the government in office. The Conservative government did not admit Chilean refugees not only because it entertained good trade relations with Pinochet's Chile (including the sales of arms to the dictatorship) but also because they shared close affinities on account of their common adoption of Milton Friedman's monetarism. The Conservative government's intimate link with the US strengthened this stance and the position of Chile, allied to Britain in the Falklands War, did so too (1982). However, Britain's historical relationship with Argentina made it practically impossible for Argentinian refugees to be accepted even under a Labour government. Criticisms of the Argentinian regime were only uttered when Britain saw its territorial and colonial interests directly threatened in the Falklands. More generally, Britain's privileged ties with Commonwealth countries made it difficult for Commonwealth citizens to be accepted as refugees in Britain (Joly, 1987b; Kay and Miles, 1992). The same situation prevails in France where citizens of ex-colonies with a friendly regime are concerned. This may be one factor accounting for discrepancies in the acceptance of particular groups of refugees in Europe; why, for instance, the percentage of Sri Lankan asylum-seekers being granted refugee status is much higher in France than in Britain (Joly with Nettleton and Poulton, 1992).

Relationship with third parties

However, matters are not resolved by a mere equation between the refugees' country of reception and country of origin. Broader international relations come into play. In the first place the relationship of the receiving country with the USA contributes heavily to its policies and attitudes towards particular groups of refugees. For instance, France, which was more distant to the USA than Britain (especially after de Gaulle had expelled NATO forces from French territory), did not find any difficulty in accepting thousands of Chilean, Argentinian and Uruguayan refugees even under a Conservative government. Secondly, the geopolitics of the region and relationships with neighbouring countries may also constitute a determining factor. Australia's decision to resettle Vietnamese refugees was largely motivated by its preoccupation with the stability of the region and its friendly relationship with ASEAN countries which were countries of first asylum (Cox, 1979). It thus took into account Malaysia's concern for preserving its ethnic balance and at the same time paid attention to China's role towards ethnic Chinese from Vietnam and the possible intentions of China and Vietnam in the region (Suhrke, 1983). Its alliance with the United States in the Vietnam war was also of major importance.

The interplay of foreign policy factors is very complex and it has been shown that a change of government may entail a change of policy without a change of regime. But 'international' pressure through international agencies also plays a part (this is examined below). Moreover, the foreign policy of a country may muster a general consensus at home but often displays divergences on specific issues, and pressures are brought to bear on the government to modify it. In the United States a clear-cut cleavage existed between President Carter and Senator Edward Kennedy regarding foreign policy towards Latin America and particularly Chile. Letellier's growing popularity and his assassination within a few miles of the White House while he was a refugee in the United States brought this conflict of view to a head (Letellier was the Allende's government's ambassador in the USA when the *coup d'état* occurred in Chile). Organized sectors of the population and eventually the majority of the population may also disagree with government and promote a change of foreign and asylum policies.

Diplomacy and refugees

Even if it is assumed that human rights violations will secure a positive attitude from the receiving country towards nationals of the country seeking asylum, one impediment is the sources of information. The absence of a proper mechanism offering reliable information on refugees' countries of origin is compounded by what serves as a substitute. As a consequence the first source of information on a country's human rights record is often the foreign embassy of the country from which a refugee seeks asylum. The result is bound to fall short of what is required as an embassy is poorly equipped to fulfil such tasks since its brief is to maintain good relations between the two countries, not to find fault. This is another evidence of the role played by foreign policy in asylum policy.

At the end of the eighties the parameters of the Cold War began to crumble. A realignment of powers and a global reformulation of policies is currently in process. This will have a profound impact on refugee policies. It is already possible to observe that asylum-seekers from Eastern Europe do not enjoy the same preferential treatment as before. Few countries agreed to accept victims of the civil war in the former Yugoslavia despite the well-publicized atrocities taking place which affect several groups. The process is only beginning and it remains difficult to anticipate the ways in which refugees of non-European origin will be affected.

ETHICAL FACTORS

This is not the place to develop a general discussion on ethical dilemmas regarding immigration policy; we shall refer the reader to Zolberg, exploring the cosmopolitan and the national ideals in the light of 'social justice at an international level' (Zolberg, 1987, p.262). It will suffice to mention here the points most relevant to our discussion. In the views of liberal theorists, two main reasons are advanced for the granting of priority in admission to refugees: 'the priority attributable to freedom (Carens), and the impossibility of exporting relief in the case of the refugees (Walzer)' (Zolberg, 1987, p.292). In this light the main conjuncture which could justify restriction is when a large-scale influx might destabilize and cause chaos in the receiving society (Zolberg, 1987).

The ethical issue regarding refugees and receiving states is a complicated one and rests on an inherent tension between the sovereign state and its universalist obligations. On the one hand it could be argued that ethical factors are the only ones which must and should be taken into account. States are bound by the international conventions to which they are signatory and they do not have the freedom to decide on criteria for the granting of asylum. In principle each case must be determined according to its merit as defined by the relevant conventions: the moral claim of the applicant is overriding. On the other hand international practice demonstrates that states are jealous of their sovereignty and especially control over their borders, and are overwhelmingly guided by their national interest, expressed through their foreign and domestic policies rather than by moral imperatives. If this is the case there is no reason why they should worry about total strangers in need. However while admitting that domestic and international policy interests are the determining criterial in the formulation of policies on asylum and refugees I will now analyse the modest role played by ethical factors.

It has been argued that for refugees more than for any other migrants ethical factors cannot be totally ignored by policy-makers (Loescher and Scanlan, 1985). There exist international bodies and conventions dealing with the question of refugees which go beyond narrow national interests. And there is also a degree of consensus in the world and among industrial countries in particular indicating the unacceptability of ruthless policies devoid of any moral justification. Moreover, '*l'Etat de Droit*' within a given state can prevail even when it runs counter to specific interests and it is sometimes difficult to flout it openly.

Refugees, human rights and international conventions

Issues concerning refugees who have lost the protection of their state of origin have been exacerbated in the twentieth century with the consolidation of the nation state and its boundaries. This has meant that people deprived of the protection of a state did not have any place in society and in any state (this was at least the case in Europe); hence the need for another state than their own to offer asylum and award its protection. It is in the twentieth century that the question of refugees has been politicized and internationalized (Bettati, 1985). However, the notion of asylum has existed for millennia, from ancient Egypt with Sinuhe through the Middle Ages and sanctuary offered by the Church. Sympathy and interest for refugees and for particular types of refugees changed through times and was modified by historical events. For the period that concerns us, events leading to the Second World War and the war itself are still prevalent in European outlook. The general guilt generated throughout Europe as a result of the millions of victims of fascism and Nazism, many of whom were refused entry visas and asylum in other European countries, led to a special treatment being awarded to 'political refugees', i.e. persons in fear of persecution for reasons of race, religion, nationality, membership of a particular social group or political opinion as enshrined in the 1951 Geneva Convention. It was also motivated by Cold War objectives (Salomon, 1991). In addition, where historical experience has brought out other features of the plight and causes of refugee movements this has been reflected in collective awareness and conventions. For instance, in Africa where refugee movements have also been caused by generalized violence, recognition and assistance have been extended to several additional categories of refugees (OAU Convention).

The question of refugees clearly pertains to the whole area of human and democratic rights. Since the First World War, when the tackling of refugee issues became internationalized, a broad sensitivity to refugee and human rights issues has grown considerably. This process was precipitated by the atrocities condemned as crimes against humanity which took place prior to and during the Second World War. The reaction against these barbarous acts and concern for human and democratic rights were translated in a number of international conventions and declarations in the second half of the twentieth century. The Universal Declaration of Human Rights was adopted in 1948, stating *inter alia* the right of everyone to seek and enjoy in other countries asylum from persecution. The 1951 Geneva Convention defines refugees and stipulates the obligations of states towards them, in particular the interdiction of *refoulement*; it was thereafter completed by the 1967 Bellagio Protocol which removed the time and geographical limits imposed by the Geneva Convention. The United Nations 1984 Convention against Torture and other Cruel Inhuman or Degrading Treatment or Punishment is also of relevance for refugees. The awareness of human rights extending beyond the civil and political rights led to the adoption of instruments to protect the 'second generation' of human rights (Jaeger, 1991, p.20). These include the International Covenant on Economic, Social and Cultural Rights (1966) and the International Covenant on Civil and Political Rights (1966). In 1981, the Executive Committee of the UNHCR endorsed a list of some sixteen 'basic human standards' which should govern the treatment of refugees and asylum-seekers admitted temporarily in a situation of mass influx (Goodwin-Gill, 1986). As wider concepts of human rights have developed, more aspects of human life and human activities are considered at present to be human rights (Jaeger, 1991). This is illustrated by the Universal Declaration on the Eradication of Hunger and Malnutrition (1974). These international instruments represent an internationally accepted ethics of human rights consensus and are a gauge of the level of awareness surrounding these issues. Indeed human rights and fundamental freedoms also apply to refugees and asylum-seekers (van Boven, 1991). Moreover, there are regional conventions and declarations; in Europe this comprises the European Convention for the Protection of Human Rights and Fundamental Freedoms and several recommendations from the Council of Europe. But it is not only that refugees are to be extended support and protection. It is also the case that states have an obligation to other states not to create refugees and are expected by the international community to accord their nationals a certain minimum standard of treatment in terms of human rights and fundamental freedoms (Goodwin-Gill, 1983). These international instruments can play an important part in influencing asylum policies.

What needs to be considered however, is what additional factors might lead policy-makers in a particular country to pay

attention to moral arguments where refugees are concerned.
It has been argued that political systems leave room for moral
considerations in immigration and particularly asylum policies
even within a Hobbesian perspective (Scanlan and Kent,
1988). The duty to admit refugees can also be derived from
Shue's triad of duties and Rawls's natural duties as described
by Goodwin-Gill (1986).

Widely shared values

The tradition of asylum was made morally compelling through
religious protection for centuries. Asylum had its place in
ancient Greece thanks to the inviolability of sanctuaries. The
Bible develops the right of asylum internally and in exile, and
the medieval Church also offered asylum and protection
(Bettati, 1985). One major reason for the strength of ethical
factors promoting asylum would be the role that ideological
and symbolic modes of representation play in government as a
result of widely shared systems of belief. As Gramsci explained,
those in power would find it extremely difficult to govern
without open coercion if they blatantly flouted the values held
and shared by the majority of the population (Gramsci, 1971).
For instance, in the USA the popular assumption posits a land
where freedom is extolled and defended, where a variety of
immigrants and refugees have been welcomed through more
than two centuries (i.e. since the *Mayflower*) and where racial
discrimination has become unspeakable (even if it happens in
practice). The desire to flatter or conform to this accepted
moral norm accounts for Ronald Reagan's speech when he accepted his nomination as president:

> Can we doubt that only a Divine Providence placed this
> land, this island of freedom here as a refuge for all those
> people who yearn to breathe free? Jews and Christians en-
> during persecution behind the Iron Curtain; the Boat
> people of Southeast Asia, Cuba, and of Haiti; the victims of
> drought and famine in Africa; the freedom fighters in
> Afghanistan. (Quoted in Scanlan and Kent, 1988, p.81)

Such declaration does not commit Reagan to implement what
he claims but is designed to please his audience; he tells them
what they want to hear and what they like to believe is right.

When these moral concerns are strong and broad among the population they lend support for the enactment of laws and explicit policies in conformity with these ideals. This is how Senator Edward Kennedy explains the 1980 Refugee Act:

> This Act gives statutory meaning to our national commitment to human rights and humanitarian concerns – which are not now reflected in our immigration law. (US Senate Committee on the Judiciary, Review of US Refugee Resettlement Programs and Policies (report), 96th Congress, 2nd Session, 1980, p.80, quoted in Scanlan and Kent, 1988, p.84)

The Australian Statement on Refugee Policy and Mechanisms presented to Parliament in 1977 outlines as one of its principles a humanitarian commitment and responsibility to admit refugees. In France *Liberté, Egalité, Fraternité* are still the main motto of the Republic. The 1793 Constitution proclaims that the French people grants asylum to foreigners banished from their motherland for the cause of liberty (Bettati, 1985). The image of France *terre d'asile* was preserved in the preamble of its Constitution until 1994. In the past foreigners were granted the right to take part in the National Assembly if they had fought for liberty (Thomas Paine was a member of the 1892 Convention). In Germany the inheritance of guilt from the Holocaust contributed to the writing of the right to political asylum in the Constitution (Grundgezetz, Article 16) maintained until 1993.

The political system will allow attempts to change this widely shared system of values. For instance, Truman at first encountered resistance from the population when he promoted the view that refugees from communist countries should be received without restrictions although it had become clear to the political leadership that this furthered the US foreign policy objectives. But a favourable public opinion was secured by sustained and carefully organized campaigns. There are numerous instances showing how the dehumanization and criminalization of certain categories of people through intense propaganda made their unequal treatment acceptable: the colonized inferior status at the time of colonial empires, and the witch-hunting of communists in the MacCarthy era in the USA, for example. It is argued that it has become more difficult to disprove the equal moral worth of individuals at the present time (Shacknove, 1988). And there exists a bottom-line limit to the sole use of practical considerations. If a refugee policy runs counter to the nation's most deeply rooted moral values it may encounter opposition or rebellion (Scanlan and Kent, 1988). Pure selfish interest can only be accepted as justifiable to a certain extent. For instance, the sanctuary movement in the USA and in Switzerland demonstrates that citizens are ready to challenge the law in order to protect asylum-seekers in the name of justice and human rights. Moral and religious authorities stress that some values supersede state or national interest. One strand of Protestantism puts forward the view that religious duty falls into the category of ultimate duty ante-dating the civil authority. The Catholic theology of liberation contests the sovereignty of the state when it runs counter to its conception of religious duty (Nichols, 1988).

Participation in the political process

A variety of bodies and interest groups participate in the political process and sometimes put forward an agenda guided by moral considerations. Their views might not be at one with the government's (as is often the case where refugees are concerned) but their political influence ensures that such views cannot merely be brushed aside. There can be a cooperative venture between the state and moral authorities and this frequently implies that the state authorities cannot simply discard the opinions of their moral counterparts. For instance in the United States religious bodies seem to have been prime movers behind the US acceptance of responsibilities for refugees (Nichols, 1988). They have assisted in the resettlement task of refugees generally according to the principle of subsidiarity[1] but the execution of this task gave them an additional lever to influence the state. An important conference called by the State Department and a new religious advisory group discussed the role of religious and moral traditions in US refugee assistance (Nichols, 1988). Other religious bodies may also have an input in policies such as the Jewish Council before and after the Second World War. This is equally the case for refugee agencies and other humanitarian NGOs making representation to the government on behalf of refugees and asylum-seekers; for example, in Britain they helped to bring about changes to the proposed bill on asylum (1992). Moreover, these NGOS and religious organizations have links with international bodies concerned with human rights and trying to bring pressure to bear on their governments, as in the British case when international bodies criticized its EVW programme (Kay and Miles, 1992). Other organizations or groups may intervene on behalf of refugees and put forward a moral point of view differing from governmental policy: for instance, in several European countries communist parties, socialist parties and trade unions supported the acceptance of Chileans after a bloody *coup d'état* brought down a government held and supported by fraternal organizations in Chile. There are multiple examples in Western Europe of the advocacy role played by organized sectors of society and of their successes regarding policies on refugees (Joly with Nettleton and Poulton, 1992). Reports in the international courts on human rights leading to the condemnation of states for their violation of human rights constitute good levers to influence policies. Discussions and resolutions from the United Nations can also play a significant role.

In addition, pressure groups at home often draw support from some international bodies such as the UNHCR, the International Labour Organization, the Council of Europe and all fora relevant to asylum-seekers and refugees or human rights in general, which can put on the agenda of governments the relevant conventions discussed above.

CONCLUSION

It is well known that foreign policy plays a part in the determination of asylum policy but it seems to weigh most heavily in a system of hostile international relations. This is evidenced by the significance of foreign policy considerations in determining refugee policies during the Cold War. The existence of two blocs poised against each other in which the whole world was enmeshed dictated a bias favourable to refugees escaping from the 'enemy's' territory. It helped to vindicate the righteousness of one's ideology and system and to condemn the opponent's, particularly so among Western states. As a corollary a ricochet system of alliances following the axiom that the enemy of my enemy is my friend and, vice versa, the friend of my enemy is my enemy, embroiled asylum policies *vis-à-vis* an increasing number of refugees into the net of foreign policy. The impact of foreign policy issues on asylum policy is also demonstrated by other small-scale instances of hostile international relations. Despite the Geneva Convention premise that recognition of refugee status must not prejudice the diplomatic relations between countries, practice shows that the relationship between a country of reception and country of origin largely influences decisions on specific groups of refugees. For instance, in the case of colonial powers in conflict with colonies or ex-colonies, political, economic and ideological interests embedded in foreign policy directly determine the policy of the former towards refugees from the latter.

Finally, foreign policy considerations assume considerable influence if it is perceived that international or regional security are jeopardized by asylum issues. The reaction of countries in South-East Asia including Australia to 'boat people' from Vietnam spilling out into neighbouring countries is a good example of this point.

Generally the factors which seem to have the greatest influence on asylum policy are those pertaining to domestic issues. These encompass not only economic matters but also cultural and ideologico-political questions. Domestic considerations tend to weigh against a generous asylum policy in situations of internal difficulties: an economic recession compounded by unemployment and threats to the standard of living, loss of confidence in the government and uncertainties about the future combined with anxieties about minorities and outsiders among the majority society as demonstrated by the situation in Western Europe in the nineties. Among Western liberal democracies it appears that the ones more open to refugees are those which are least conflict-ridden and which enjoy a good deal of internal harmony and stability, particularly in situations of economic prosperity.

With regard to specific groups of refugees it is clear that those most welcome are those who are perceived as having affinities with the country of reception or sections of that society whether they be of a historical nature, cultural, linguistic, religious, ethnic or ideological. Another feature propitious to their acceptance is noticeable when refugees are construed as a potential asset to the country of reception. The end of the Cold War has freed asylum policies from the strait-jacket of the two blocs, thus in principle removing the general bias favourable to refugees from communist countries and less favourable to the others in the Western world. One could expect as a consequence a more balanced asylum policy. However, the end of the Cold War coincides with a period of economic recession and grave societal problems. On the one hand foreign policy factors have decreased, while on the other domestic considerations have increased within a context of crisis. This has rendered the latter almost overriding and has led to a restrictive asylum policy in most of Western Europe. Moreover, the end of the Cold War also seems to have opened greater possibilities of international action in the countries of origin against violations of human rights, generalized violence and severe deprivations, as international co-operation is not as in the past hampered by the two blocs jealously guarding their sphere of influence. The US intervention in Haiti in 1994 testifies to this, as they displaced a regime which generated a mass influx of refugees attempting to find asylum in the USA. This can also be used as a legitimation for a less open asylum policy. It also facilitates helping the refugees *in situ* or in close neighbouring countries.

Conflicts in Eastern Europe illustrate this trend. Western countries are offering development/democratization packages to Eastern European states. They poured humanitarian aid into former Yugoslavia and endeavoured to end the war, which proved a protracted process. But they have proved extremely reluctant to open their door to refugees. This reaction can be accounted for on several grounds to which governments are sensitive:

— The recession and unemployment combine with the fear that refugees will be a burden to the nation;
— Xenophobic and racist feelings already rampant are deemed to be exacerbated by a mass influx of refugees;
— This ran the risk of leading to the permanent settlement of large numbers;

— It could have been perceived as an invitation to come to people from other conflict areas in Eastern Europe;
— The fact that the vast majority of these refugees were Muslims worked against their admission. Indeed the hostile relations of Western states with several Muslim countries or organizations are compounded by a growing anti-Muslim feeling in European societies with Muslim minorities.

It remains difficult to evaluate the role played by ethical factors in asylum decisions as they depend heavily on a complex network of circumstances. They generally play some part when supranational values are accorded sufficient importance or when a particular conjuncture allows the refugees' interest to coincide with other interests at stake in the variegated fabric of national and international factors at play.

However, it appears that if one concession is made to ethical grounds some sense of justice can succeed in prevailing. At the time of the Cold War the acceptance of refugees from communist countries provided a hinge for the enhancement of ethical factors; in the name of parity most countries also had to grant recognition to other refugees or found it difficult to justify their action. The normative influence of ethical factors is strengthened by the international instruments to which advocates of refugees can appeal. But they are best taken into account when supranational bodies intervene directly to promote them, as shown by current UNHCR actions with regard to former Yugoslavia. There also seems to exist a bottom line to selfish and pragmatic interest which cannot be transgressed in violation of human rights. This perception is changing through time, but despite their attempts at reducing the numbers of asylum-seekers by all kinds of means, European states have not dared to renege on international conventions embodying inalienable human rights including the rights of refugees. At the end of the day the plight of the needy carries a moral weight which is difficult to ignore totally. For instance, in spite of their great reluctance, all European States have eventually given admission to the most extreme cases of persecution and violence in former Yugoslavia.

Perhaps the conclusion must be that the influence of ethical factors about asylum issues is proportional to the awareness of and respect for other democratic and human rights globally and in a particular country and to the 'degree of solidarity of a society' (van Boven quoted in Rudge, 1989).

NOTES

1. Pope Pius XI in the 1931 Encyclical *Quadragesimo Anno* provided a rationale for Catholic institutions to enter into a dialogue with modern governments. Nicholls (1988) summarizes subsidiarity as the delegation by a larger institution to smaller institutions of the tasks which those lesser institutions were best suited to perform.

3 Cracks in the Wall: European Harmonization on Asylum in the Nineties[1]

INTRODUCTION

It is not possible to speak of a 'European policy' on asylum and refugees prior to the mid-eighties. What could be identified in the way of such a policy was only a conglomeration of different national policies among European states. There existed substantial differences between one country and another and little in the way of harmonization. Admittedly there were common trends to be found among the respective states' policies but these did not result from a concerted effort.

After the mid-eighties a process of harmonization of policies on asylum began from within the EU, but at intergovernmental level. Two major events precipitated this process: the imminent Single European Act which *inter alia* prepared for the abolition of EU internal borders, and the dramatic increase of asylum-seekers arriving in Europe at a time when the economic recession made newcomers unwelcome. The initiatives taken in the wake of this were several and far-reaching; indeed they were still being pursued and expanded in 1993. Convergence, restriction and secrecy is the paradigm prevailing in this phase of European policies.

It has to be noted that the question of asylum, hardly raised at intergovernmental and international meetings in Europe, has grown to become one of the central issues deserving special declarations, resolutions and policy formulation. All the main European fora have taken it up and some were created specially for that purpose. It also occupies a prominent place on the agenda of human rights organizations and churches.

The first body set up to harmonize policies on asylum, namely the Schengen Agreement, became a magnet and generated a centripetal movement. All the twelve members of the EU developed similar initiatives which former EFTA

44

countries are presently eager to join. It means that all the European countries which do not produce refugees at present and are not likely to do so in the foreseeable future are to be associated in this harmonization process.

However, another twist in the evolution of the EU[2] may modify the democratic deficit of the intergovernmental treaties mentioned above, and the consequences of the Treaty European Union still remain to be seen.

At the very beginning of the nineties a major upheaval altered the map of Europe and had a profound impact on asylum issues, namely the dismantlement of communist regimes and the end of the Cold War. On the one hand it produced the lifting of exit controls in Eastern European countries. On the other hand the crises and conflicts which ensued entailed a mass refugee movement from former Yugoslavia and the threat of further population movements from other parts. This has prompted a variety of initiatives. In the first place negotiations have been initiated with some Eastern European countries towards a better control of potential refugees and immigrants. Several programmes have also been launched for assisting those countries. In addition several fora have been formed, bringing together Western and Eastern European countries, some of which have taken on board the question of asylum. However, the bases for discussions are necessarily very different from those of bodies such as the Schengen group or the EU as countries are now involved which are potential producers as well as receivers of refugees. Will this mean a modified or a more liberal regime?   *Major role*

Finally, the UNHCR has been brought into the discussions increasingly. Where the former-Yugoslav crisis was concerned it played a decisive role, and new concepts and policies have emerged.

This chapter examines the trends in European policies on asylum and refugees. It demonstrates that the lead still rests with EU states with a prevailing restrictionist approach: intergovernmental harmonization, convergence and restrictions are still on the order of the day. However, two new undercurrents, possible harbingers of the future are already present in the European arena:

—   The secrecy presiding over agreements on asylum is partly relinquished, giving way to a greater involvement

Secrecy.

of public bodies and NGOs as the main arena of discussion moves away from intergovernmental agreements;
— Selective and temporary admission will in the long term replace pure restrictions, together with a more comprehensive approach on asylum and migration issues.

FROM UNCOORDINATED LIBERALISM TO HARMONIZED RESTRICTIONISM

Too open policy

In the early seventies European states were implementing a fairly open policy with regard to asylum-seekers. However, this resulted from general circumstances producing lax immigration controls. There does not seem to have been any coordination among European countries about their asylum policy and vast discrepancies in procedures existed between one state and another. The 1951 Convention had gradually been ratified by European states; 16 ratified it before 1960 (Jaeger, 1992) and they then proceeded to ratify the 1967 Protocol. Nevertheless in many cases there was no special mechanism to deal with asylum applications. These were introduced through the seventies and the eighties. It appears that in those years the trend in asylum law was a liberal one incorporating the principles of the 1951 Convention and 1967 Protocol (Jaeger, 1992). Refugees from Eastern Europe were almost automatically recognized within the Cold War context. The 1967 Protocol had been recently adopted which made it possible to grant refugee status to non-European asylum-seekers as well.

These were arriving in relatively small numbers and they were little mentioned in the media or in politicians' declarations apart from a few large movements which spilled into Europe: the Chileans in 1973 were escaping from a bloody dictatorship and arrived with other Latin Americans as dictatorships flared up throughout the continent in Argentina, Uruguay and elsewhere; the arrival of East African Asians culminated with the mass expulsion of Ugandan Asians by Idi Amin in 1972; from 1975 onwards the Vietnamese were the next important group. This does not mean that there were no other refugee movements occurring in the rest of the world, but only a small fraction of them reached Europe. On the whole they clearly corresponded to the Convention definition or were deemed to do so. Moreover, until the mid-seventies European countries were still welcoming foreign labour to meet the needs of stable economies. As a consequence many refugees from the Third World entered Europe either as immigrant workers or as students, as was then made possible by loose immigration controls (Blaschke, 1989).

The only Europe-wide body which concerned itself with asylum issues as early as the sixties was the Council of Europe. It is also the first one which broached the question of harmonization of policies and practices. The Council of Europe produced its first Recommendation on Harmonization in 1976 and a second on the Harmonization of National Procedure Related to Asylum in 1981. The latter does not propose any formal system, but invites European states to check that their procedures and practices meet with standards recommended by the Council of Europe, which require: an 'objective and impartial judgement'; referral of the decision to a 'central authority'; 'clear instructions' to immigration officers against *refoulement*; and permission for the applicant to remain while the asylum request is being examined. The Council of Europe has continued to issue declarations, reports and recommendations on refugees to the present time. However, it has lost the lead in these matters which were taken over by EC states' intergovernmental groups. The discussions on refugee protection have thus been moved from a human rights platform in the Council of Europe to a platform concentrating on political and economic preoccupations in the region.

In the mid-eighties the whole matter of European policy on asylum began to change. The trend started to revert in several ways: policies which were liberal became increasingly restrictive, a process of convergence replaced the separate policy-making which had obtained until then. The question of asylum which had remained pretty uncontroversial also became more and more debated. This whole process started at the initiative of a few EU countries. It resulted from a combination of circumstances but was prompted by new developments in the EU. In the first place the boom years had come to a halt in the seventies and Europe fell into an economic crisis triggered off by the increase in oil prices. As a consequence labour immigration was stopped. Secondly the number of requests for asylum started to increase not only because air travel became more accessible but also because it was difficult to be granted admission in other ways. This coincided with the eruption of conflicts which failed to attract much international humanitarian attention, such as the revolution in Iran, the Iraq–Iran war, the escalation of civil wars in Lebanon and Sri Lanka. This meant that refugees from those areas had only one option open to them: to make their way to Europe on their own initiative and apply for asylum (Kjaerum, 1993). It could be argued that the migratory pressure has to a large extent been caused by the closing of borders (Tapinos, 1992) but the fact is that there were some 13 000 asylum applications in Europe in 1972 and by 1980 numbers had risen to 158 500 (Joly with Nettleton, 1990). In 1990 there were 425 100 and in 1991 some 550 625 (France Terre d'Asile, June 1992). The Single European Act was in the offing and was ratified in 1986 with the promise that internal borders to the EC would be abolished to allow for free movement not only of goods and capital as stipulated in the Treaty of Rome but also of people. This raised concern among the so-called Northern EC countries which became preoccupied with a variety of issues including security, drugs and immigration once internal border controls would be abolished. The Benelux countries, France and Germany were the recipients of the largest proportion of refugees in the EU. In the years 1988–90, about 80 per cent of all asylum applications lodged in the European Community were submitted to two countries: Germany (60 per cent) and France (20 per cent) (Commission of the European Communities 1992). Southern countries such as Italy, Greece, Portugal and Spain were perceived as transit countries from which asylum-seekers travelled on. It was argued that the greater prosperity and social benefits available in the north attracted the bulk of asylum-seekers. Northern states felt that this trend would be facilitated and precipitated by the implementation of the Single European Act.

This gave rise to the Schengen Agreement between Belgium, the Netherlands, Luxembourg, France and Germany in 1985. Where refugees are concerned it was to have far-reaching consequences and signified a harmonization of asylum policies to make them more restrictive throughout the Schengen territory. Restrictive policies and practices implemented previously in individual countries were brought together in the Schengen Agreement, which reinforced and streamlined them. The four main components of the Schengen Agreement asylum policy are the following: the state responsible for examining the asylum application, the procedure, exchange of information and the circulation of foreigners.

Although the Schengen group was the first to take that road it was soon followed by other intergovernmental initiatives among the twelve EC members. The Trevi group had already been set up in the seventies to look into the question of drugs, terrorism and immigration and comprises the Ministers of Justice and Interior of the Twelve. The Ad Hoc Group on Immigration formed in 1986 included a subgroup on asylum created to examine 'the measures to be taken to reach a common policy to put an end to the abusive use of the right to asylum' (quoted in Joly, 1989, p.367). It prepared a report and a programme of work for the Maastricht European Council on 9 and 10 December 1991 (Maastricht Summit), and continued to play a prominent role in drawing up conventions and agreements related to asylum in the EU. The Group of Coordinators or Rhodes Group (from the EC summit in Rhodes, 1988) prepared the Palma Document which proposed a programme of actions towards the harmonization of policies. The European Commission sat in the meetings of the two latter groups but does not seem to wield much influence, as indicated by their proposal for a Directive which was not taken up (Joly, 1989). Although all member states of the EU are involved these initiatives did not fall within the remit of the EU as they remained purely intergovernmental. It has meant the exclusion of the European Parliament and Court of Luxembourg.

The Convention applying the Schengen Agreement of 14 June 1985 was signed on 19 June 1990 by the founder members and instruments permitting accession to the Treaty were signed by Italy on 27 November 1990, by Spain and Portugal on 25 June 1991 and Greece on 6 November 1992. The Convention had to be ratified by all member states before it could become operational and prior to this national laws had to be modified to make implementation possible. The Schengen Convention which came into force on 1 September 1993 was to be applied as from 26 March 1995. At the time of writing in January 1996 this has not yet happened, mostly on account of France's concerns over security issues and its

requests for enhanced police cooperation as a sine qua non.
Negotiations are taking place on the joining of Nordic countries (Norway, Iceland, Denmark, Finland and Sweden).

The twelve states of the EU have prepared conventions which
taken together include very similar provisions to the Schengen
Convention. The first is the Convention determining the state
responsible for examining applications for asylum lodged in
one of the member states of the European Communities
(Dublin Convention) which was signed in Dublin on 15 June
1990. It will only come into force three months after all twelve
states have ratified it and in October 1995 it still lacked the
ratification of Belgium, Ireland and the Netherlands. The
Dutch Parliament insists that the European Court of Justice be
competent to give preliminary rulings on the interpretation of
the Convention before it agrees to ratification, which is likely to
entail further delays (*Migration News Sheet*, October 1995, no.
151/95–10). The Convention of the member states of the
European communities on the crossing of their external frontiers (Convention on the Crossing of External Frontiers) has
not been signed as yet because of a disagreement between
Spain and the UK over Gibraltar but European states seem to
feel confident that it will eventually be signed and they are
laying the ground for its implementation, as examined below.

Between them, the Schengen Agreement, the Dublin
Convention and the Convention on the crossing of external
borders cover the following main areas:

—   *The state responsible for examining the asylum application*
    One of the main purposes of harmonization has been to
    prevent multiple applications for asylum in several states, si-
    multaneously or successively. The Schengen Agreement
    and the Dublin Convention are both stipulating the follow-
    ing guidelines: each application should be examined by
    one single state and that responsibility would rest with the
    state which had the main role in authorizing entry either by
    issuing a visa, or having issued the visa of longest duration,
    or by not requiring any visa. The notion retained is that of
    first country of asylum, so that in a case of irregular entry
    the first border reached would determine which state was
    responsible. An additional criterion was introduced relating
    to close family links and it is also rendered possible for a

state other than the one deemed responsible to examine an asylum request if it has special ties with the applicant or for humanitarian reasons (Dublin Convention Article 9); or for reasons relating to national law (Schengen Agreement 1990 Chapter 7). To ensure the efficient implementation of these guidelines, states are committed to expel asylum-seekers refused status, and a readmission clause is added to enforce the responsibility notion.

— *The procedure*
On the question of procedure, all the states concerned in the Schengen and Dublin documents agreed to maintain their national procedure for the handling of applications.

— *Exchange of information*
The exchange of information was considered paramount in both the Schengen Agreement and the Dublin Convention. This includes general information on national procedures, statistical data on the monthly arrival of asylum-seekers and their breakdown by nationality, the emergence of significant increases of certain groups, information on countries of origin and more specific information on asylum-seekers; the latter covers information on members of the family, documents, itineraries and decisions taken about their cases. Computerized databases will be set up for that purpose. This is planned by the Schengen Agreement and the Dublin Convention. Moreover the Convention of the Twelve on the crossing of external frontiers proposes a computerized list of *personae non gratae* on EC territory.

— *The circulation of foreigners*
The issue of circulation of foreigners is dealt with by the Schengen Agreement and the Convention of the Twelve on the crossing of external frontiers. A discrepancy exists between these two documents.

The Schengen Agreement proposes to treat *refugees* in the same way as other aliens holding a residence permit from one of the contracting states: they will enjoy freedom of movement within the Schengen states but will have to declare themselves to the competent authorities on arrival or within three days of entry, while *asylum-seekers* will not be allowed to move out of their country of application.

According to the Convention on the crossing of external
borders, *refugees* will be able to move and stay in another EU
state for up to three months, and it is *asylum-seekers* who will
have to register with the police within 72 hours of arrival, while
being able to stay up to one month. However, both documents
agree to introduce sanctions on transporters and the carrying
of undocumented aliens and to harmonize the policies and
practices of the states concerned on the question of visas, with
the aim of issuing common visas. A more detailed study of these
texts can be found in Joly with Nettleton and Poulton (1992).

THE AD HOC GROUP ON IMMIGRATION IN THE NINETIES

The Ad Hoc Group on Immigration (Ad Hoc Group) continued and intensified its work and came up with recommendations for approval by the Ministers for Immigration. There
is a marked contrast between the laboriousness associated with
the drawing up and signing of the Conventions mentioned
above and the speed and efficiency of the Ad Hoc Group
in passing subsequent resolutions and recommendations.
Whereas the Schengen and Dublin Conventions took about
five years to come to fruition and are not yet implemented at
the date of writing, several resolutions and conclusions have
been agreed with great diligence since 1991 and were approved by the Council of Ministers. They do not have the same
status as the Conventions mentioned above and are not legally
binding but Ministers agree to incorporate them into their national legislation and guidelines. This is a much speedier
process than the process leading to the ratification of a
Convention and requires no discussion at all in national parliaments. Again the character of the Ad Hoc Group did not
make it answerable to any EC institution.

The Ad Hoc Group submitted a programme of work which
was approved at the Maastricht Summit and they have been
following it through. Fundamentally the immediate aim of the
Ad Hoc Group is to take the steps they consider essential to
enable the free movement of persons within the Union, which
in their view means guarding external borders on questions of
security and immigration (European Council 1992c). In

practice it has meant that priorities were largely dictated by measures believed necessary for the implementation of the Dublin Convention and the Convention on the Crossing of External Frontiers. In effect these Conventions directly placed a number of issues on the agenda which needed to be resolved before their implementation could even be considered as those are written in the very text of the Conventions; this is the case for manifestly unfounded applications, host third country, countries where there is no serious risk of persecution, expulsions and visas, as they require clarification and agreement. Others, such as a clearing house and a centre for information, discussion and exchange on the crossing of frontiers and immigration (CIREFI), follow from the tasks stated in the Conventions and in this instance the collecting of information. All these are examined in more detail below.

These Conventions have brought about mighty consequences: 'apparently of only limited scope the ultimate effect of these Conventions is much greater than was perhaps originally expected' (Ad Hoc Group on Immigration, 1991).

The progress made in the ratification of the Dublin Convention was regularly monitored by the Ad Hoc Group as noted in the Press Release of Ministers of Immigration (European Council, 1992b) which also noted 'with satisfaction' its report on the aspects linked to practical arrangements for implementing the Convention. These include for example the Conclusions on the transfer of applicants for asylum under the provisions of Articles 11 and 13 of the Dublin Convention (Ad Hoc Group on Immigration, 1992i). The way is also being paved for the implementation of the Convention on border controls as demonstrated by the Conclusions regarding the implementation of control on persons on the basis of the Draft Convention between the member states of the European Communities on the crossing of their external frontiers (Brussels 21 May 1993 Ad Hoc Group). In addition other resolutions have been approved.

The Resolution on manifestly unfounded applications for asylum (see appendix, p.85)

This Resolution was approved at the meeting of the ministers responsible for immigration (London 30 November–1 December 1992) and states that applications for asylum will be considered as manifestly unfounded when they raise no substantive issue under the Geneva Convention and New York Protocol for one of the following reasons:

— 'there is clearly no substance to the applicant's claim to fear persecution in his own country'(1a);
— 'the claim is based on deliberate deception or is an abuse of asylum procedures' (1a).

The first refers to grounds falling outside the Geneva Convention such as economic reasons for departure, where there is no indication to show fear of persecution or lack of personal detail in the dossier, or where the story manifestly lacks credibility. It may also be deemed to apply to cases where fear of persecution is extant in one area of the country of origin if effective protection is available in other areas of that country (paragraphs 6–8). Moreover, a general presumption may be established if the applicant comes from a country where there is in general terms no serious risk of persecution.

The second may result from an application based on a false identity or on forged documents, or deliberately made false representations about the claim, documents relevant to the claim having been destroyed or damaged in bad faith. It also includes cases where the applicant submitted an application to forestall expulsion measures and where he submitted applications in other states (paragraphs 9 and 10).

All these applications will or may be fed through an accelerated procedure under which may also come cases involving reasons of public security or where the applicant has committed a serious offence in the state concerned. The Resolution adds that a member state may not examine an application which falls under the resolution on host third countries (2b). Ministers also pledge to seek to ensure that their national laws are adapted to incorporate its principles (paragraph 12).

Some safeguards are fed into the Resolution such as taking into account information received from UNHCR (paragraph 7) about areas of a country where effective protection is available, but also stating clearly that factors linked to abuse of procedure 'cannot in themselves outweigh a well-founded fear of persecution' (paragraph 10). Finally a number of procedural guarantees are given including that of the opportunity of a personal interview with a qualified official. Appeal or review procedures are also mentioned although they may be 'more simplified than those generally available' (paragraph 3). In considering this Resolution the key question to be asked is whether *bona fide* refugees are given real opportunities to be recognized even though they may find themselves channelled into an accelerated procedure because their application appeared to be manifestly unfounded. Only practice can truly tell this. If the Resolution were to be implemented with depth of understanding, real attention to fairness and in total good faith the answer to this question might be positive. However if an overwhelming interest in reducing the entry of refugees were to underpin implementation this Resolution would give the authorities plenty of opportunities to invalidate an application on grounds of form rather than content.

But what already raises concern is the spirit which seems to have presided over the writing of this Resolution and the complete lack of understanding of the refugee's situation as indicated by a previous draft of the Resolution (Ad Hoc Group on Immigration, 1992f, p.6). The whole preamble betrayed an overriding desire to keep out asylum-seekers, pulling in a battery of ill-thought-out arguments to achieve this aim. It argued *inter alia* that applicants needed to seek a remedy to their plight in their own country and deserves to be quoted in full:

> those who fear violations of their human rights should if possible remain in their own countries and seek protection or redress from their own authorities or under regional human rights instruments. (Ibid.)

There is a history to this part of the preamble; it was leaked to the BBC and strong protests were levelled from various quarters. It was being withdrawn anyway because of more 'internal' criticisms, as indicated in a Note by the Presidency:

> It is apparent from the comments already received that a number of Member States are concerned about the presentational impact of the preamble and will be looking for significant changes (Ad Hoc Group on Immigration, 1992f, p.2) and possibly as a result of consultations with UNHCR.

A more detailed study of this draft reveals additional alterations. In general the final text has more nuances than previous versions: for instance, in several places the necessity for the applicant to provide 'evidence' about his case (paragraphs 6 and 8 in earlier draft, Ad Hoc Group on Immigration 1992f) is replaced by 'indications' (paragraphs 7 and 9 in the final text). The final text also makes specific references to the UNHCR in the Preamble stating 'Inspired by Conclusion No.30 of the EXCOM of the UNHCR' and to the Article 1C(5) of Geneva Convention (paragraph 9) which did not appear in the previous version.

On the other hand a list of grounds is added to those previously quoted under 'deliberate deception or abuse of asylum procedures' (paragraph 10 in final text). A direct reference to the Dublin Convention is made in the preamble to this resolution.

The Resolution on a Harmonized Approach to Questions Concerning Host Third Countries

This Resolution was adopted at the same time as the previous one, which makes a clear reference to it (paragraph 1). According to this Resolution the country which can be identified as a third host country must meet a number of criteria. The basis for it is that the applicant has already been granted protection in another country or had an opportunity in another country or at its borders to present an application for asylum (paragraph 2c). Furthermore in such a country the applicant must not be in fear of persecution 'within the meaning of Article 33 of the Geneva Convention' (paragraph 2a) or exposed to torture or inhuman or degrading treatment (paragraph 2b). The latter is an implicit reference to the European Convention on the Protection of Human Rights (Article 3). Finally the returning of an applicant to a third host country must not entail *refoulement* and he must enjoy effective protection against it (paragraph 2d).

The substance of an applicant's claim does not enter into the matter (paragraph 1). Cases will be channelled into the accelerated procedure and the application may not be examined at all if a third host country is identified. However, states have the possibility of not removing the applicant for humanitarian reasons (paragraph 1e). In this Resolution the application of the principle of host third country is also developed within the context of the Dublin Convention (paragraph 3). The final text of this Resolution introduces a reference to Conclusion No. 58 adopted by the EXCOM of the UNHCR at its 40th session (1989) absent from earlier drafts.

The initial text of this Resolution entitled it 'Definition and harmonized application of the principle of the first host country' (Ad Hoc Group on Immigration, 1992b); this was changed to 'host third country' because the Dublin Convention is supposed to regulate first host country issues within the EU after it has been determined whether a third host country exists to which the applicant could be returned. In this instance 'third country' means that it is not a member of the Dublin Convention. This notion of first host country is not completely new in Europe and several states, such as Denmark and Switzerland, have been implementing it for a few years. It was generally referred to as country of first asylum. Past practice has already demonstrated that great caution must be exercised in this matter. It remains to be seen whether this resolution offers enough guarantees against grave mistakes (Melander, 1992). Several areas involve risks for the asylum-seeker. For instance the fact that a country may have signed the Geneva Convention or intends to sign it does not offer a guarantee against *refoulement* (Joly with Nettleton and Poulton, 1992). Moreover the statement that the applicant must have had an opportunity to request asylum in the third host country is so broad that it allows for a variety of interpretations. Would it prevent the practice of considering as acceptable within the meaning of the resolution a country where the applicant has only been in transit, as was done by Denmark (Joly with Nettleton and Poulton, 1992)? In many instances the returning of asylum applicants to a 'third host country' has resulted in their *refoulement* to the country where they feared persecution, and ultimately in their death, disappearance or persecution (Joly with Nettleton and Poulton, 1992).

The final paragraph on future action stipulates that ministers will seek to ensure that their laws are adapted accordingly and mentions regular reviews of the situation in cooperation with UNHCR (paragraph 4).

The Conclusions on countries in which there is generally no serious risk of persecution

These Conclusions are also brought about by the Resolution on manifestly unfounded applications which includes a reference to this concept. They appear to have given rise to controversies and disagreements. In the first place the intended plan was to establish a common list of such countries for all the Twelve and it was abandoned because 'the majority of delegations voiced misgivings for political or diplomatic reasons, or because absence from a list might imply that the country was unsafe' (Ad Hoc Group on Immigration, 1992e). Instead the Conclusions provide guidelines to each individual state in assessing which particular country could be considered as one where there is generally no risk of persecution and will aim through an exchange of information to reach 'a common assessment of certain countries' (Conclusions on Countries). The latter phrase replaced the earlier formulation of 'safe country' which was considered as possibly 'misleading'. It is defined as:

> a country which can be clearly shown, in an objective and verifiable way, normally not to generate refugees or where it can be clearly shown, in an objective and verifiable way, that circumstances which might in the past have justified recourse to the 1951 Geneva Convention have ceased to exist (Ad Hoc Group on Immigration, 1992e, p.5).

The elements to be considered in the assessment of a country in this context 'should be taken together', and include:

— previous numbers of refugees and recognition rates;
— observance of human rights, formally and in practice;
— democratic institutions;
— stability.

A previous draft indicates the documents considered in the discussion preparing the Conclusions and specifically mentions UNHCR paper on the 'safe country concept' (Ad Hoc Group on Immigration, 1992e Annex A 1). But a paragraph referring to a UNHCR veto was removed in the final text and a statement on the desirability to include UNHCR in the assessment process was replaced by giving a 'specific place' to information from UNHCR (paragraph 5 in final text).

The final draft of this Resolution attenuated some of the more adverse elements where asylum-seekers are concerned. As noted above, a common list of countries was not pursued and the terminology of 'safe countries' was dropped altogether. The numbers of refugees and recognition rates are considered one of a number of elements in the assessment in the final text, while they were called the 'most appropriate criterion' in a prior version of the Conclusions. This would have led to grave risks of error as it could become a tautology; a state having awarded low rates of recognition to nationals of a particular country (erroneously, for lack of information, for instance) would then solidly place it in the category of countries where there is generally no risk of persecution and this would make it difficult thereafter to correct the situation. Equally if bad faith governed the operation, a state intent on reducing the number of asylum-seekers to be examined and/or recognized would only need to grant them a low recognition rate and assess the country of origin on that basis.

The Resolution on Harmonization of National Policies on Family Reunification

This Resolution was adopted by the Ministers responsible for immigration at Copenhagen (1 and 2 June 1993). It applies to persons who are lawfully resident with the expectation of a long-term stay but not to refugees under Convention status for whom national guidelines generally already exist. However, it concerns many other refugees granted another status. It appears very severe and seems to reduce the possibility of family reunification to the most restrictive practices existing in Europe.

Conditional admission will be granted to spouses and children of the resident; the maximum age of the children admitted is not fixed clearly but can range 'between 16 and 18' if they have not formed an independent family or an independent life; the criteria determining the exact maximum age are left out. Whenever the family link of the children is not absolutely conventional and biological, admission can become problematic: where, for example children are adopted or the offspring of only one member of the couple. For a spouse to be admitted, the marriage must be recognized by the host member state. It is not stated whether such arrangement as a common-law marriage is considered. Moreover, an unspecified waiting period can be imposed by states as well as other conditions such as the availability of adequate accommodation, sufficient resources and even the existence of sickness insurance (paragraph 16). The British 'primary purpose rule' about marriage and adoptions is envisaged (paragraph 4) thus making it possible to refuse entry if they are deemed as 'solely or principally' contracted to enable entry and residence. Some measure of discretion is none the less left to states to exercise more flexibility in granting admission to family members.

Expulsion

The 'Recommendation regarding practices followed by member states on expulsion of people unlawfully present in their territory' was approved by the ministers responsible for immigration (London 30 November, 1 December 1992). It is not specifically designed for asylum-seekers but may apply to them in some cases. This Recommendation caters for people who 'have entered or remained unlawfully', involve grounds of public safety or national security, or who 'have failed definitively on an application for asylum' without having any other claim to stay (Ad Hoc Group on Immigration, 1992g, 1,2). Moreover, measures are included to make it possible to restrict the personal liberty of people liable to expulsion (section II), for the identification and documentation of the people concerned (section III) and for the prosecution and sanctioning of people who facilitate and harbour illegal entrants as well as those who employ them (sections V and VI). Readmission agreements are to be considered and the agreement between Poland and the Schengen states is cited as a model (section IV).

This Recommendation refers not only to obligations under the Geneva Convention and Protocol but also under other instruments including the 1950 Convention for the Protection of Human Rights and Fundamental Freedoms (section I). It also provides for the right to be represented and an appropriate means to challenge expulsion decisions although the latter is not specified (section I, 7).

Illegal employment and expulsion

The 'Recommendation concerning checks on and expulsion of third country nationals residing or working without authorisation' (Ad Hoc Group on Immigration 1993e) was approved at Copenhagen (1 and 2 June 1993) and again does not specifically tackle asylum-seekers but could affect them greatly. The strongest impact of this resolution is probably the checks it introduces on persons who are 'known or suspected of working without authority including persons whose request for asylum has been rejected' (paragraph 3). Asylum-seekers themselves may be concerned at least in so far that they are not allowed to work in several European states, despite the fact that international human rights instruments are quoted. But in any case these measures will have a profound influence on issues pertaining to personal liberty and democratic rights (Brochman, 1993).

A third recommendation was also adopted related to expulsions, the Recommendation on transit for the purpose of expulsion (London 30 November, 1 December 1992. See Appendix, p.80).

The Clearing House

The creation of a Clearing House or Centre d'Information de Réflexion et d'Echange en Matière d'Asile (CIREA) stemmed from the Ad Hoc Group report approved at Maastricht. It follows logically from the tasks the Dublin Convention sets itself, particularly with regard to the gathering of information. It is set up as an 'informal forum', without any executive powers (Groupe Ad Hoc Immigration, 1992a). It is composed of representatives of the member states dealing with questions of asylum in the Council, officers in charge of implementing policies on asylum and the Commission which is to be fully associated with this work although it is not clear how this will happen. The CIREA's brief is wide ranging and covers several categories of information (Ad Hoc Group on Immigration, 1992d). The CIREA has already made progress and in May 1993 had held five meetings (Ad Hoc Group on Immigration, 1993c). This is what has come under its remit:

(1) A first group of items were already accompanied by detailed guidelines in early documents and seem to constitute the more urgent tasks which have been partly accomplished:

— Information on member states' legislation and rules on asylum, together with national practice (in fact this applies also to some third countries), which was collected; the exchange of information on new and, in part, planned legislation on asylum has been initiated (ibid.);

— Statistics *inter alia* of monthly arrivals of asylum-seekers and their breakdown by nationality which have been to an extent compiled and exchanged but difficulties are encountered on account of diversified compilation techniques in different countries (ibid.);

— Important policy documents;

— Important case law and legal principles including judgments on asylum not only in member states but in the European Court of Human Rights in Strasbourg;

— Assessment of the situation in the countries of origin or of provenance of asylum-seekers to be based on embassies' reports and other information in possession of national administrations; three reports are in an advanced state of readiness out of the five country reports earlier requested.

A compilation of texts on European practice with respect to asylum has been prepared (Ad Hoc Group on Immigration, 1993d) which is deemed to constitute the manual of European asylum practice, but its contents somehow appear to remain limited mostly to Conventions and Resolutions passed at intergovernmental level. The UNHCR databases were examined and a UNHCR representative invited to address CIREA.

(2) A second group of items as yet unexplored include:

— indications available as on early warning;

— routes taken by asylum-seekers and the involvement of intermediaries and/or transport operators;

— matters already harmonized;

— general information on new developments relating to applications for asylum.

The clearing house also considered who should be the recipients of which kind of information. One category of information will be made accessible to the public, and covers legislation and rules on the right of asylum, court decisions, important policy documents and statistics. Others will be decided upon case by case and require a unanimous decision. Dissemination of information (Ad Hoc Group on Immigration, 1993a). Country reports come under the latter category and yet might very well be those requiring the greatest amount of public scrutiny to avoid mistakes. A number of measures related to the implementation of the Convention on the crossing of external frontiers were also taken.

In the area of information one must note the establishment of a European automated fingerprint recognition system (EUROPAC), a European information system, i.e. a computerized list of unadmissible aliens and the creation of the Centre for information, discussion and exchange on the crossing of frontiers and immigration (CIREFI).

Conclusions regarding implementation of the common visa policy were agreed (Copenhagen, 1 and 12 June 1993) and so far nationals of 73 countries require visas for all member states (European Council, 1993). On 23 November 1995 the Justice and Home Affairs Council approved a joint action on a system of airport transit visas for nationals of ten countries: Afghanistan, Ethiopia, Eritrea, Ghana, Iraq, Iran, Nigeria, Somalia, Sri Lanka and Zaire. But this was deemed to fall under the Third Pillar rather than the First Pillar on Community matters (see below) (*Migration News Sheet*, December 1995, no. 153/95–12).

The close periphery of the EU: former EFTA states

The Council of Europe had warned that the harmonization and restriction process undertaken in EU countries might divert flows of asylum-seekers into other European states. Indeed while the phenomenon of refugees in orbit might be helped within the EU it runs the risk of being transferred to third countries (Goodwin-Gill, 1993). This has entailed a protective reaction on the part of former EFTA countries, some of which receive large numbers of asylum-seekers. Sweden, Norway, Austria and Finland applied to join the EU and

referenda in Nordic countries led to the entry of Sweden and
Finland into the European Union (1995) while Norway voted
to stay out, but it could take a long time before all is concluded. In the meantime they cannot join the relevant
Conventions which are open only to EU member states. For a
speedier resolution of this question a parallel protocol is being
prepared to permit non-EU states to accede to the two
Conventions (Ad Hoc Group, 1992b). The attraction of this
harmonization goes even beyond the frontiers of Europe since
Canada expressed a strong interest in accession and contacts
have been established with the United States.

BEYOND RESTRICTIONISM AND SECRECY:
A COMPREHENSIVE STRATEGY

In the period following the Schengen and Dublin agreements,
EU states seem to be preparing a comprehensive and long-
term strategy with the aim of reducing immigration through
cooperation and harmonization of policies.

The first and main leg of this strategy relates to controls and
restrictions on entry. This is demonstrated by the list of priorities established in the Ad Hoc Group report submitted to the
Maastricht Summit and the progress made by the Ad Hoc
Group in tackling each of these. The one area selected for a
'rapid and deep-going' harmonization is that of asylum
(Ministers responsible for immigration, 1991) because it is
considered as the main channel of entry. The six headings
outlined for action in the sphere of asylum are connected with
control and restrictions and the work related to them is well
advanced, as indicated by the resolutions and recommendations studied above: the application of the Dublin Convention,
the harmonization of substantive asylum law, the harmonization of expulsion policy, a clearing house, legal questions and
conditions for receiving applications for asylum. More general
issues of immigration which have been dealt with are guidelines on expulsions, illegal immigration, visas and readmission
agreements with other countries. It suffices to look at all the
measures taken to date to notice that not one of them fails to
address the question of control and restriction of admissions.

This includes restrictions regarding access to asylum procedures. Visa requirements combine with carrier sanctions to make it extremely difficult for refugees to use their fundamental right to seek asylum. The Schengen Agreement and the Dublin Convention ensure that carrier sanctions will be introduced in all EU states and this process has already started. At the same time a common list of countries whose nationals need visas to enter all EU states does not allow for any flexibility. A tight and complete body of measures is being built up, as demonstrated by the frequent cross-references to resolutions and conventions.

Secondly, immigration over and above asylum is not completely ruled out but harmonization is envisaged for selected and controlled cases: humanitarian aims and employment 'taking account of possible requirements in Member States over the years to come' (Ad Hoc Group on Immigration, 1991, p.6) and the preparation of training and apprenticeship contracts, particularly for Eastern European and North African countries on account of their geographical situation bordering Western Europe (Euro-Mediterranean Conference, Barcelona, 27–28 November 1995).

A third area of policy is taken on board within the harmonization plan largely because of its influence on the numbers of potential asylum-seekers/immigrants. This includes the treatment given to asylum-seekers and reception facilities as well as the possibility of obtaining a *de facto* status. Indeed, as stated in the report to the Maastricht Summit (Annex, detailed note, Ad Hoc Group on Immigration, 1991), this could make some countries more 'attractive' than others.

Fourthly, additional long-term measures are mentioned which relate not so much to the limitation of entry but to the prevention of departure from countries of origin. In the report to the Maastricht Summit these are encompassed under an analysis of the causes of immigration pressure, followed by cooperation towards the removal of these pressures. The Edinburgh meeting reiterated and elaborated on the principles guiding this cooperation (European Council, 1992c Annex 5, Part A, paragraph XI). These include working towards the preservation and restoration of peace as well as the respect for human rights in order to reduce flights into asylum but also encouraging and helping displaced people to 'stay in the nearest safe area to their

home'. General aid and economic cooperation leading to social
and economic development are also considered.

This comprehensive plan tackling immigration and asylum
issues corresponds clearly to the outline discussed by the intergovernmental consultations with UNHCR (UNHCR, 1991a).
However, all the measures above, which are not directly connected with control and restrictions at entry, were not
classified as priorities by the Ad Hoc Group and only exist as
statements. It remains to be seen whether they will be concretized or stay in the shape of *voeux pieux*.

More 'openness and transparency'?

A noticeable change has occurred following the signature of
the Schengen and Dublin Conventions. The outcry caused by
both the substance of these Conventions and the secrecy
which surrounded their preparation seems to have hit home
among the governmental circles concerned. The report submitted by the Ad Hoc Group to the Maastricht Summit takes
note of the considerable and critical attention which it attracted particularly because discussions were held behind
closed doors: 'the impression remains that there is insufficient
transparency' (Ad Hoc Group on Immigration, 1991, p.17).
Its main preoccupation stems from the fact that the chances of
success of this harmonization process will be influenced by
'society's perception' of it (Ibid.).

As a consequence the Ad Hoc Group has embarked on a
public relations exercise. This coincides with a general commitment to 'openness and transparency' stated at the Birmingham
and Edinburgh European Councils (1992c) and accompanied
by a plan towards achieving it. The negative results of
Denmark's referendum on the Treaty on Political Union
(12.6.92) may also have played a role in reinforcing this
concern. For the Ad Hoc Group it has meant the regular involvement of the Commission and of the UNHCR in discussions
and in the preparation of policy proposals on asylum; this has
been done through informal consultation and official meetings
such as Troika meetings, the first of which took place on 20
December 1991 comprising representatives of the EU
Presidency, the Secretariat Council, the Commission and
UNHCR (UNHCR, 1991b). A limited audience has even been

granted to some NGOs. Both the Schengen Group and the Ad Hoc Group have invited comments from the Commission, the UNHCR and NGOs such as ECRE (Joly with Nettleton and Poulton, 1992). Contacts have also been established with the European Parliament under the United Kingdom and Portuguese Presidency (Ad Hoc Group on Immigration, 1992b). This greater openness is noticeable in the accessibility of some data and documentation to the public and the concern expressed because it 'does not entirely meet the objective of transparency' (Ad Hoc Group on Immigration, 1993a). Moreover, Resolutions and Recommendations consistently make a reference to the Geneva Convention and New York Protocol and to UNHCR documents, decisions and conclusions. Some of them also mention the European Convention for the Protection of Human Rights and Fundamental Freedoms although one might wonder if it has been carefully considered, as it appears under different names in different documents. It has been quoted also in the Treaty on European Union. The UNHCR is increasingly consulted but these very consultations are confidential so that others are excluded from knowing what either side has said. It is a delicate situation for UNHCR, which is consulted perhaps at the risk of being perceived as legitimating the decisions of Immigration Ministers.

The Treaty on European Union

The institutional framework for dealing with asylum policies in EU countries is likely to change in the future; how much and how fast remains to be seen. It appears that intergovernmental agreements will no longer be a major forum for harmonization on asylum in the EU; this has important implications for the openness of the debate. The greater measure of openness and consultation with the Commission (and to a lesser extent with the European Parliament) follows from the Treaty on European Union. The latter defines three areas of competence called pillars. The first pillar, on community matters, includes the determination of third country nationals needing a visa and the adoption of a uniform format for visas, for which the Commission has a right of initiative and the Parliament that of being consulted. The second pillar, on common foreign and security policy, does not mention

asylum and immigration issues specifically but those are likely
to be broached under its auspices. In this sphere the
Commission is to be 'fully associated' with the Council's work
and the European Parliament is to be informed and consulted
on basic choices in policy. The third pillar deals with justice
and home affairs, and devotes a good deal of attention to immigration and asylum issues. In this area the Commission has
a shared initiative with member states and the European
Parliament is to be informed and consulted. There is a possibility of transferring some questions from the third to the first
pillar, i.e. under community competence through a system of
'*passerelle*' (K9). Asylum issues occupy a privileged position in
relation to the passerelle as the separate declaration on asylum
contained in the Treaty stipulates that questions related to
asylum policies will be a priority for a transfer to Community
matters. It is difficult to surmise when this will take place and
what impact this situation will have on asylum and refugees in
the EU. One could argue that this perspective acts as a major
accelerator for the establishment of a common asylum policy
before intergovernmental hands are tied by the Commission's
interference. On the other hand it may bring about an improvement of the debate in the EU on questions of asylum
and refugees, bringing it more into the open. But what of the
involvement of national parliaments?

So far, the European Union governments seem reluctant to
bring immigration and asylum issues under the First Pillar
(Community matters). Four European Council texts (adopted
on 30 November and 1 December 1994) and two joint actions
have been agreed under the Third Pillar by the Justice and
Home Affairs Council:

— The Resolution on the admission of third-country nationals to the territory of the member states of the European
   Union.
— The Resolution on the limitations on the admission of
   third-country nationals to the territory of the member
   states for the purpose of pursuing activities as self-
   employed persons.
— The Recommendation concerning a framework text of a
   readmission agreement between an EU member state and
   a third country.

— The conclusions on the organisation and development of the Centre for Information, Discussion and Exchange on the crossing of frontiers and immigration (CIREFI).

— A joint action on travel facilities for third-country nationals' school children (30 November 1994).

— A joint action on a system of airport transit visas for nationals of ten countries (23 November 1995).

These proceedings were strongly criticised by the European Parliament, which argues that they are in breach of the Treaty on European Union. (*Migration News Sheet*, November 1995, no. 152/95–11).

The European Parliament does not intend to relinquish its right to be consulted and to have its views duly taken into consideration (Article K6). As for the European Commission it intends to make full use of its right of initiative (Article K3) and put forward a variety of comprehensive proposals on asylum and immigration (Commission, 1994). Moreover it is preparing a report to the Council on transferring at least asylum matters from the Third to the First pillar, as announced by the Commissioner responsible for immigration and judicial affairs to the European Parliament (20 September 1995). A tug of war is thus being fought among the different European Union institutions over the control of asylum issues.

In 1995, the French presidency of the European Union outlined its priorities in the field of asylum and immigration (Conseil, 1995a). These include the completion and implementation of the Dublin Convention, a harmonised application of the definition of 'refugee' within the meaning of the 1951 Geneva Convention, and minimum guarantees for asylum procedures. Other items on the asylum agenda look at the reception of refugees and asylum-seekers. A feasibility study of the European Automated Fingerprint Recognition System is being prepared (EURODAC). Under the immigration heading, admission, removal/expulsion, control of external frontiers, false documents and CIREFI are the main themes considered. The burden-sharing procedure for the admission of persons displaced as a result of conflict is being examined closely. The Spanish Presidency proposed in effect the continuation of this programme with an additional pledge to promote 'legitimacy, efficiency and transparency' in its work.

It also promised to give 'due consideration [to] close and loyal cooperation with the various institutions, especially the European Parliament'. (*Migration News Sheet*, October 1995, no. 151/95–10). The latter commitment seems to indicate that it had so far failed to deliver on transparency and consultation. What is not being pursued actively is the question of root causes of refugee movements. Progress was made in three major areas under discussion.

The Resolution on minimum guarantees for asylum procedures covers the right of asylum-seekers during the procedure of examination, appeal and revision of their application, manifestly unfounded asylum requests, applying at the border, non-accompanied minors and women (Conseil, 1995b).

ECRE and Amnesty International forwarded an immediate response to warn that the Resolution 'in some instances clearly falls short of international standards', namely in the 'exceptions' which it accommodates: on the suspensive effect of an appeal; on the principle that decisions on asylum claims must be taken by a central, competent authority; and on nationals of other EU member states. Furthermore, concern is expressed on the notion of 'safe third country' which in this instance is deemed to lead possibly to orbit situations or chain deportations (ECRE and Amnesty International, 1995). These preoccupations were shared by other NGOs and by UNHCR (UNHCR, 1995a).

The Resolution on burden-sharing with regard to the admission and residence on a temporary basis of displaced persons was adopted on 20–21 June 1995 by the Council of European Union (Conseil, 1995c). This resolution had motivated much discussion and negotiation within the EU and with other fora such as the Council of Europe. The Resolution makes provisions to take into account prior contributions made by member states in the prevention or resolution of the crisis, humanitarian aid awarded in situ, and factors which affect their capacity for reception. It broadly applies to the cases identified by previous resolutions on the acceptance of persons from former Yugoslavia (see below) but excludes those who were admitted prior to the adoption of this resolution. It does not apply to those having committed a crime against peace, a war crime, a crime against humanity or serious common crimes. Despite the limitations of this resolution and its lack of more concrete guidance towards implementation, it establishes the long-term position of the EU on temporary protection and is clearly designed to cater for possible crises to come in Eastern Europe. However, it could be applied also to crises on the southern shores of Europe such as the Algerian situation. This remains to be seen.

Finally, the most prominent measure taken by the European Union is the Joint Position defined on the basis of article K.3 of the Treaty on European Union on the harmonised application of the definition of the term 'refugee' in Article 1 of the Geneva Convention of 1951. It deals inter alia with the determination of refugee status, i.e. criteria and individual/collective determination, the establishment of evidence, the meaning and origin of persecution, situations of civil war and internal conflicts, relocation within the country of origin, refugee *sur place*, conscientious objection, cessation of refugee status. This document and the drafts which led to its finalisation have attracted many comments and criticisms from various bodies such as the UNHCR, ECRE and the Standing Committee of experts in international immigration, refugee and criminal law. They challenge the limitation awarding refugee status only to persons suffering persecution at the hands of the state or with the state's tolerance or complicity. The EU does not accept the claim of somebody who is persecuted by a third party and whom the state is unable to protect. UNHCR demonstrates that this notion is nowhere stipulated by the 1951 Convention (UNHCR, 1995b), while ECRE and the Standing Committee give examples of five European countries where the jurisprudence has not adopted this interpretation (ECRE, 1995; Standing Committee, 1994).

Another contentious question is that of relocation within the country of origin, and it is pointed out by critics that safeguards need to accompany this notion: it cannot apply in the case of state persecution, the route and escape must be safe and accessible, but it must also offer a durable solution with the possibility for the people concerned to settle down and earn a living (ECRE, 1995). UNHCR also warns that a decision concerning the existence of an internal flight alternative 'should be based on a profound knowledge and evaluation of the prevailing security, political and social conditions in that part of the country' and should not be applied in the framework of accelerated procedures (UNHCR, 1995c, pp. 3–4). With regard to civil war and other internal or generalised armed conflicts, UNHCR and ECRE stress that the determining factor must always be that the asylum claimant has a well-founded fear of persecution based on one of the reasons stated in Article 1(a) of the refugee definition, independently of the state of peace or war in his country of origin. A final remark must be made concerning this harmonized application of the definition: it nowhere refers to 'de facto' refugees, nor does it open the possibility of an additional text concerning them, while permitting the heterogeneous practices of states in this respect.

THE EU AND EASTERN EUROPE

Eastern Europe represents a much greater challenge where asylum is concerned. The situation which prevailed in the eighties has altered dramatically. On the whole Eastern European borders were closed under communist regimes and only a small number of people succeeded in getting out. The dominant Cold War ideology made it easy for those to be recognized in the West as refugees. In the nineties all this has changed. The dismantlement of communist regimes had enormous consequences for refugee and asylum issues in Europe. When the demise of these governments started, mass movements of refugees crossed borders or took refuge in foreign embassies (Joly with Nettleton and Poulton, 1992). Borders are now open and Eastern Europeans can travel out of their countries. But Western countries are much less keen to accept them as their numbers have risen dramatically and as no ideological gain can warrant their acceptance now that the Cold War has ended. Their concern is enhanced by the realities and threats which ethnic strife and general upheavals pose in terms of population movement in these regions.

Several initiatives are being taken to deal with this problem: one question is that of asylum-seekers arising from countries bordering the EU or EU-EFTA states who might cross into the latter countries. Another issue is that of asylum-seekers originating from further on and passing through an Eastern European state before entering a Western one.

One measure designed to control entry has been to impose visas on nationals of Eastern European countries, in particular when they are producing or likely to produce movements of population. One critical example is that of former Yugoslavia. In 1993 Greece and Ireland required visas for all citizens of former Yugoslavia; Luxembourg and the Netherlands for all except Slovenians; the UK for all except Croatians and Slovenians; Germany for nationals of Macedonia, Serbia, Montenegro and Bosnia Herzegovina. Among Western European countries, only Italy, Portugal and Spain do not request visas from people from former Yugoslavia (UNHCR, 1993c). Where other Eastern European countries are concerned the imposition of visas keeps increasing. In June 1992, it was announced that a number of countries had been added to the list of those whose nationals needed a visa to enter the EU: Armenia, Azerbaijan, Belarus, Georgia, Kazakhstan, Kyrgyzstan, Moldova, Uzbekhistan, Russia, Tajikistan, Turkmenistan and Ukraine (European Council, 1992a).

Another initiative has been to prepare agreements with those countries. Under Germany's leadership the Schengen Group has already taken measures to deal with these possibilities and has a Protocol of readmission with Poland (March, 1991). The EU states are planning similar agreements in either a bilateral or a multilateral form and quote the Schengen/ Poland agreement as a model:

> Insofar as re-admission agreements do not already exist, consideration should be given to establishing them with appropriate States.[...] In the case of multilateral agreements, these might be along the lines of that between Poland and the Shengen States... (Ad Hoc Group on Immigration, 1992g, p.6).

To deal with countries of origin some limited aspects of policies addressing the causes of population movements are also implemented at EU level:

— the PHARE Democracy Programme is designed to support the process of economic and political reforms
— the Europe Agreements provide for the establishment of political and economic systems based on 'pluralist democratic procedures and practices'. The EU offers the

possibility of Associate and Co-operative membership,
this   has   been   awarded   to   Poland,   Hungary,
Czechoslovakia and Romania *inter alia*
— the Tempus Programme addressed at higher education
aims to help prepare people 'for a market economy'.
(Statement of a Representative of the European
Commission on Preventing Involuntary Migration, CSCE
Human Dimension Seminar on Migration)

The crisis in former Yugoslavia

Where former Yugoslavia was concerned more specific decisions were taken. However, the level of coordinated response
and burden-sharing for the admission of refugees from that
region has remained disproportionately low and slow relative
to the amplitude of the crisis.

At the end of November 1992 EU states adopted a 'Conclusion on People Displaced by the Conflict in the Former
Yugoslavia' (London, 30 November 1992). It is worth noting
that by then more than 90 000 former Yugoslavians had
already applied for asylum in Germany (ECRE, October
1992). Moreover this Conclusion happened after the High
Commissioner for Refugees convened the International
Meeting on Humanitarian Aid for victims of the Conflict in
Former Yugoslavia which endorsed a seven-point humanitarian response plan on 29 July 1992.

In the middle of 1993 EU states adopted a 'Resolution on
certain guidelines as regards the admission of particularly vulnerable groups of persons from the former Yugoslavia' (1 June
1993 Copenhagen). By then there were three million refugees
from former Yugoslavia, the vast majority of whom had remained within ex-Yugoslav territory (more than two million)
while 650 000 were outside the territory of former Yugoslavia.
It is clear that the initiative and the relief efforts have rested
overwhelmingly with the UNHCR and NGOs, despite the
European character of the crisis which could have warranted
decisive action from the bulk of Western European countries
and particularly from the EU states.

The crisis in former Yugoslavia and its three million
refugees brought about a new arsenal of concepts and practices among Western countries' asylum policies.

Internalization

The notion of internalizing refugees meant maintaining them within their area of origin, in Bosnia Herzegovina (Suhrke, 1993); 'safe havens' were created to be guaranteed by and under the supervision of the UN although it initially had not favoured this option. The UNHCR feared at first that this would result in the creation of 'Bantustans' under international military protection; later it felt that the existence of safe havens in Bosnia would help to increase the involvement of NGOs, thus providing more humanitarian aid and human rights protection (ECRE, 1993c). And presently 'safe havens' were proved to be terribly unsafe, as shown in Srebrenica (1995). In both the EU states documents it was declared and then emphasized that displaced people should be encouraged and helped to stay in the 'nearest safe area to their homes' (Conclusion on People Displaced) while assistance would be given to make this possible; any other alternative was to be envisaged only if this proved impossible.

Containment

If internalization was not possible, EU states promoted containment, i.e. a narrow interpretation of regionalization, whereby refugees should remain within the territory of former Yugoslavia. They would make 'provisions to assist with material assistance in supporting reception centres in the former Yugoslavia' (Conclusion on People Displaced). Indeed, large resources in cash and material assistance were sent out for humanitarian purposes in former Yugoslavia (ECRE, 1993a). This circumscribed regionalisation has attracted wider interest and was pursued also by the Inter-governmental Consultations in a substantial working paper on reception in the region of origin (Secretariat, 1994). A trend appears to be setting in.

Temporary protection

Finally, the main concept adopted and implemented was that of temporary protection as stipulated in the Conclusion on people displaced by the conflict (30 November, 1 December 1992), whereby EU states undertook to respect a number of guidelines including: 'Readiness to offer protection on a temporary basis to those nationals of the former Yugoslavia...'

Who was deemed to benefit from temporary protection? According to the Conclusion it must be people coming 'direct' from combat zones, who are 'within' an EU state border and cannot return to their homes 'as a direct result' of the 'conflict and human rights abuses'. This limited considerably access to temporary protection.

Moreover, positive action could be taken to offer temporary protection to 'vulnerable groups' defined as follows by the resolution on certain common guidelines (Copenhagen, 1 June 1993): detainees as prisoners of war in internment camps who are at risk for 'life or limb', people in critical need of medical treatment who cannot obtain it *in situ,* those who have been subjected to severe sexual assault with no assistance possible near their home and generally those who are 'under direct threat to limb or life' and who cannot be protected otherwise. All these categories broadly met UNHCR recommendations although they did not include specifically 'children at risk' (UNHCR, 1993a, p.6) or 'persons who for other reasons specific to their personal situation are presumed to be in need of protection' (UNHCR, 1993b, 5, p.2) but these two groups could be deemed to be covered none the less. The one innovation in this list was that of persons subjected to sexual assault, thus creating a totally new category of people worthy of protection.

This type of temporary protection differs somewhat from the temporary protection awarded in other regions of the world in situation of large-scale influx and for which the UNHCR drew up recommendations: EXCOM Conclusions No.19 (XXXI) on Temporary Refuge in 1980 and Conclusion No.22 (XXXII) on the protection of asylum-seekers in situation of large-scale influx in 1981. As pointed out by Kjaerum (1993) temporary protection had previously been perceived as an intermediate step towards a durable solution, i.e. in the country of entry or as resettlement in a third country. In the case of former Yugoslavs there was no such perspective as the only plan seriously considered was to return refugees to their country of origin as soon as possible. Burden-sharing has proved impossible and this is evidenced by the distribution of refugees whereby 3–4 countries bordering the region host

50–60 per cent of some 600 000 refugees not living in an immediate neighbouring country (Kjaerum, 1993). This was reinforced through the introduction of visas for nationals of former Yugoslavia by most Western European states and by returns to 'first host countries' if the refugees did not arrive directly from their country of origin.

Whereas most European countries made offers of temporary protection, the implementation of temporary protection in Europe was extremely varied. Sometimes new procedures were introduced to deal with it but in the majority of countries some contrivance of existing procedures was used. Moreover, large discrepancies exist where the situation of people benefiting from temporary protection is concerned. Not only does it differ according to the country of reception but conditions of reception may also vary within the same host country as a result of a motley and arbitrary selection of factors such as whether the person has been admitted under a 'vulnerable group' quota or has arrived spontaneously, whether accommodation is provided in a refugee centre or with hosts. Even access to the asylum procedure was not uniform, some countries making it available immediately upon arrival, others suspending it for a few months as in Holland, or two years like Denmark, some refusing it altogether and making it incompatible with a temporary protection status (UNHCR, 1993b).

This raised concern among UNHCR and NGOs as it was felt that temporary protection may in practice entail the withholding of refugee status and exclusion from an integration programme. Particularly sensitive issues are those related to the access to asylum procedures, the right to family reunion, the right to work and training and to education (UNHCR, 1993a). The more general risk involved is that of constituting a precedent which creates second-class refugees, which would also lower protection standards for others (ECRE, 1993a).

Finally, the UNHCR examined the position of refugees from former Yugoslavia *vis-à-vis* the Geneva Convention definition and concluded that many would qualify for refugee status. It recommended applicability of the definition to deserters and war evaders in this particular context. It refuted the argument that the situation of civil war turned people into simple war refugees, as the movements of population were not just the consequences of the war but one of its goals for the purpose of ethnic cleansing. It also argued that even if civilians were the perpetrators of these crimes the persecution was not invalidated by the fact that the legal or *de facto* power was not directly responsible as it either tolerated them or was incapable of preventing them (HCR, 1992). This meant that people under temporary protection would most probably have obtained Convention status if they had been put through the procedure and it was presumably one reason why they were discouraged from so doing. However, those who would not meet the Convention criteria would be entitled to protection on humanitarian grounds. Temporary protection dealt with both categories in the expectation that the conflict would be ended promptly. But what would happen if this were not the case or if the new mapping of the region created problems for returnees?

Already before the negotiation of the peace settlement in Bosnia Herzegovina at the end of 1995, the General Affairs Council of the European Union had stipulated that good will on the part of countries of origin to accept the return of refugees was to be one of the criteria for the granting of reconstruction aid to states of former Yugoslavia (30 October 1995). (*Migration News Sheet*, November 1995, no. 152/95–11).

The Conference on Security and Cooperation in Europe

The EU states have taken the lead in establishing exclusion and control zones. Former EFTA states are taking the hint and frontline Eastern European states are drawn into agreements to further this strategy.

One must ask, however, how far back exclusion and control zones can be pushed. It seems difficult to envisage that any country will accept being the last post, settling all the asylum-seekers who might arrive. It is therefore likely that a consortium of more vulnerable countries will pressurize for a more equitable burden-sharing attitude. There are two possible fora for such a route. One is the Council of Europe which so far has made reports and recommendations on these issues even before governments took much interest in a European view and which has integrated more and more European states. The Council of Europe includes 26 members in 1992, four of which are Eastern European states. In the 1990s, the Council of Europe has raised its profile on asylum issues particularly with regard to Eastern Europe. It has produced numerous reports and recommendations on asylum and refugees, and engaged in discussions with other fora. Its Parliamentary Assembly adopted an extensive Recommendation on the right of asylum which proposes an amendment to the Convention for the Protection of Human Rights and Fundamental Freedoms to include the right of asylum (Council of Europe, 1994). The accession of Russia to the Council (1996) enhances its prominence and it will deserve closer examination where asylum is concerned in the future. However, another more comprehensive forum is the Conference on Security and Co-operation in Europe (CSCE), renamed Organization for Security and Co-operation in Europe (OSCE) since 1995, which augmented its interest in refugee issues with each of its meetings as the developing situation demonstrated the salience of refugees for general security and stability.

The final Act of the CSCE was signed in Helsinki by the High Representatives of 35 European and North American States in 1975. It includes three main areas of co-operation: security and military matters, economy, science, technology and environment, and finally human rights and humanitarian issues. Refugees and asylum do not appear at all in this document. But at the time of the Cold War the CSCE's main goal and responsibility were to regulate a major structural conflict in East–West relations, between the NATO and Warsaw Pact blocs (Lawyers' Committee for Human Rights, 1992).

In the late eighties transformations in the political map of Europe produced new impetus and breadth to the CSCE. Its membership has risen dramatically and in 1993 included 52 states. The dismantlement of communist regimes and the end of the Cold War made it possible and also necessary to take on new issues so that the human dimension of the CSCE has been enhanced. For instance, the so-called Moscow mechanism (1991) enables ten states to act in a case of violation of human rights, and in 1992 a 'consensus minus one rule' was adopted so that the CSCE can take political measures against and without the consent of a state involved in massive violations of human rights (Gibson and Niessen, 1993). The political organs and offices of the CSCE were strengthened and currently comprise: a two-yearly meeting of heads of states, a yearly meeting of the Council of Ministers taking decisions, a trimestrial meeting of the Committee of Senior Officials (CSO) and a Parliamentary Assembly composed of members of national Parliaments meeting once a year. Those are serviced by a Secretariat in Prague, a Conflict Prevention Centre in Vienna and an Office for Democratic Institutions and Human Rights (ODIHR) (Gibson and Niessen, 1993). CSCE documents and agreements are not legally but politically binding on its signatories and have a normative influence (Leite, 1991).

The progress made by issues connected with refugees can be seen over the years. The Paris Charter (CSCE, 1990) lays down an important set of human rights objectives and the Copenhagen document on the human dimension states that the participating states will consult and cooperate in dealing with problems that might emerge as a result of the increased movement of persons but neither mentions refugees as such (Joly et al., 1992). Refugees appear for the first time in the Vienna Concluding Document with a promise to ensure that no one will be subject to exile and that a safe return home will be allowed for refugees (Gibson and Niessen, 1993). Finally, the 1992 Helsinki document (*'The Challenges of Change'*) devotes a section to refugees and displaced persons (clauses 39 to 46 inclusive). It stresses the link between human rights violations and refugee movements, the need to identify and address the root causes of involuntary migration with a view to prevent them and the importance of international cooperation. It recognizes international instruments, in particular the Geneva Convention relating to the status of refugees and the Protocol and makes a specific mention of the work of the UNHCR and NGOs. Finally, it directs the ODIHR to organize a Human Dimension Seminar on Migration, Including Refugees and Displaced Persons which took place in April 1993 in Warsaw. The seminar tackled three themes: preventing involuntary migration, protection, and institution building. The main substantial discussion took place in connection with issues of protection and focused on the question of temporary protection. It was found to be a useful notion if it was combined with burden-sharing. The EU was taken to task about questions of resettlement and aid (ECRE, 1993c). The crisis in former Yugoslavia informed much of the debate.

The theme of migration and refugees is destined to occupy a key position in CSCE discussions as they relate so closely to both human rights and security concerns. The CSCE has the unique advantage of bringing together so many Western and Eastern European states at a time when refugee issues are exacerbated in Europe. It is a flexible mechanism with a tradition of openness; it has in the past relied on publicizing its debates widely for maximum impact through public support (Lawyers' Committee on Human Rights, 1991). It has also given a specific place to NGOs and the UNHCR. This is evidenced by the incorporation of NGOs' submissions to the Helsinki document, albeit not in their entirety (Rudge, 1991). The fact that the CSCE comprises countries of reception, transit and origin (ECRE, 1993c) gives it more balanced orientation than that of, for instance, EU states and offers 'a particularly appropriate platform for a comprehensive approach to the search of durable solutions' (NGO, 1993). The seminar seems to have revealed three groups of countries. The EU states received strong criticism from other states. The former EFTA/Nordic states in part have a more open view on refugees and asylum; such as the Swedish government which submitted a proposal on temporary protection. Central and Eastern European states are concerned about bearing the brunt of the refugee crisis in Europe. The Hungarian delegation for instance calls for more burden-sharing:

With the escalation of the tragic armed conflict in the former Yugoslavia, and the reduction of chances for safe return, tens and tens of thousand of refugees has [*sic*] come to Hungary. We have come to the limits of our economic [*sic*] possibilities, to the limits of our capabilities to shelter more refugees. In this moment it is mandatory to develop a new system of co-operation for international migration (Istvan Komoroczki, 1993, p.3).

It also makes a reference to the refugee definition to be found in the Cartagena Declaration (in addition to the Geneva Convention definition) to which EU states take care to avoid referring as it is much broader than the Convention definition.

The CSCE had been posited in 1991 as one organization which had potential for dealing with asylum and refugee issues

(Joly with Nettleton and Poulton, 1992). This had been confirmed by the Warsaw human dimension seminar examined above. But it is only a first step concretized into mere statements. The role of the CSCE is not yet clear when it comes to practice and implementation.

CONCLUSION

The main trend in Europe, particularly in Western Europe, is still that of increased restrictions on asylum. EU states have kept their lead and march on with an accelerated process of harmonization of their policies. These are taking the shape of a coherent and watertight body of policies which not only indicate general guidelines but also define concepts precisely and give detailed instructions on implementation. It was clearly stated that practices will have to be harmonized alongside procedures. Former EFTA states are following in the wake and will soon accede to the relevant Conventions through supplementary accession instruments. Those which join the EU will have to take on the *acquis communautaire*, thus making their own all the restrictive measures discussed in this chapter. Moreover, readmission agreements with front-line Eastern European countries establish a *cordon sanitaire* preventing entry into Western states. As several of those are queuing to join the EU, the *cordon sanitaire* would presumably be pushed further back.

Is one therefore to conclude that pure and simple restrictionism has won the day in Europe? There are indications that this is not the end of the story, and that it does not present a complete picture of the situation.

In the first place, in the EU, a '*communautarisation*' of policies on asylum is going to take place within the framework of the Treaty on European Union, moving away from intergovernmental agreements. This will entail a greater involvement from the Commission and perhaps more consultation with other bodies such as the European Parliament, the UNHCR and NGOs. Most probably this will open the possibility of greater accessibility to information. One can already notice an effort on the part of the Ad Hoc Group on Immigration to consult with the Commission and the UNHCR and a rapprochement with the European Parliament. But this is a protracted process and despite the reluctance of the European Union Council to make a place for the European Commission and the European Parliament, those have intensified their concern with asylum issues through numerous reports and resolutions. They will undoubtedly continue to press for their increased involvement.

Secondly, it is not excluded that non-Convention refugees will find a place within the harmonization process. Under the terms of the Schengen Agreement and Dublin Convention the possibility of their existence was not even envisaged. But in the report approved at the Maastricht Summit and in several subsequent resolutions and recommendations a commitment is made to the 1950 Convention for the Protection of Human Rights and Fundamental Freedoms (in particular Article 3), while the discretion of states in granting admission for 'humanitarian reasons' is acknowledged. 'This is however not pursued in the harmonised application of the definition of the term "refugee"' (November 1995). Addressing the root causes of movements of populations is now being considered as part of a strategy to reduce immigration. The closer partnership with former EFTA countries certainly runs the risk of bringing every member state down to the lowest common denominator but it could also lead to a more nuanced asylum policy as some of these differ with EU states in their approach.

However, the greatest source of pressure brought to bear against Western states restrictive policies comes from Eastern European countries, as they are potential countries of origin, transit and settlement for asylum-seekers. They might not be placated forever into readmission agreements by development programmes. And they are deeply concerned by potential influxes of population. Their views are best conveyed when they are gathered in a forum which puts EU states in the minority, such as in the OSCE, where they also receive a certain measure of support from some former EFTA countries.

The crisis in former Yugoslavia was a good example demonstrating the utmost reluctance to admit refugees on the part of most Western countries and their shying away from burden-sharing. However, EU states eventually had to pass resolutions committing them to accept certain categories of refugees from former Yugoslavia. Other European states had done so too.

Temporary protection has entered the European scene *à l'Européenne*, that is, with the sole prospect of return as soon as the situation permits. This concept was the answer to the crisis in former Yugoslavia when admissions could no longer be avoided. But it has come to stay. One can already note that it tallies with the stated plan (in the Ad Hoc Group report approved at Maastricht), to allow temporary stays for work, and for training programmes within the framework of a controlled immigration policy in agreement with future labour needs in host countries. Demographers have already noted and mapped out such needs and governments have to take these factors into account. Temporary protection and temporary stays will enable states to allow entry while continuing to pander to some sections of the electorate demanding immigration controls.

The initiative for European coordination on asylum issues has shifted from human rights platforms like the Council of Europe to EU states' intergovernmental groups. Although the former is continuing its work the views of the latter prevail. This has led to concentration on one aspect of asylum policy, namely control at entry and restrictions, away from a comprehensive plan. Sooner or later the limitations of such an approach will be rendered evident, as it can be safely predicted that even the most efficient restrictive practices cannot stop the flight and arrival of desperate people. UNHCR, NGOs, the Council of Europe, the OSCE and some Western European states are preparing the ground for such a development (Christensen and Kjaerum, 1990).

Finally, the central role of UNHCR has been evidenced throughout the crisis in former Yugoslavia alongside NGO contributions. Governments cannot help paying heed to UNHCR and will do so whenever a large-scale crisis arises, because they rely heavily on its services. Inevitably, it also means that UNHCR will keep some influence in European debates on asylum.

NOTES

1. An earlier version of this chapter was published in the *International Journal of Refugee Law*, Vol. 6, 1994, pp.159–193 under the title 'The Porous Dam: European Harmonization on Asylum in the Nineties'.
2. To avoid confusion the EC/EU has almost invariably been referred to as the European Union throughout this volume.

APPENDIX

Ministers Responsible for Immigration
London, 30 November 1992

Recommendation regarding practices followed by Member States on expulsion of people unlawfully present in their territories.

Recommendation on transit for the purposes of expulsion.

Resolution on manifestly unfounded applications for asylum.

Resolution concerning host third countries.

Dublin Convention determining the State responsible for examining an application for asylum submitted in one of the Member States of the European Communities.

Draft Convention parallel to the Dublin Convention.

Draft Convention between the Member States of the European Communities on the crossing of their external frontiers.

4 Reception and Settlement Policies:
A Comparative Study

INTRODUCTION

Most of the attention devoted to refugees in Western Europe tends to focus on asylum issues rather than the question of settlement. However, once refugees have been admitted their situation will be heavily determined by reception and settlement policies in the country of exile. The 1951 Geneva Convention makes a number of recommendations regarding employment and welfare which include rationing, housing, education, public relief and all aspects of health and social security. On an international level, the Universal Declaration of Human Rights advocates satisfactory conditions of living for all (UNHCR, 1979, p.102); in Europe itself statements from the Council of Europe and the European Parliament stress the importance of good conditions of settlement which, it is argued, benefit both the receiving society and the refugees themselves (Bohm, 1985).

Little coordination has taken place in European fora regarding reception and settlement and comparative research remains sparse in this area. The documents dealing with this question tend to focus on a single group of refugees or perhaps several groups but in a single country (for Britain see Joly, 1988a and Srinivasan, 1994). Some comparative studies stretch over Britain and North America (Majka, 1991) but few take in the European experience (Joly and Cohen, 1989; Muus et al., 1993; Joly with Nettleton and Poulton, 1992). This chapter endeavours to fill the gap as it examines reception and settlement policies *vis-à-vis* two substantial groups of refugees, Chileans and Vietnamese in two European countries, France and Britain. These groups and countries were selected so that a comparison would make sense on the basis of the following data: they were admitted in substantial numbers in the two countries; in all four cases the issue of status did not pose a problem so that variables pertaining to the uncertainty of asylum-seekers' situations were eliminated; they were all recipient of a reception and settlement programme. Finally, these factors make them also suitable for a comparison dwelling on the refugees' point of view which is developed in Chapter 7.[1] The present chapter concentrates on reception and settlement so the processes and mechanisms of admission such as the Office Français de Protection pour les Réfugiés et Apatrides (OFPRA) are not considered in any detail. Its data are drawn from the study of refugee agencies' archives, government policy documents and interviews with individuals involved in refugee reception and settlement.

BACKGROUND

The overthrow of Salvador Allende's government by a bloody *coup d'état* in 1973 attracted much sympathy for the thousands of Chilean exiles it engendered. The story of the massive killings, torture and imprisonment is well known. From the early days the French embassy in Santiago opened its doors to refugees for whom the first safe-conducts were negotiated in November 1973. In the first few months following the *coup d'état*, Chilean nationals, who did not need a visa to come to France, arrived at the rate of over two hundred a month (Cimade, 1975); later in 1974 the number of arrivals decreased but remained steady. When visas became necessary in the eighties they were obtainable without difficulty for the purpose of claiming asylum. Chileans benefited from a favourable presumption on their status and from a large movement of support among the French population owing to the existing sympathy for Allende's democratically elected socialist government and because of the brutality of the repression. It soon became clear that a mechanism had to be set up for their reception. It is estimated that 15 000 refugees from Chile settled in France (Bolzman, 1993).

In the UK the situation was more complicated. In 1973 the Conservative government of the day refused to accept Chilean refugees; the British embassy in Chile became notorious for shutting its doors to anyone running for his or her life at the time of the coup and no Chilean was accepted as refugee at UK borders (Joly, 1987b). This action was even justified by Alec Douglas Home who argued in Parliament that no cases had occurred in Chile whereby individuals had been 'under immediate threat of death or injury in the vicinity of the embassy' (*Hansard*, Lords, Vol. 347; *Hansard*, Commons, Vol. 863, Written Answers). It was not until the Labour government came to office in the spring of 1974 that Chilean refugees were accepted. On 27 March 1974 the Secretary for Foreign and Commonwealth Affairs announced in the House of Commons that the Home Secretary would consider applications from Chilean refugees sympathetically (*Hansard*, Commons, Vol. 902, Oral Answers). However, long delays were often experienced before 'letters of consent' and visas could be issued as a 'security clearance' was deemed necessary. Selection criteria for the granting of visas included giving the UK as first choice of country of settlement, knowledge of the English language and ties with the UK as it was considered that those gave individuals 'the greatest claim to come here and [they] can most easily be assimilated' (Browne, 1979, p.29). The condition stipulating links with Britain which would have excluded most applicants was circumvented by the 'adoption' of individuals by trade unions, churches, etc. In Britain too, a broad movement of support emanated from some Christian circles, the Left and the trade unions. Altogether it is estimated that about 4500 refugees arrived and 3000 remained in the UK. By 1979 the Conservative government returned to office and made it very difficult for Chilean refugees to be admitted in Britain.

With the defeat of the USA in Vietnam in 1975 France received a first wave of refugees from Indo-China. Their rate of arrival reached 1000 a month between May 1975 and December 1978 (Masse, 1992) and between 1983 and 1986 a quota was set at about 700 a month. By 1987 there were 115 906 refugees (Assemblée Nationale, 1987) from Cambodia, Laos and Vietnam, out of which 30 000 came from the latter country and more were likely to follow. Priority criteria for the selection of people in camps included having relatives in France, services rendered to France, links with France and knowledge of the French language (de Wangen, 1980) but many others were accepted who did not meet any of these conditions. In 1984 quotas were abandoned in favour of eligibility criteria which prioritized family reunion and humanitarian cases (Fabre, 1984) bringing in between 350 and 400 a month (FTDA, 1984).

In the UK a few hundred refugees had arrived following sea rescues by British ships (there were 650 in 1978). But it was in July 1979 that Margaret Thatcher promised to resettle 10 000 Vietnamese refugees from camps at the conference called by the United Nations Secretary General in Geneva. Subsequently this quota was increased through the acceptance of family reunions. Today there are over 20 000 refugees from Vietnam in the UK altogether with a large majority of ethnic Chinese (Jones, 1983) but practically no Laotians or Cambodians.

In both France and Britain and for both the groups the legal situation was favourable. In Britain Chileans were easily granted either Convention status or Exceptional Leave to Remain without restriction while all the Vietnamese were granted Convention status. In France the Chileans were granted Convention status without difficulty. No quota limited the number of arrivals. Refugees from Vietnam as well as Laos and Cambodia were all granted Convention status or were later accorded preferential treatment for rights of residence, work and social rights on a par with nationals even while keeping their national passport (Masse, 1992). In addition they were granted the right to apply for French naturalization on arrival without any minimum length of residence (Ministère du Travail, 1975).

The fact that the status of these groups did not pose problems has great significance for the process of settlement in several ways. Resources were more readily obtained towards a reception programme and entitlements to social rights concomitant with refugee status were rapidly awarded. From the point of view of the refugees it relieved the individuals from the anxiety which stemmed from uncertainty about being allowed to stay. Chileans had no links with Britain or France prior to their exile and people from Vietnam did not have any relationship with Britain either. However the latter had a long historical association with France where an established community from Vietnam existed prior to their arrival.

This chapter examines the actors involved in receiving and resettling the refugees, the mechanisms created to organize this work, the policies adopted and their implementation.

MAIN CHARACTERISTICS

Reception mechanism

When Chilean refugees arrived in France and Britain there was no established mechanism for the reception of refugees in either country. Refugees had come in earlier periods, sometimes in large numbers, but they had always been perceived as a temporary and unique event. In the seventies a greater awareness developed about the structural nature of the refugee phenomenon and the need for reception provisions in Europe. In both France and Britain structures were set up to deal with the Chileans but each was destined to a differentiated fate. In France it marked the beginning of an institution and a policy which were designed to last. Reception structures were formulated with a view to mapping out the reception of other refugees and asylum-seekers to come; they remained permanent and although thereafter they underwent modifications and elaborations there was no fundamental change. From then on France was equipped with a long-term mechanism for the reception and settlement of refugees. Indeed, it is the same basic structure which catered for the reception of refugees from Indo-China.

In Britain, however, an *ad hoc* scheme was devised for the sole purpose of dealing with the reception of Chilean refugees. For the arrival of refugees from Vietnam yet another mechanism was established with a fairly short-term perspective. Timothy Raison rationalized and justified these *ad hoc* responses to successive waves of refugees, emphasizing the unique character of each event: 'Each refugee situation has its own characteristics and our response has to be geared to these... It would be entirely inappropriate to try and impose a uniform pattern on how each situation is dealt with or to imagine that one could set up permanent machinery to deal with a series of separate and unrelated situations'. (Quoted in Edholm et al., 1983, p.42). Over the years the Vietnamese programme and the agencies handling it changed a great deal and eventually evolved into a more long-term structure: the British Council for Refugees (1981), called Refugee Council since 1993, working with other NGOs.

Central government

In France and Britain central government played an important role in the funding of reception programmes but they did
not assume a direct involvement in the actual reception work.
Government representatives were more heavily committed in
France, administratively, politically and financially. They even
directly intervened on numerous occasions through circulars,
recommendations and instructions to the various bodies concerned. In the UK there was definitely no reception programme defined or directed by the government. One reason
suggested was that it would have implied 'a formal plan, and
therefore goals, standards and commitments' (Refugee
Council, 1989, p.2). Local government remained marginal
and was not awarded central government funding earmarked
for refugees despite the fact that refugees technically fell
under its remit as soon as they were housed in a particular locality. The low profile of local authority initiatives in settlement is more noticeable in Britain where decentralization
endows the local government with a large budget together
with enormous responsibilities and areas of action.

The main actors to be considered with regard to reception
and settlement are undoubtedly the NGOs, as they carried out
the bulk of the work. This is one important common and characteristic feature of the British and French situations. It represents one widespread model of operation but is not a
generalized pattern throughout Europe, as for instance the
central and local states take full responsibility for the reception and settlement of refugees in the Netherlands and
Sweden (Hammar and Lange, 1989; Sayers, 1989). In the USA
the federal government funding to NGOs in charge of those
tasks is complemented with funding to local states and authorities (Zucker, 1983). In addition, solidarity committees for the
Chileans and support committees for the Vietnamese existed
in both national contexts but on the whole British NGOs
relied on them far more than the French ones. Two main
reasons can be advanced to account for this difference: one is
the British tradition of do-gooders and charities; this approach
was actively promoted by at least one of the main NGOs involved (Ockenden Venture, see Levin, 1981). Secondly, the

limited resources released by government made it imperative
to rely on volunteer help while the level of funding was more
generous and more long-term in France.

Coordination committees

In both countries a coordination committee was created to organize the reception of Chilean and Vietnamese refugees.
This proved necessary because of the involvement of several
organizations. In France one NGO whose main concern was
the fate of Chilean refugees, France Terre d'Asile (FTDA), put
forward a plan for their reception and the government accepted the funding of it. A coordinating committee was set up
by the Ministry of Foreign Affairs at the initiative of France
Terre d'Asile which put forward an emergency plan resting on
three components: reception in reception centres (*centres
d'hébergement*) for six months, free medical care according to
an emergency procedure and French language classes
financed by the Fonds d'Action Sociale (FAS) for 180 hours
with audio-visual methods (Cimade, 1975). The coordination
committee, Comité de Coordination pour l'Accueil des
Réfugiés du Chili included official bodies responsible
for refugees in France, that is, UNHCR and the Office
Français pour la Protection des Réfugiés et Apatrides
(OFPRA), the Service Social d'Aide aux Émigrants (SSAE),
NGOs such as France Terre d'Asile (FTDA), La Cimade, Le
Secours Catholique, Le Comité Juif d'Aide Sociale et de
Reconstruction (COJASOR), le Centre d'Orientation Sociale
and representatives of the ministries of Health, Labour and
Finance. Several smaller committees and associations joined
in so that it included altogether over 25 organizations (de
Wangen, 1980). This structure was conceived as a long-lasting
one so that a coordination consisting of the same basic organizations took on the reception of refugees from Vietnam. The
coordination became systematized and formalized as the organizations involved signed a *protocole d'accord* (agreement)
where they shared out responsibilities (de Wangen, 1980):
FTDA was in charge of transit centres (which were introduced
in addition to reception centres), of opening reception
centres and overseeing initial settlement, La Cimade of
French language classes, La Croix Rouge of reception at

airports and Le Secours Catholique and SSAE of individual solutions and unaccompanied minors. A Comité de Liaison coordinated the work (in May 1975) being augmented with the Comité National d'Entraide Franco-Cambodgien, Franco-Laotien Franco-Vietnamien (created by the Ministry of Foreign Affairs) and other committees dealing with medical care, training or other relevant questions. There was no interruption of continuity and this general set-up still obtains today. In addition the NGOs also cater for spontaneous asylum-seekers including those who are not resident in reception centres and campaign on a variety of issues to do with asylum and reception.

In Britain the first Chilean arrivals had been met on a small scale and as more were expected a number of initiatives were taken by several NGOs and sympathetic groups. Initial provisions and monies were provided by NGOs (Christian Aid, British Council for Aid to Refugees (BCAR) and the Ockenden Venture) and the government was prevailed upon to release some funding through two different channels: the voluntary service unit of the Home Office and the Overseas Development Ministry (ODM) operating through the World University Service (WUS) (JWGCh, 1975). The Joint Working Group for refugees from Chile (JWGCh) created in 1974 was responsible for coordinating the work and its broad brief was 'to assist refugees from Chile with reception and resettlement in the UK' (Hutchinson, 1985). In reality it fulfilled a multiplicity of functions and was an active campaigning organization attempting to influence policies of admission as well as settlement and 'publicising the situation in Chile from which the refugees have fled' (JWGCh, 1975, p.35). The JWGCh was composed of NGOs and solidarity committees and included the following organizations: Christian Aid, BCAR, the Chile Committee for Human Rights, the World University Service and the Ockenden Venture, with the subsequent addition of the Chile Solidarity Campaign. It became the Joint Working Group for Refugees from Latin America in 1978. The closure of the Chilean programme was announced on 29 November 1979 by the Home Secretary, William Whitelaw, and the JWGCh was given until March 1981 to wind up (Joly, 1987b).

When a few hundred refugees from Vietnam were brought in, mostly from ship rescues (650 in 1978), they were taken care of by the Ockenden Venture. But the institutional vacuum resulting from 'the failure to develop an institutional memory' (Jones, 1982, p.49) became evident when Margaret Thatcher's government promised to take in 10 000 more in 1979 following appeals by the High Commissioner for Refugees at a United Nations conference (Geneva, 1979). The Joint Working Group for refugees from Vietnam (JCRV) was set up in October 1979 at the initiative of the Home Office and comprised the Ockenden Venture, Save the Children Fund and BCAR. It was a completely new structure and differed from the JWGCh in its membership and mode of operation although some of the NGOs remained in the arena. It was composed of representatives of each NGO with a secretariat of two Home Office staff but within this framework each agency retained its operational independence. Its functions were to manage the selection of refugees from Hong Kong, coordinate the agencies' policies and operations, liaise with local authorities and monitor the progress of the programme of reception and settlement (Refugee Council, 1989). The three agencies divided the work according to geographical areas: BCAR was in charge of the southern third of England and Wales, Ockenden of the Midlands, the North, North and Mid-Wales; Save the Children Fund, later replaced by its daughter organization Refugee Action, took care of Scotland, Northern Ireland, the North-East, East Anglia and part of the Midlands. At the end of the Vietnamese programme the whole structure was modified and became the basis of a structure which is continuing in 1994: the British Refugee Council (today Refugee Council) resulting from a merger between the Standing Conference on Refugees (SCOR, an umbrella organization) and BCAR.

It is interesting to note that the bases of support for the Chileans and for the Vietnamese share the same broad character in France and Britain: in the case of the Chileans the committees which sprang up in both countries drew from numerous sectors of society and organizations of a broad democratic complexion displaying a deep commitment; for the Vietnamese it had a narrower base and its strength lay among a reduced number of Christian and humanitarian organizations and sympathies. The one feature unique to Britain is that of WUS action for Chilean refugees, which was unmatched in other countries.

Reception and settlement policies

Framework

In the first place it is necessary to note that France and Britain are endowed with a developed welfare state and that in both countries refugees from Chile and Vietnam enjoy social rights broadly on a par with nationals in the spirit of the 1951 Convention. Indeed, a similar trend developed in the two countries where until the eighties welfare protection and rights became gradually more comprehensive as gaps were identified by NGOs and refugees' associations (Guillon, 1992). One example will demonstrate this: in France the rule limiting a non-national lecturer's contract to three years (in a university) was waived for Convention refugees. In Britain from 1980 onwards refugees did not need to meet the three years' residence rule before being entitled to a grant for undergraduate studies. From the mid- to late eighties a reversal of the trend took place, reducing refugees and asylum-seekers' social rights (Guillon, 1992) in parallel with the introduction of restrictive asylum policies. Within this general framework the British and French situations differed in several ways.

In France the NGOs which launched reception programmes for the Chileans had a long-term vision and clearly stated the philosophy underpinning this reception: refugees were not to be or made to feel that they were the beneficiaries of charitable individual or local initiatives: they were to be taken on by the national collectivity, that is, fully funded by central government departments; the government accepted '*une prise en charge totale de la part de l'Etat*' (Dienesch, 1973; Ministère de la Solidarité Nationale, 1981). Secondly, the principles and structures forged for the Chileans were conceived to become applicable to all other current and future refugees in France and even to asylum-seekers (de Wangen, 1980). The latter were deemed potential refugees and according to NGOs must enjoy the same social rights so that their integration would not be postponed (Guillon, 1992) on the assumption that their settlement began with their arrival and not when they were to be granted status. Thirdly, refugees were clearly placed in a much better position than labour migrants with regard to their entitlement to all sorts of provisions, even when the latter had had a long residence in France. From the end of the seventies the refugees' legal and social status was far superior to that of labour migrants and it was perceived as such by French people and by the refugees themselves. In France the distinction between nationals and foreigners is a watershed where most things are concerned, including social benefits, as non-nationals enjoy only a limited amount of social rights; refugees are almost the sole exception to this rule (together with European Union nationals).

In Britain, on the other hand, most social benefits were available to foreigners who obtained a long-term residence permit after three years (now four years) of residence. Refugees became entitled to these benefits as a matter of fact by virtue of their long-term residence status like any other foreigner in a similar situation. They were, however, granted some rights from the day of entry, such as the right to work without restriction and the right to receive supplementary benefit (JWGCh, 1975). However, they were no better off than immigrants and were even disadvantaged compared with Commonwealth citizens (and their descendants) who in Britain form the bulk of labour migrants. These could benefit from a substantial amount of funding and provisions specifically destined for them from local and central sources (Candappa and Joly, 1994).

Moreover, although central government funding was granted for reception programmes in both countries the differences in their modalities had a great influence on the implementation of these programmes. In France the government's financial commitment was more secure and longer term: after the guidelines had been agreed by all the parties concerned funding was virtually expandable according to the increase in the number of refugees who had arrived. In Britain funding was negotiated for a fixed amount and a fixed period (six months) and nobody knew what would happen after it elapsed. This made planning very difficult and a long-term vision impossible and led to pragmatic, temporary solutions. In Britain the measures taken were to a large extent resource-led while in France resources followed from the plan. This tends to be in keeping with national models of operating.

It is difficult to find a statement expounding fully the settlement policy adopted in France and Britain. Often this policy derives from practices, and trial and error methods which become policy after the event. It is possible, however, to elicit partial statements and to bring out some of the features which characterize the reception and settlement of the refugees concerned.

'Front-end loading'
In the first place the reception programmes in the two countries could be called 'front-end loading' as resources were made available for a relatively short period after arrival, without planning for 'post-settlement' work. This differed from US front-end loading which could be better described as 'tapering' since the major part of funding was spent early on but was followed by a lighter programme assisting settlement (Majka, 1991). In both the European countries under study, however, some sort of post-settlement provisions were eventually made as an afterthought.

Accommodation or accommodation-employment
Reception was organized in the following manner for the groups under study. When the Chileans arrived in Britain the JWGCh decided not to receive them in camps (JWGCh, 1975). A small reception centre was created in London and subsequently one created in the Midlands but on the whole the refugees were immediately sent to live with British families who offered to have them for a time or to accommodation wherever it could be found through a variety of means. As a consequence the pattern and modes of settlement were dictated by the housing that was available, which in this instance meant mostly the regions where Labour councils, trade unions and other solidarity committees existed (JWGCh, 1975). It also meant regions with a high rate of unemployment. Medical check-ups, language classes and introduction to British society were to be organized (or not) on a local level in a very haphazard fashion. Chileans in France were dealt with in a different manner; the backbone of a policy of settlement was created for their benefit: reception centres were set up in Paris initially and then throughout France by FTDA where the length of stay was targeted as four months for single persons and six months for families. During that period French language classes, a medical check-up, and some introduction to French society/culture were to take place and the

administrative situation (i.e. status) was to be sorted out. The plan was to enable the refugees to find accommodation and employment by the time they left the reception centre; it was clearly stated that the settlement task included finding both a house and a job (Circulaire, 25.01.74). The same model was followed for refugees from Vietnam with a slight modification: from 1976 the newcomers were received in a transit centre for one week or two before being distributed in reception centres throughout France. In Britain refugees from Vietnam were received in reception camps in different regions which performed similar functions to the French CPHs: medical check-ups, language classes, introduction to British society (Refugee Council, 1989). The length of stay in centres was meant to be three months and resettlement was considered as accomplished when accommodation was found for the refugees.

Dispersal

In both France and Britain some kind of dispersal policy was implemented. With regard to Chileans in Britain, dispersal was not the product of a deliberate plan; it happened as a result of the availability of solidarity groups and accommodation, to distribute the Chilean refugees where they were most wanted. Where Vietnamese are concerned, dispersal took place by design as the Ockenden Venture had drawn the guidelines of not more than ten and not less than four [families] in a single locality' (Barrie Denton quoted in Joly, 1988b). This policy was underpinned by three main assumptions: the need to avoid ghettos, better possibilities of local integration for the refugees and more chances of obtaining local authority housing (Jones, 1983). In France dispersal resulted from the distribution of reception centres throughout the country around which refugees where resettled. This initially was not a thought-out strategy: it soon became obvious that the Paris region could not cope with any more refugees from Chile and after 19 centres had been in operation around Paris, ten more were opened in different regions (Cimade, 75). When refugees arrived from Indo-China more centres were created in provincial localities. This time it made part of an overall plan of decentralization (de Wangen, 1980). But this kind of dispersal created clusters of refugees in different localities.

Following this broad outline of settlement policies, I shall now turn to a more detailed examination of their implementation.

IMPLEMENTATION OF POLICIES

Reception and reception centres

It has already been said that reception centres did not play any significant role for Chilean refugees in Britain: the London centre was more of a transit centre with a very reduced capacity, where people stayed a few days or a week on arrival; the Sutton Coldfield centre was also very small. They were found useful but their reduced capacity allowed only a minority of the newcomers to make use of them (JWGCh, 1975). The Chileans' settlement was organized straight away and consisted mostly of finding accommodation. Later on, as it became evident that problems were still unresolved, regional workers were funded to help the refugees with administrative and everyday difficulties, that is, how to claim social security, register with a general practioner, etc. There were 13 staff in the whole of Britain in 1975 including head office staff (JWGCh, 1975).

Reception centres were created for refugees from Vietnam only. There were over forty throughout Britain from 1979 to 1982 (Hitchcox, 1987). Their size ranged from a capacity for 20–700, altogether catering for some 4000 people at any one time. The length of stay went far beyond the projected three months and extended to one year (Jones, 1982). The policy on running the camps was not determined centrally but varied according to which of the three NGOs was responsible as each had a clearly defined outlook and past experience. BCAR mostly ran large centres, offering 1621 places, while Ockenden catered for 997 people in small centres and SCF had centres of about 70 places for 1233 residents in all (Levin, 1981). Staff–inmate ratios differed as did salary levels for two reasons, lack of funding and ethical grounds, as Ockenden for instance promoted a volunteer spirit throughout its work while the Save the Children Fund (SCF) emphasized the professional social work dimension. Two of them (Ockenden and BCAR) separated out neatly reception and settlement as two distinct operations handled by different staff and in different geographical areas. Refugee Action, which took over from SCF, adopted another approach: the very same team which took care of the refugees in the reception camp also settled them. This was also the practice in all the French centres. The outlook and functioning of SCF is closest to that of the French NGOs organizing reception.

In France reception centres or *centres provisoires d'hébergement* (CPH) were created for the benefit of refugees from Chile and thereafter became accessible to other asylum-seekers and refugees. CPH were set up on the basis of an extension to refugees of the social protection usually available to nationals within the spirit of the legislation governing social protection according to Article 185 of the Code de la Famille et de l'Aide Sociale and under instruction from the Ministry of Health and Social Security (Dienesch, 1973). Suitable establishments, that is, existing social institutions such as *foyers de jeunes travailleurs* (young workers' hostels) were 'identified' by FTDA and expanded to become CPH, with the agreement of the local authority, the *préfet*. The reception was to be collective, that is, keeping the families together and two budgetary guidelines were agreed, one for adults and one for children, which meant that funding increased according to the number of residents in CPHs. However, their budget was entirely the responsibility of central government and not of the *département* (French local authority). Towards the end of 1974 there were about thirty CPH, half of which were in the Paris region. Between May 1975 and February 1980 their number rose to 136 in 71 *départements* and they accommodated *inter alia* 39 910 refugees from Indo-China (de Wangen, 1980). Split centres (*centres éclatés*) were created in premises granted by the HLM (social housing) (Circulaire 25.1.74. Annexe l).

It is worth mentioning that transit centres were introduced to cope with the large numbers of refugees from Indo-China in the mid-seventies. In 1980 there were about ten of them, all in the Paris region, where people stayed a couple of weeks before being distributed to reception centres or being settled. In the transit centres basic information was taken down about the refugees and each case examined, noting family groups and departure groups for a CPH; a systematic medical check was also introduced in 1976. Refugees from Indo-China were often in an advantageous position compared with other refugees as an established community already existed in France which enabled about a third of the refugees to find individual solutions with the help of family or friends when they left the transit centre (de Wangen, 1977). Those were assisted by SSAE.

Initially all the CPHs were run by FTDA but from mid-1975 onwards a decentralization took place and a great number of associations were created locally to run the centres (de Wangen, 1980). This entailed variations in their mode of operation. In most cases centres were accessible to other refugees than Chileans and Vietnamese but in a few cases they had residents from Vietnam only (for instance, one CPH near Grenoble). Within the general guidelines of the policies described above (accommodation and employment-led) it is possible to note considerable variation in their implementation. Some CPHs considered that priority must be given to finding employment and accommodation strictly within the six-month length of stay and impressed this upon their residents; a letter was sent every month to the CPH residents letting them know how many months were left before they had to leave (Barrou et al., 1988). Other CPHs were not so concerned about lengthening the stay in order to consolidate the refugees' situation on a broader front: health, training and language (Barrou et al., 1988). Staff and resources effectively differed between one CPH and another as priorities varied and extra funding was sometimes awarded by local authorities. But salaries were comparable throughout on a par with salaries in social institutions. Sometimes the CPH were deliberately 'open' to facilitate contacts between their residents and life outside. This was in the first place determined by the location of the CPH (in a city or in the country), but also by mixing its population; either taking in refugees from a variety of origin and/or sharing premises with residents of the institution used such as young workers (Fle, 1988). Residents could be encouraged to travel on their own to other sites and to organize their administrative errands themselves. In contrast to this, one centre lived in a kind of autarchy owing to its isolated situation and to the fact that it only took in refugees of the same origin (Barrou et al., 1988).

The analysis made by practitioners and researchers in France and Britain is remarkably similar where reception

centres are concerned. Their benefits are acknowledged on
both sides of the Channel as helping the refugees to take stock
of the situation, understanding and regularizing their position, receiving systematic help in a number of areas (health,
language, introduction to the society of reception, finding accommodation and, in France, employment), and also getting
to know their fellow refugees. Reception centres are deemed
essential for a planned settlement and in the case of the
Chileans in Britain the lack of sufficient centres was deplored
(JWGCh, 1975). Indeed, it is argued that the stay in a reception centre is one of the positive factors facilitating settlement
and integration (Simon-Barouh et al., 1992) However, in both
countries NGOs warn about the critical length of time to be
spent in a centre (about six months), beyond which pro-
longed residence may lead to a dependency feeling and a
transit mentality. Other pitfalls are indicated such as the attention which needs to be paid to staff–resident relationships.
Everywhere the family-type relationship sometimes called pa-
ternalistic seems to work best and this militates against large
centres (Barrou et al., 1988). But large centres may have other
advantages such as better language-teaching facilities, making
the acquaintance of a greater number of people and so on.
The issue of staff salaries crops up regularly and presents problems, as in Britain, where there are discrepancies or when they
are too low; discrepancies between one agency and another,
between the centre's staff and the teaching staff (employed by
the LEA at professional rates), between social workers in
centres and their peers in local authority employ (Edholm,
1983). It appears that the continuity between reception and
settlement work is most beneficial as demonstrated in Britain
with SCF centres and in France. Finally, while the flexibility
derived from agencies' autonomy seems valuable, a rational
division of tasks is preferable to a geographical distribution
and it needs to be guided by a clear central policy and long-
term core funding.

Medical care

In France and Britain an initial medical check was performed
in reception centres and proved extremely useful, as conta-
gious and serious illnesses were thus detected from the start;

4–5 per cent of refugees in France from South-East Asia were hospitalized on arrival (Bourdillon, 1986). The two main illnesses screened were tuberculosis and parasites; a general examination was also given. This screening was systematically performed in transit centres in France (de Wangen, 1977) and this was all the more necessary as a good number of refugees did not go through a CPH but joined family or friends soon after arrival. In France a Comité Médical pour les Exilés was created in 1979 which saw some 800 persons a year until 1982 and it became a permanent structure in 1983; 20 per cent of those had been victims of torture (Olcese, 1986). In some of the French reception centres an in-house medical officer nurse or doctor was recruited to follow up the refugees' psychological and physiological condition and give them relevant advice. The success of this provision is always stressed by the staff and residents and this further underlines the importance of adequate and appropriate medical care for refugees. In many instances the settlement difficulties such as language acquisition, coping with studies, work and everyday life can be attributed to health problems and result from specific traumas involved in exile (World University Service, 1986; ADRI, 1988). On the whole there are not sufficiently specialized staff and facilities available to deal with the refugees' health problems and long-term attention is needed in this area. Care must be taken however, to develop a sensitive service adapted to the specificity of the refugee situation and the cultural characteristic of the groups (Gold, 1992).

Language classes

Most of the refugees considered in this study had little knowledge of the language of the country of reception with the exception of a proportion of refugees from Vietnam in France. The acquisition of the language is a *sine qua non* for everyday life and for satisfactory settlement, all the more acute when there is no established community in the country of exile. In France French language classes formed part of the package agreed for the reception of all new refugees, fully financed by the Fonds d'Action Sociale. They were initially organized by La Cimade everywhere through an audio-visual course. Later on there was some diversification according to the centre

involved and several formulae were adopted. When the
Chileans arrived they were awarded between 180 and 240
hours of teaching and subsequently 520 hours were offered in
CPH (UNHCR, 1985b); in some cases up to 650 hours were
financed by the region. In addition to La Cimade specialized
bodies took charge of language teaching and refugees who
did not stay in CPH could obtain coupons entitling them to
attend classes provided by the Alliance Française, the university and others. In Britain there were no language classes
organized or financed centrally for the Chileans, so attempts
at setting them up by settlement workers were described as
'without exaggeration a nightmare' (JWGCh, 1975, p.26).
Provisions were totally dependent on the goodwill of some language schools and local authorities making a few places available free of charge. In British reception centres for
Vietnamese refugees, language classes were taught under the
auspices of the local education authorities (LEAs).

On the whole two remarks can be made which derive from
the French and British experience equally. Whatever language
classes were provided proved insufficient and this is mentioned by all the refugees and agencies concerned; it did not
enable the refugee to learn enough to be competent in other
than manual jobs or to be able to attend advanced courses
(Fle, 1988: Joint Committee for Refugees from Vietnam,
1982). This is particularly the case for refugees from Vietnam
whose mother tongue is very distant from European languages. Moreover the refugees' motivation to learn the language often remained limited on arrival and during their stay
at reception centres for a variety of reasons: health problems,
concern about finding a job and a place to live, culture shock,
trauma of exile, etc. Generally refugees became more aware of
the necessity to learn French or English and much keener to
do so after they had left the centre (JWGCh, 1975; Edholm,
1983; ADRI, 1988; Barrou et al., 1988). Unfortunately at that
point language tuition is not provided on a statutory basis and
the refugees must find individual solutions to improve their
proficiency. It has been noted that in many instances their
level of language considerably regressed after they left the reception centre (Edholm, 1983). Other problems plagued language tuition: the disparate levels of education and aptitude
of the refugees, some of whom had postgraduate education

while others were illiterate even in their mother tongue; in this respect large centres were advantaged in being able to set up classes of different levels (Barrou et al., 1988). One problem confronting teachers and refugees alike was that language acquisition was only one aspect of the task; at the same time refugees also had to learn a culture and its institutions (Hall, 1981). In Britain large discrepancies existed in the nature of the courses themselves as no common scheme was made available.

Housing

It almost goes without saying that a roof over one's head is one foremost priority for refugees in the country of reception. In Britain refugees were considered resettled once accommodation was found, while in France accommodation constituted one of the two requirements to be attained when they left reception centres. As most Chileans did not come through a reception centre in the UK the urgency of the question led to the adoption of *ad hoc* immediate solutions which involved little planning and were often temporary. They mostly had to rely on offers made out of solidarity whether from sympathetic individuals or local authorities (in some London, Northern and Scottish Labour councils). No instructions were issued by central government to local authorities regarding the attribution of social housing to the refugees. A number of units were obtained from housing associations. As a consequence two-thirds of accommodation was found in the private sector with high rents and deposits (JWGCh, 1975). This created serious problems as housing benefits set an upper limit on the rent they would fund and this often entailed the acquisition of inadequate accommodation. Equipment such as furniture and curtains were covered by the special needs social security clause which at that time made it possible for the refugees to obtain a sum on installation.

In the case of the Vietnamese the stay in reception camps made some planning possible and the NGOs extended much effort in obtaining housing; despite the positive effect of the media campaign favourable to Vietnamese refugees, settlement workers had to spend a good deal of time cultivating contacts and negotiating with local authorities to convince them to provide accommodation. This paid off, as figures for 1976–82 show that out of 6255 refugees 4921 were housed by local authorities and 950 by housing associations (Jones, 1982). Thus initial responses were good. Some local authorities were helpful and came forward but as numbers increased there were long delays and sometimes procrastinations which amounted to refusals. By then it was said that housing shortages 'bedevilled' the programme (Jones, 1983, p.448).

The issue was not solely that of accommodation, and concern was raised over the social burden involved once needy populations were settled under the remit of local authorities which were not granted a budget for that purpose. Indeed this state of affairs contributed to the dispersal policy adopted which aimed to avoid overburdening any one local authority, thus hoping to obtain more offers of housing. Some problems resulted from the poor quality of the homes provided (hard-to-let accommodation) but more serious were the effects of the dispersal policy and the accommodation-led settlement programme. Loneliness and isolation ensued, to be compounded by unemployment. As a consequence the refugees regrouped in a few large cities without assistance (Manchester, Birmingham and London) and this led to overcrowding (Robinson and Hale, 1989). As early as 1980 the refugees often expressed their unwillingness to be dispersed (Refugee Council, 1989): they wanted to live in large cities where a Chinese/Vietnamese community existed. NGOs referred to the JCVN for advice but the refugees' wishes still remained unheeded. It was in 1985 that the Home Affairs Committee recognized the failure of the dispersal policy. Competition and problems also developed as a result of the geographical division of responsibility between NGOs, for instance if one NGO was successful in obtaining housing in an area which was not under its remit. More than ten years after the beginning of the programme regroupings have taken place through secondary migration. The main location for refugees from Vietnam is London where housing conditions are far from satisfactory. Apart from overcrowding other problems arise which are typical of those found in large run-down estates: damp, poor heating and ventilation, poor state of repairs and a lack of security. Moreover they are often situated in localities with a high incidence of vandalism, crime and burglary, where the most important issue is fear of attacks and racism (Bell and Clinton, 1992).

In France housing was found by the reception centre staff in the same locality. In the seventies, at the time of the Chileans' arrival social housing (HLM) was systematically provided without problem. This became increasingly difficult since the mid-eighties and delays are often experienced in most regions, particularly in areas where the prosperous economic situation attracts more people, such as the Rhône-Alpes region. These difficulties are compounded by a change in the policy of social housing which aims to avoid 'ghettos' and improve social housing (ADRI, 1988). Where the private stock is concerned high deposits and guarantees combine with expensive rents to make their access difficult. The CPHs have developed a variety of strategies to assist the refugees. To help the refugees save the sum required for deposits they may put aside a proportion of their daily allowance, or allow them to live in the CPH free of charge one month after finding a job. They bring in organizations to offer subsidies and guarantees (DDASS, charities, etc). For the initial expenses of installation some funding is obtainable through the Fonds d'Installation Locale des Réfugiés (FILOR). The existence of an established community has greatly helped the refugees from Vietnam who in one third of cases organized their own accommodation. In general the main problems mentioned were that accommodation was sometimes too dear or too far from the place of work (Barrou et al., 1988).

Along the same lines as mentioned for SCF-Refugee Action, all accommodation was found in the areas surrounding the CPH. Effectively it has meant that the refugees were dispersed throughout France in substantial clusters around the CPH; there were at one point 136 CPH in 76 out of 95 *départements* (de Wangen, 1980). In only very few cases did the *préfet* refuse permission for the establishment of a CPH in his *département*. It appears that CPH have played a role of 'fixation' (Mignot, 1983) and secondary migration has not cancelled this out except in the central region of France (Ajchenbaum, 1981). However, it is worth noting the special attraction of Paris for refugees from Vietnam as '*il n'y a qu'à Paris que l'on peut obtenir tous les loisirs vietnamiens*' (Le Huu Khoa, 1985, p.83). (It is only in Paris that one can find all the Vietnamese leisure activities).

Employment and Training

Although employment is perhaps the one factor with the
strongest bearing on settlement, in Britain it was not incorporated in settlement programmes for refugees. Britain had already
been hit by the economic recession when the Chileans arrived
and this rendered the task of finding a job all the more difficult
as they were left to their own devices. In some cases trade unions
and Labour local authorities provided assistance. What acted as
a compensatory measure was the large programme of further
education funded by the Overseas Development Ministry
(ODM) through WUS. Academics for Chile (a solidarity group)
and WUS approached the ODM for funding in March 1974. The
presence of Judith Hart, Government Minister for the ODM,
who had a special interest in Chile, constituted a decisive factor.
The ODM already had a scheme of grants and fares for govern-
ment-sponsored students from some developing countries and
their families and Chile was one of those countries. This provided the technical lever which was to channel funding for 900
grants to Chilean refugees (WUS, 1986). A grants award committee assessed candidates on the basis of three criteria: they had
to be Chileans in social need, that is, expelled from Chile and in
danger, of a satisfactory educational level, and in a development-
related area (this was left out in practice) (JWGCh, 1975).
Priority went to Chileans in other Latin American countries and
in Chilean prisons. WUS estimated that 63 per cent completed
their course but it warned of the pitfalls which they encountered: grants were approved on a yearly basis and too late in the
year, which made planning difficult and did not leave time for
students to pursue adequate language tuition before starting
their courses (WUS, 1986). The absence of appropriate counselling and specialized health provisions meant that many of the
refugees could not cope and failed to receive the assistance necessary to enable them to succeed.

The refugees from Vietnam were supposed to receive advice
on seeking employment during their stay in the reception
centres. However, they received little help in the concrete task of
looking for a position once they were settled and this coincided
with a period of high unemployment. A number of studies indicate that employment figures are discouraging, particularly for
refugees from Vietnam: an average of two-thirds were unem-

ployed in the South and in the Midlands while this figure rose to 90 per cent in the North (Hitchcox, 1987). Altogether it is estimated that only 16 per cent were employed in 1983 (Jones, 1983). The difficulty in finding employment was aggravated by the accommodation-led settlement policy, as housing was generally provided more readily in areas of high unemployment. The training courses which they could have taken up often required a level of English which the refugees could not meet.

In France the settlement policy aimed to find employment before the refugees left reception centres. The securing of accommodation was linked to employment, as a regular income often had to be demonstrated before housing was offered. This has led several reception centres to employ officers whose task was to prospect for jobs, establish links with employers and sometimes organize a campaign of information for employers in the region (Barrou et al., 1988; Fle, 1988). Some CPH established links with employers which became a regular outlet for refugees leaving the CPH, such as in Rennes and in Grenoble. In addition the positive expectations of employers *vis-à-vis* refugees from Indo-China worked in their favour (Gomane, 1992). The success rate of employment was heavily dependent on the economic buoyancy or slackness in the relevant regions: very good results came from the Rhône-Alpes region, for example, against poorer results in the west (Barrou et al., 1988). However, within this general framework it has been shown that specific measures taken by CPHs to actively seek out positions made a noticeable difference, as in Rennes (Fle, 1988) while in the few cases where the reception centre was simply referring the refugees to structures existing for French people (Agence Nationale pour l'Emploi, ANPE), it did not yield very positive results (Nantes) (Fle, 1988). It is estimated that in 1988, 66 per cent of refugees from South-East Asia had found employment or paid training (Training and Employment, 1987). Other problems involving employment pertain to the type of jobs found which were often low paid, precarious, unpleasant and/or requiring low qualifications (ADRI, 1988). Frequently the first posts taken up meant a downward move in social mobility (Field, 1985) but pressure was put on the refugees to accept them. Some of the refugees were hoping to obtain subsequently a place on a training course or a better job, while others remained resigned to the situation (Barrou et al., 1988). But all of

them stressed that their lack of proficiency in French constituted a major handicap in attaining both these objectives. The
staff of the CPH noted that refugees were less selective in the
kind of employment which they were ready to take up if this was
proposed soon after arrival; if this was delayed they preferred to
wait for a better offer or a place on a training course.

A variety of schemes for all kinds of training are available in
France targeting particular groups of people: young people,
unemployed, women, specific sectors of the economy; for instance the 1984 plan included electronics, crop-farming,
building and foreign trade (Training and Employment, 1987).
The schemes are accessible to nationals and refugees. In addition there are courses and provisions specifically designed
for refugees (Granet and Dijoud, 1975) towards language
proficiency, socio-professional adaptation, and courses to
reach recognized standards for graduates (in their country of
origin); in the paramedical and social work careers a special
course was set up to enable qualified Latin American refugees
to practise (Circulaire, 21.1.74. Annexe IV). A number of state
bodies and NGOs offer financial assistance towards training
and refugees seem to make full use of these facilities.
Nevertheless the employment situation seemed to have wors-
ened in the mid-eighties (FTDA, 84).

Many problems persist in the search for employment which
are also quoted in Britain: language, know-how in job-hunting
techniques, lack of references, poor knowledge of national
idiosyncrasies and cultural difficulties in understanding the
system and its channels, non-transferability of skills, and non-
equivalence in qualifications (Training and Employment,
1987). In France, moreover, there are limitations imposed on
a number of careers: for instance, a quota is imposed on the
number of foreign dentists, doctors and pharmacists (Training
and Employment, 1987). All the civil service careers are also
barred to non-French citizens and this covers an enormous
range, including school teachers. In this respect the British
system of recruitment is more flexible and less plagued with
bureaucracy. It is clear however, that refugees benefit from
help and advice in seeking employment and/or training not
only in the first few months after arrival but for a longer
period of time. A mechanism needs to be set up and developed to provide such a service. Prospecting for jobs demands

proactive dynamic initiatives and a sustained effort on the part of settlement workers. To obtain the best results they must be careful to take into account not only the situation in the particular region of settlement but also the wishes of the refugees themselves.

Post-settlement work

After the initial period of reception and settlement, Chileans in Britain and France fared for themselves. With regard to the Vietnamese (and particularly in Britain) it was shown that they still encountered great difficulty with managing everyday life after leaving the reception centre. Support groups could not cope with the task as they were already overburdened with immediate settlement duties. Severe problems were identified (Refugee Council, 1989 est.); debts, rents arrears, ill-understood DHSS claims, mental illness, serious health problems, neglect of children, wife battering and low school attendance. A formula for 'post-settlement' work was proposed by the British refugee council and some funding was provided. The plan included the appointment of an education adviser and a development officer for Great Britain and the creation of regional refugee councils. The key concept became 'community development' as it had become clear that refugees could find good sources of support among their own community, but this had been hampered by the dispersal policy employed with the Vietnamese (JCVN, 1982). In France several reception centres took it upon themselves to carry out post-settlement work and the settled refugees seem to have greatly benefited from this situation (in the Rhône-Alpes and Rennes for example; Barrou et al., 1988; Fle, 1988). This action was facilitated by the continuity between reception and settlement work which stands out as the better formula.

In France and Britain it is underlined by the parties concerned that there needs to be an official policy taking post-settlement work in its stride and making provisions towards it. The rationale behind front-end loading is supposed to make the refugee ready for work and able to manage rapidly. It has been argued that this might be valid for an educated and skilled population. And it probably also requires a buoyant economic situation where jobs and opportunities are plenty.

This is not the case in the Europe of the eighties and nineties. Post-settlement must be systematized and include provisions for language teaching, retraining, assistance in looking for employment, and specialized medical care.

RECOMMENDATIONS

Although the settlement of refugees in the country of exile is influenced by several factors this chapter has shown that policies of settlement and reception can play a major role in this process. For instance, it is clear that the availability of substantial resources in terms of finance, provisions and staff on a planned, long-term basis makes a difference to the refugee's prospects of successful installation. A number of comments arise from this study on reception programmes and their methods.

Reception programmes were created in France and Britain for refugees from Chile and Vietnam. These programmes remained mostly limited to assistance during the first few months, but sometimes lasted for a year after arrival. The fact that each of these two countries has a fairly broad welfare system that could be extended to refugees awarded these indirect benefits and offered some compensation for the limitations of the programme: benefits included social security allowances, allowances for pensioners and the handicapped, family allowances, study grants, free or subsidized medical care and housing allowance. In both countries the state was mostly involved as a funder while NGOs were contracted to carry out the work.

There is much room for improvement in all the four case-studies examined but features to be retained can be summarized as follows:

— It is imperative that a clear-cut policy of settlement and integration guides the work and determines the resources devoted to these tasks. One mistake must be avoided: an accommodation-led policy should give way to a more comprehensive approach. Strategies have to be developed that build on previous experiences to ensure that lessons are drawn and to avoid repeating mistakes.

— It is essential also that long-term funding must be secured for the agencies which perform the tasks and also the local authorities where refugees settle. Funding has to cover initial reception *and* post-settlement work.

— The principles laid down by France Terre d'Asile that refugees must be taken on by the nation collectively are a *sine qua non* in fostering the best statutory and public attitude to refugees.

With regard to specific areas of reception and settlement, the following is to be noted.

Reception centres

These play a major role in the reception of refugees. Attention has to be paid to the optimum size and length of stay involved (medium to small size, for about six months). Salaries awarded for reception staff have to be on a par with professional rates in the area. A special in-service training has to be incorporated for these staff. The relationship among the staff and between staff and residents must be carefully cultivated. Finally, refugees themselves have to be involved in the work to ensure that their viewpoints are taken into account and that they are not treated as passive victims.

Medical care

It is necessary that medical care should be available free of charge. Appropriate and sensitive medical provisions are needed *in situ* (in reception centres) and in post-settlement situations. The staff involved needs to have specialized training and awareness to deal with refugees and different cultures.

Language

The acquisition of the language of the society of reception is a top priority. The availability of language classes is central to a good settlement policy. These have to be proposed in reception centres but also afterwards as it appears that the need for them continues long after arrival. Language teaching has sometimes to be coupled with training. Classes of different levels are necessary and coaching on the culture and institutions of the society of reception should be incorporated in the programme. Finally, a formula has to be worked out so that an income enables the refugees to sustain themselves while attending courses.

Accommodation

In the field of accommodation, wide dispersal should be abandoned totally and replaced by substantial clusters. When selecting or accepting houses, the situation of the locality and the district have to be kept in mind, paying attention to the employment situation and the state of repairs or dereliction. Accommodation should not be the sole factor included in a settlement policy.

Employment

Employment is another key factor which will determine the success of settlement. Employment officers must be contracted to prospect for jobs and promote the refugees to employers. This is needed before residents leave the reception centres and afterwards. It is not only necessary to be clear and well informed on the region's potential but also on the refugees' skill and aptitudes. Most of all, their wishes have to be taken into account as much as possible.

Post-settlement

Post-settlement work is absolutely necessary to give refugees who need it assistance and advice in a variety of fields: health, housing, employment, language learning and training, education, and everyday life. A strategy for this has to be developed which also takes on board the needs of women, the elderly, children and youths.

The lack of post-settlement work is noticeable in the programmes studied and adversely affects the refugees, especially in the present conjuncture characterized by economic recession, unemployment and a growing public hostility to refugees.

Refugees and community

The refugees' point of view is rarely taken into account and they are little involved in the tasks of settlement. This must be corrected, as evidence suggests that it is an effective factor of success (Gold, 1992). There is a place for positive action towards community formation and the creation of refugee associations in a strategy of settlement.

CONCLUSIONS

Comparative research makes it easier to attain some understanding of the factors underpinning the policies and their implementation. Decisions concerning the programmes rested on assumptions made about the refugees and their relationship to the society of reception. Gaining a better understanding of these interconnections is essential for a critical analysis of the reception policies and structures. For instance, the *ad hoc* approach adopted by Britain results in large part from the fact that each wave was considered as a unique and temporary occurrence. This is one of the factors underpinning the lack of official commitment to a reception mechanism. The French NGOs correctly assessed that a need for reception structures was to endure and this led to the creation of a positive infrastructure. Consequently one contribution to the improvement of reception programmes will be to establish the structural nature of the refugee phenomenon in Europe (despite all attempts to curtail it) and convince decision-makers to take it into consideration.

Many features of the programme in France and Britain followed from a failure to grasp the characteristic features of refugees as distinct social groups and often simply treated them as one would labour migrants. This is demonstrated in both France and Britain by the front-end loading approach devoid of post-settlement provisions. More assistance is needed for refugees than for labour migrants as the former have been totally disempowered, but assistance must also be made available at the right time. The trauma of the flight and exile often produce a temporary state of shock and anxiety which makes it difficult for refugees to be able to function totally on their own after a relatively short period, as one would expect labour migrants to do. It has to be said that reception centres go some way towards facilitating the process of settlement as they give the refugees some time to take stock of their situation. But it is also clear that this is not sufficient: a consistent medical follow-up, organization for the teaching of language and other provisions are necessary for a longer period than so far allowed, as refugees need time to collect themselves before they can take full advantage of these facilities. Other areas of policy would benefit from taking into account the specificities of the refugee situation: the dispersal policy for instance was misguided because its promoters failed to understand the dramatic dislocation of the refugees' social world and hence their acute need to be near their own community. The refugees have lost control over their life perhaps more than any other social group and it is important to enable them to regain this control rather than unwittingly reinforce the 'powerless victim' syndrome. This was often overlooked and thus also the significance of involving them in the reception process, of paying attention to their views and of promoting the formation of communities and their associations. The treatment of refugees as labour migrants may also explain why Britain did not incorporate employment in its settlement policy. Consequently it is not only necessary to carry out research on reception and settlement policies but on the refugees themselves in their diversity and complexity in order to develop appropriate policies in this field.

Finally, the programmes are determined by the government commitment to asylum and refugees which in turn is dependent upon political considerations and ideological conceptions. In Britain humanitarian objectives seem to be pursued as charitable enterprises while in France they are embedded in a universalist philosophy. The latter also incorporates a vision of the integration of refugees into the national collectivity. In both national contexts there are tensions between the refugees' interests on the one hand and the majority society viewpoint on the other. The French and British approaches to the reception and settlement of refugees display differences underpinned by cultural and political characteristics.

The British reception programmes considered in this study are characterized by a pragmatic, *ad hoc* approach. They developed empirically, building over the previous six-month period for which funding had been approved. No grand plan was elaborated but a policy of small steps was adopted. This corresponds to a typically British approach which is expressed through its philosophical tradition of empiricism and its legal system based on custom and practice (case law and precedents). The longstanding tradition of NGO involvement in humanitarian and social work provided a blueprint for the reception of Chilean and Vietnamese refugees. The advantage of such a formula is its flexibility and adaptability but it fails to compensate for the shoestring budget awarded (even if NGO work is reputed to be less costly) and for the impossibility of planning ahead. As a result it led to the repetition of mistakes as the turnover of structures hampered the development of an institutional memory. The Chilean programme in 1974 does not seem to have learned from a previous settlement programme, that of the Ugandan Asians in 1972, and little reference is made by the Vietnamese programme to the Chilean programme.

The reduced level of resources gives rise to additional comments. What is apparent is that it reveals a low level of commitment to asylum and refugees who are powerless in the political structure. This stands in contrast with the resources released for Commonwealth immigrants as these gained political clout through their political rights (the right to vote and to be elected) which they exercised dynamically (Joly, 1995). Undoubtedly the government feared a political backlash if refugees were seen to benefit from special favours. When the Chileans arrived the question of funding could be perceived as sensitive as resources had recently been deployed for Ugandan Asians who despite their British passport had not been welcome in all sectors of British society. When the Vietnamese came, the Conservative government was committed to the halting of immigration and did not wish to be seen as privileging refugees at the expense of British tax-payers. A reception budget was allocated under tight and regular review which was to stop as soon as the refugees fell under the remit of local authorities, on a par with other residents.

One negative result of this approach was that settlement strategies were largely resource-led rather than policy-led and also majority society-led rather than refugee-led. For instance, a strong component of the dispersal policy was the fact that local authorities were more likely to offer social accommodation if they did not feel that they would be overburdened by needy populations without funding to match the extra facilities required. This entailed a serious mistake in the Vietnamese refugee settlement programme. Research and practice have now found that refugees more than any other group need to be near their own in order to cope with their new situation. Researchers spoke of the ethnic group as a 'resource' (Sayfullah Khan, 1977; Dahya, 1974) and practitioners started to work towards 'community formation' (Risdale, 1994). This follows an earlier focus on ethnic group deprivation through discrimination and the redressing of this situation through measures addressing 'social disadvantage' (Candappa and Joly, 1994). Another serious problem is the accommodation-led practice and policy which made the refugees more prone to unemployment. It is not clear why assistance towards employment was not incorporated more decisively into the reception and settlement programme but it constitutes a significant weakness. Perhaps it was simply that the lack of long-term vision of integration only allowed a concentration on immediate needs, which were obviously a place to live.

In France the Chilean programme constitutes a watershed as it ushered in a long-term structure for the reception and settlement of refugees. The French government of the time demonstrated a greater commitment to asylum and refugees, not merely through the funding of a substantial reception programme but also through its consistent administrative and political involvement: instructions through numerous letters and circulars were addressed by the relevant departments to the varied bodies concerned with reception, including local authorities. It sometimes dealt with fairly detailed aspects of refugees' settlement, as for instance the recommendation to avoid settlement in rural areas where jobs outlets were few. It could be argued that the heavy bureaucratic machine intrinsic to the French system required such state interventions to make the programme operable. It does not detract, however, from the state's readiness to foot the bill. This commitment was consolidated and amplified with the admission of a considerable number of refugees from Indo-China. The political conjuncture was also more favourable than in the UK. When the Chileans arrived the recession had not yet set in as severely as in Britain and measures to curtail immigration had not yet been introduced. Moreover the great sympathy of the French population for the Chileans was matched by a government desire to distance itself from the US position. With the Vietnamese other processes of sympathies were activated pertaining to Vietnam's colonial association with France which ensured that the expenses laid out for them did not come under question.

The NGOs nevertheless took the initiative in matters of reception and seem to have negotiated from a position of parity with the government. They are also the major agents which established the principle underlying the position of refugees in France on a par with French citizens in matters of social rights.

At the same time they reflected a traditional French approach to the integration of foreigners (Lapeyronnie, 1993). French NGOs are registered under the Loi 1901: some of them are powerful institutions and in receipt of state funding especially if they are recognized '*d'utilité publique*' (of public interest) as for instance the SSAE. The reception programme formulated in a consensus between NGOs and the government derives from a vision for the integration of the refugees which comprises status, language, health, accommodation and employment. In this national context resources followed from policy and planning. This is no surprise in a country where Descartes expounded the *règles de la méthode* and where plans are part and parcel of government objectives and procedures in the economic and other domains. As a consequence less reliance and dependence were placed on volunteer support, which was welcome when it came forward but did not provoke anxieties when it waned as a solid infrastructure existed. Another characteristic feature of the French programme was that measures to encourage community formation did not form part of the overall plan but were left to local initiatives. This illustrates the discrepancy between the official position on minority communities which it tends to ignore and the changing social practice of sectors of civil society and the minorities themselves. However, this process has a much lower profile than in the UK. The situation has changed considerably in the nineties as separate centres receive refugees and asylum-seekers in a less sympathetic public mood towards the latter, and under a government which is far more hostile to immigrants and refugees. In France strong measures of deterrence were adopted in the late eighties and early nineties. It is becoming increasingly difficult in both France and Britain to maintain and expand the existing reception structures as governments display their reluctance to fund them. This directly follows from deliberate policies to curb the arrival and admission of asylum-seekers/ refugees which is the prevalent trend in Europe in the nineties.

NOTE

1.   Chapter on refugee associations in France and Britain.

5 Local Authority Policy on Refugees: The British Case

INTRODUCTION

A great variety of components contribute to shaping the settlement policies of a particular country towards refugees and it is not the aim of this chapter to enter such a discussion. However, one factor needs to be mentioned which has a direct bearing on the treatment of refugees by local authorities and it pertains to the conception one has of refugees. Are they considered as capable survivors anxious to regain control over their own lives, or as disadvantaged persons unable to cope with their new environment without a lengthy period of public support (Zucker, 1983)? These are two polarized views and there are a number of intermediate positions. The relationship between refugees and local authorities is underpinned by such an understanding; in Britain it has reflected the government's position which, through the media, portrayed the Ugandan Asians as an educated group requiring little assistance (Ward, 1973) and the Vietnamese as possessing useful transferable skills. One must ask whether this was genuinely believed by policy-makers or was directed by the wish to placate hostile voters concerned that extra provisions for refugees might reduce the resources they themselves could call upon (Bristow, 1976). One significant result was that local authorities were broadly asked to take on refugees as though their situation and needs were comparable with that of the majority population.

The relationship between local authorities and refugees in Britain rests on a contradiction. In the first place refugees are implicitly recognized as a population which is likely to draw heavily on local authority provisions because of their particular situation. This assumption has led settlement practices and policies such as the specification of red and green areas for

Ugandan Asians (Bristow, 1976) and the dispersal policy for Vietnamese (Joly, 1988b). The stated aim was to avoid over-burdening local authorities with needy populations, in partic-ular those which were already taxed by a large number of immigrants and ethnic minorities. In some European coun-tries this notion is formally incorporated in the settlement policy so that special provisions and mechanisms are set up to service refugees at local authority level, as in the Netherlands (Sayers, 1989), Denmark (Kormendi, 1989) and Sweden (Hammar and Lange, 1989). It is significant that in those countries specific funding is allocated to local authorities for that purpose. In Britain, on the other hand, while in some cases central government invited local authorities to offer ac-commodation to some programme refugees such as the Ugandan Asians and the Vietnamese, it failed to award con-comitant funding. On arrival or after leaving the reception centre as the case may be, refugees became the responsibility of local authorities in the same way as the majority population. No account was taken of the fact that they often found them-selves in difficult situations and needed additional or differen-tiated assistance. In terms of accommodation this possibly exacerbated the problem as local authorities were under no obligation to offer housing. It could be argued that they might have hesitated to come forward with offers because of the financial implications for other services and departments.

The crux of the matter is the political significance attrib-uted to public assistance to refugees. Refugees had the worst of both worlds. They suffered from being identified as labour migrants (later called ethnic minorities) in the eyes of the public. The large groups of the new refugees (from the Third World) arrived in Britain at a time when politicians feared a white backlash if 'immigrants' were seen to be granted special benefits. As a consequence benefits to refugees were carefully measured for fear that they would be perceived by the public in the same manner. However, for a variety of reasons most refugees could not achieve nor officially share in the special provisions enjoyed by ethnic minorities. The 1966 Local Government Act incorporated a section (Section 11) which made it possible for local authorities to obtain additional funding if they had a substantial number of immigrant resi-dents from the Commonwealth, who constitute the majority of labour migrants in Britain. Urban programmes and inner-city partnerships also made funding available to local authorities largely to meet the needs of ethnic minorities, without naming them. In 1988 there were 57 Urban Programme authorities and 110 authorities receiving Section 11 grants (Home Office, 1988). Moreover, Section 71 of the Race Relations Act stated that local authorities had a duty to make arrangements towards the elimination of 'unlawful racial discrimination' and the promotion of 'equality of opportunity, and good relations between persons of different racial groups'. This was seriously taken up by local authorities in the eighties as it became apparent that an ethnic minority vote had to be taken into account at least on local level; the legacy of empire meant that Commonwealth citizens resident in Britain enjoyed all the political rights of British nationals. The multiplication of community organizations acting as pressure groups and the presence of ethnic minority councillors enhanced this realization (there were 250 councillors and six MPs from the ethnic minorities in 1993). If this was not sufficiently convincing, the urban riots taking place in several British inner cities in 1980, 1981 and 1985 spurred the local authorities into action towards ethnic minorities (Candappa and Joly, 1994). As most refugees do not come from the Commonwealth they did not have the political clout of ethnic minorities and failed to qualify for most of the funding destined specifically for Commonwealth immigrants. This condition was removed from Section 11 criteria in 1993 but at a time when this source of funding had been considerably slashed.

While some refugees first attracted much public attention through the dramatic media coverage of their flight (as with the boat people), others have arrived discreetly and remained unnoticed. But altogether none have been perceived as the special responsibility of local authorities. Front-end loading of the funding devoted to programme refugees and the handing over of the resettlement task to voluntary agencies has made them appear as the sole responsibility of those agencies. On the whole, local authorities often remained unaware of refugees as residents in their locality or as a specific client group. They tended to be confused with other ethnic minority people. Local authorities are ill informed about the refugees' specific character and rights; this is aggravated by uncertainties on their status where asylum-seekers are concerned.

Yet refugees constitute a vulnerable section of the population likely to be in need of public services. Most refugees tend to have arrived in Britain through the whims of fortune and not as a result of a chain migration, as is the case for labour migrants. Consequently they often cannot rely on an already established community to help with their understanding of and adaptation to British society. Few had prior links with Britain in the way of language or culture. This is compounded by the trauma resulting from the circumstances of their flight and exile (Joly and Cohen, 1989). Front-loaded policy proved insufficient and the needs of refugees endured for a longer time than was envisaged, to be met by local authorities (Refugee Council, 1989).

Moreover, the task of local authorities has been rendered more difficult: as refugee populations are newer and in smaller numbers, their existence has not yet attracted attention in many localities. Lack of information on their specific characteristics has prevented the development of appropriate services, particularly as there exists a great diversity among the refugee groups and within the groups which affects the process of adaptation and needs to be taken into account in the delivery of services: language, culture, socio-economic level, level of education, history and reasons of exile, etc. In addition local authorities received almost no central government instructions or recommendations about refugees, with few exceptions: the designation of red and green areas for Ugandan Asian where they respectively should not and could settle, one general policy of dispersal for Vietnamese refugees and an announcement to local authorities that the Vietnamese programme was coming to an end in 1985 which meant that Vietnamese were becoming the entire responsibility of local authorities. To this the Association of Directors of Social Services (ADSS) answered that it was unrealistic (Chant, 1983). As far as non-programme refugees are concerned they are simply meant to fend for themselves. Whereas funding was specifically destined to ethnic minorities from the New Commonwealth under Section 11 of the Local Government Act 1966, most refugees have not been able to benefit from these provisions. Neither were they generally included in the

Equal Opportunity Policies adopted by many local authorities since the early eighties. Refugee agencies became aware of these problems and proposed an extension of the Vietnamese programme specifically to prepare local authorities to provide for refugees.

A survey was carried out in 1988 and early 1989 in conjunction with Sean Risdale from the British Refugee Council when refugees from Vietnam were to be handed over to local authority responsibility. Questionnaires were sent out to all the local authorities with the help of the Association of Metropolitan Authorities. This report analyses the data from all the metropolitan authorities and London boroughs, over 75 per cent of which answered the questionnaires. A few authorities included detailed reports and minutes of meetings about refugees. In addition to this survey, a number of directly relevant documents were consulted (see bibliography). The statistical data quoted in this chapter come from this survey unless indicated otherwise.

AWARENESS OF REFUGEES

There is a noticeable discrepancy between local authorities' awareness of refugees from Vietnam and all the others. All the authorities which stated that they had Vietnamese refugees in their municipality quoted the exact number of families or individuals (except for two London boroughs). The numbers mentioned ranged from 2000, as in Birmingham and Tower Hamlets, to as low as three families, in Oldham. Some authorities provided an extremely detailed demographic breakdown of the refugees from Vietnam together with an exact mapping of their location; one additional report also analysed the characteristic of these populations in one borough, their level of education, the rate of unemployment and the respective groups' aspirations according to their ethnic and geographic origin after providing numerical data (Vietnamese, Chinese, from North and South Vietnam). A large number of authorities appeared to be aware of the distinction between Vietnamese and ethnic Chinese as was generally made evident whenever interpreting was specified. It comes out clearly that the information kept on Vietnamese was detailed. Some authorities even note the movements of the Vietnamese out of their localities and into others; for example they left to go to Leeds, Manchester or 'south', that is, Birmingham or London. In one instance 19 people are said to have moved back into a northern authority (Wirral) because of the cost of houses in the south.

The level of information gathered on refugees from Vietnam stands in contrast with the scarcity of data on other refugees. Seven authorities declared that they did not have any Vietnamese or other refugees; 16 authorities said that they had other refugees including people from Turkey, Iran, Cyprus, Sri Lanka, Africa, Iraq and Eastern Europe (Poles, Hungarians and Czechs), as well as Kurds, Chileans, Bolivians, Ugandans, Somalians, Eritreans and Afghans. But only three of the authorities seemed to know how many these were. In several authorities there appears to be some confusion about the term 'refugee', either being taken to mean purely Vietnamese or to cover all the main ethnic minority groups existing in the UK, that is, Pakistanis, Indians and West Indians.

A number of authorities do not have or know of any refugee in their locality, so that all the answers they give are not applicable, and in one authority only the leisure and community services returned the questionnaire. As a consequence the data retained for analysis in the rest of this chapter concern 40 authorities. A list of authorities is given in Appendix A (see p.139).

SPECIAL POLICY ON REFUGEES

It was in the eighties that local authorities paid heed to Section 71 of the 1976 Race Relations Act and seriously considered the issue of ethnic minorities. From 1981 onwards most local authorities adopted an equal opportunities policy, encompassing two features: as it applied to the authority as major employer, and as provider of services. Several authorities (generally in Labour-controlled councils) also created special structures to ensure that the policy would be carried out (Candappa and Joly, 1994). Since refugees were often an unknown quantity for local authorities, it seemed pertinent to investigate how they serviced such populations; did they treat refugees under general provisions? Did they assimilate them with ethnic minorities under equal opportunities policies? Or did they find that an additional special policy was needed?

Local authorities' approach to refugees is characterized by vagueness and disparity. One could almost argue that it is mostly noticeable through its absence. *Ad hoc* responses rather than a concerted policy appear to be the prevailing trend in all but four of the authorities considered. Three authorities stated that they had a special policy for refugees and one more noted that a policy was being formulated. The purpose of one of the policies is explained as follows: '1. to inform members on the problems facing Refugee Communities in Islington; 2. to recommend that the Council endorse the Refugee Charter for Europe [See Appendix B] and request the Government to implement its proposals; 3. to make proposals for a Council-wide review of services for refugee communities in the borough.' It then proceeds to state the problems facing refugee communities as well as the rights of refugees and asylum-seekers. The issues that the Council could address are listed as: '1. Review by the Council of the accommodation needs of refugee and migrant groups. 2. Remind Council Officers that it is Council policy not to ask for passports when people seek services and that officers should not make assumptions that people from refugee and immigrant communities are "illegal immigrants". 3. The need for greater awareness by Council members and officers of refugee, migrant and immigrant issues.' This indicates to what extent even local authority services are influenced by the tightening up of immigration policies. It is then suggested that the Race Relations Unit be authorized to arrange a public consultation meeting with all the refugee and migrant communities in the borough to discuss key areas of Council services.

Two authorities made it clear that they refused to establish a distinction between government programme refugees and non-programme refugees and treated all equally. However, in at least one case the policy makes a poor attempt to explain in what way they differed. They cast doubt on the legitimacy of non-programme refugees without any grounds, as there is certainly no legal distinction between their respective entitlement to local authority provisions. Some mention a specific effort or/and policy in the initial stages of settlement of specific groups in housing and social services, or simply for the Vietnamese. One authority makes a point of including refugees in its interpretation of the Housing Act and the Voluntary and Community sectors legislation. But the vast majority of authorities have *no* policy on refugees although several refer them to equal opportunity policies or mention being 'sensitive ' to the needs of Vietnamese and of refugees.

Local authorities were asked if general provision or a specific equal opportunities policy would be best where refugees were concerned. In the first place, authorities noted that at the time refugees were mostly serviced by general provisions. This does not come as a surprise since central government encouraged this view and resisted pressure to yield funding for refugees over and above mainstream budgets. But the majority of local authorities argue that refugees should be dealt with both through general provision and *within a specific equal opportunities policy,* including some which propose general provision with special measures for some areas of service such as language teaching or joint work with voluntary agencies for what is more specific. A few make a point of stating that general provisions are inappropriate. On the whole the question of refugees has begun to be incorporated with existing equal opportunities policies; where refugees had not become part of equal opportunities policy, it was felt that such policy was 'sufficiently flexible to accommodate them', as one local authority officer said. However, a substantial minority of authorities (nine of them) make it clear that refugees should be treated under general provisions only. It is no surprise to find that these very authorities do not have an equal opportunities structure and/or equal opportunities officers (mostly Conservative councils but also two Labour) and display consistency in their approach to labour migrants and refugees. Among those which advocate an equal opportunities policy for refugees, three do not possess any such policy but the data do not yield any explanation for this discrepancy. Perhaps it is yet to come. The most common view appears to be that race relations/equal opportunities units are a suitable home for the development of refugee-related policies.

The necessity for a contact person or structures to tackle refugee issues has been emphasized both by the Standing Conference of Local and Regional Authorities of Europe

(SCLRAE) which recommends the appointment of 'a member of the local and regional executive specifically to deal with the problems of refugees resident in the municipality or region' (SCLRAE, 1984, p.3). The Strathclyde study (McFarland and Walsh, 1988) also recommends the creation of a refugee coordinating committee. On the whole, most authorities studied have some sort of contact reference point or mechanism to deal with Vietnamese refugees and much fewer to deal with other refugees. There is a heterogeneity of mechanisms which act as 'contact point'. Several authorities already use their Race Relations and Equal Opportunities Units for this purpose; one has a Vietnamese member on its Advisory Committee for Ethnic Minorities and one authority is considering a refugee unit. In at least two authorities the Race Relations Unit has been active and instrumental in requesting reports from departments and from the Council on refugees; it subsequently drew up recommendations to be acted upon. For some authorities the contact point may be the Community Development Unit or the Grants Unit. For others an *ad hoc* arrangement is worked out according to which a particular Vietnamese/Chinese local authority employee in a department or a liaison teacher in a college is used as a general contact person. In one case various departments have their own contact point and in one housing department several staff are involved in working with refugees. Otherwise, a particular project worker such as the Asian community coordinator or a post funded by Youth and Community Services in the voluntary sector constitute a reference point. Finally, several authorities just use the voluntary sector when need arises.

As refugee agencies have played such a central role in the reception of 'programme refugees' and often assist spontaneous refugees, it is worth investigating the relationship between local authorities and NGOs in this matter. The vast majority of local authorities say that they have been in touch with refugee agencies, naming Refugee Action, Ockenden Venture, Save the Children Fund, the United Kingdom Immigrants Advisory Service (UKIAS), the Joint Council for the Welfare of Immigrants (JCWI) and the British Refugee Council, the last four being mentioned mostly in the London boroughs. Local authorities add that contacts were more intense at the beginning of the Vietnamese settlement and some refer to the seminars organized jointly at the initiative of refugee agencies, as part of the extended programme on Vietnamese. Refugee agencies clearly took the initiative for such links: indeed, refugee agencies consistently approached local authorities at the beginning of the Vietnamese settlement in order to obtain council accommodation. Under the 1984–8 Vietnamese programme they took on the task of mobilizing local authorities and approached them with a view to organizing regional seminars to discuss the issue of Vietnamese refugees (Joly, 1988b).

There is less evidence of such widespread liaising with refugee associations. Many authorities state that they have such contacts when needs arise, adopting a fairly passive attitude towards the refugees and responding when clients come forward seeking services. However, a substantial number, 18 local authorities, have had links with Vietnamese associations (which are deemed to include Vietnamese support groups), as against seven local authorities which have had contacts with another four refugee populations including Iranians, Latin Americans, Tamils and people from the Horn of Africa. This seems to reveal an under-use of the help and provisions that refugee associations could provide, as formulated by one local authority's equal opportunities committee, arguing that one should 'assist self-help community development as one of the most effective ways of settling refugees'. For this reason, it recommended the creation of two community development posts. The key role of refugee associations is also underlined by the SCLRAE, which calls upon local and regional authorities to 'encourage refugees to form associations locally and regionally' (SCLRAE, 1984, p.3). 'Community development' has now become one of the key notions advanced by agencies dealing with the settlement of refugees.

SERVICE DELIVERY

The question of communication is an important one in the delivery of services, and local authorities were asked how they dealt with it given the fact that most refugees speak little or no English. The survey showed that when written translations were needed, a central translation agency was in charge of it or, more frequently, outside services were brought in. They appeared to find this formula satisfactory. Interpreting posed more of a problem and was further commented upon by the authorities. Altogether *ad hoc* solutions were found through a variety of means or the problem was simply left unresolved. Most local authorities rely heavily on people from the Vietnamese/Chinese associations or from refugee agencies on either a volunteer or a paid basis. It brings out the dire lack of provision in this respect. In other cases, a particular employee in a department is able to act as interpreter and may even service other departments' needs. In one situation an original solution was found whereby one of these council employees is paid an allowance to be 'on call' for other departments. This task may occasionally be entrusted to a Manpower Services (MSC) community worker. One authority obtained a post funded under Section 11 of the Local Government Act 1966 in the interpreting unit. In the North, a few authorities made use of services available in neighbouring authorities. The benefits of a joint pool of interpreters to service several contiguous authorities among which Vietnamese are fairly dispersed has led to planning the setting up of one co-financed central interpreting service. As was noted before, refugees who were not from Vietnam were less prominent and only two authorities made use of interpreting services for other groups of refugees. One is left to wonder how communication difficulties were overcome in those cases.

The issue of interpreting is a very serious one and grave problems may result when no interpreter is around; for instance, a social worker found that one Vietnamese mother was giving her contraceptive pills to her new-born baby as she had not understood the doctor's prescription. Moreover it is not sufficient to enrol whoever speaks the language, as appears clearly when, for example, young children were called upon to interpret for the parents in a discussion over their severe marital problems. In some cases refugees have complained that the police or court interpreters had not translated well enough what had been said. Bang (1983) and Finlay and Reynolds (1985) analysed in detail the pitfalls involved in using an untrained amateur interpreter, and the SCLRAE recommends that interpreters must be trained concerning the nature and limits of their role (SCLRAE, 1984). In addition, where refugees from Vietnam are concerned, two entirely different languages are at stake, Vietnamese and Chinese; this has by now become clear to most local authorities. Clearly, many more languages are involved in dealing with other refugees.

EDUCATION AND EMPLOYMENT

Education and employment are two key areas of settlement which may determine its outcome. If these are resolved satisfactorily it may mean that the burden incurred by local authorities is greatly reduced. One could thus assume that they have paid special attention to these questions. This survey reveals that provisions remain patchy and completely inadequate in this sector. Where children are concerned, refugees seem to have been assimilated with other ethnic minority children and made use of general English as a Second Language (ESL) provisions in primary and secondary schools or initially joined a special language centre. Where a substantial number of ethnic minority people were already settled in the municipality some level of ESL provision appears to have been available. But knowledge about the linguistic difficulties of Vietnamese or Chinese speakers was lacking. In localities where no such provisions existed children were simply incorporated into mainstream classes.

For adults, measures have been more disparate despite the fact that this issue is of paramount importance. Interviews with refugees make it clear that the teaching of 'tourist English' is unsatisfactory (McFarland and Walsh, 1988). One council found a part-time English teacher but it appears that this was insufficient. In several cases, the refugees either joined lessons organized by the industrial language unit or by further education colleges. In February 1982, one Education Department took the decision to provide for the needs of the Vietnamese and it was approved: 'a) that provision be made for one hundred hours a week teaching time and b) this was to include ten hours for coordination and liaison.' But this is a rather exceptional measure. Outreach classes were created in some areas as the Vietnamese population was widely dispersed but often had to be cut for lack of funding. Some need for

language classes for the elderly was mentioned and one
request for mother-tongue teaching to children. This applies
mostly to people from Vietnam as little was said concerning
the others. In one case a combined language and vocational
training course was developed. There is certainly a pressing
need for this as illustrated by a sad incident where a new skills
training scheme led to a Vietnamese student having his face
burned because he did not understand safety regulations in
English. Youth Training Scheme (YTS) courses and access
courses for skill-based training had been attended by refugees
including courses in motor mechanics, catering and hairdress-
ing. It was pointed out by one authority that counselling on
the choice of training courses was necessary if it was not to
lead to disappointment because there were no jobs available
in a chosen area. People also needed to be encouraged not to
lose interest in job centres.

The key role of language acquisition and employment have
been amply documented (Field, 1985; McFarland and Walsh,
1988). Employment is not the sole responsibility of councils
but they had helped with a few projects: three fish and chip
shops, a bakery and a couple of restaurants, sometimes using
the enterprise allowance scheme for business start-ups.
Surprisingly enough, several authorities (seven) did not
mention anything under this heading as though no special
need had arisen. Given the high percentage of unemployment
among refugees from Vietnam (between 60 and 80 per cent
according to two local authorities' figures; this is corroborated
by refugee agencies), it seems that education and employment
ought to be paid more attention. Little is said about other
refugees and no employment figures were forwarded by the
survey. However, some studies reveal that other refugees are
not faring very well either (McFarland and Walsh, 1988).

HOUSING

Housing is the one single area where there has been the
largest local authority involvement. Three areas are commented upon by local authority answers to this survey: the provision or non-provision of accommodation to refugees, the
type of housing needed, and communication with refugee

tenants. The Home Office appealed to local authority associations, asking for help in providing accommodation for Vietnamese refugees, and refugee agencies repeatedly contacted housing departments to obtain houses for the refugees. The policy adopted was that of dispersal throughout the country and within authorities. As a consequence a good many local authorities of those surveyed allocated a quota of houses to refugees from Vietnam (21 authorities) but only a few mentioned other refugees. One authority helped to set up a Vietnamese hostel with spaces for relatives on a visit from other cities. The problem has been more acute in London where refugees have in some boroughs been treated under the resettlement of homeless persons programme and under the Homeless Persons Act. The shortage of accommodation in the capital has been compounded by the secondary migration of Vietnamese and Chilean refugees.

In several authorities throughout the country housing departments have appointed an adviser to deal with Vietnamese or other refugees, and this measure appears to be considered by several more as necessary. In one authority the housing department made a successful bid for a housing post for a refugee from Vietnam within the positive action training scheme under section 37 of the 1976 Race Relations Act. The main specific needs noted are primarily linguistic and cultural: communication and requests for big houses to accommodate large families. One particular authority sought to solve the problem by setting an upper limit to the number of families accepted and received a great number of single men; it still had to find accommodation for seven families with more than six members each. Another authority offered nuclear family accommodation units which compelled elder children in the family to live five or ten minutes away. A few authorities note that the lack of suitable and sufficient council accommodation has led to overcrowding through multi-occupancy and has left the refugees at the mercy of unscrupulous landlords. In one case, in 1983, one local authority decided to take into account those cultural needs and endeavoured to offer large houses, stating 'this sub-committee will take into account fully the cultural background of the applicants concerned'. It also made it possible for people to obtain transfers in order to live near one another: 'a conscious effort has been made to house the

Vietnamese families in a cluster pattern so that a group of Vietnamese families residing in the same area could support each other socially and culturally and particularly when they are faced with racial harassment.' It is worth noting that the dispersal policy has been unanimously denounced as a mistake by NGOs and government. Measures to facilitate reunions are a further testimony to this. One authority recommended the adoption of the National Mobility Scheme for those who wanted to change towns to be nearer relatives. Even more serious has been the problem of racial harassment which in several instances has caused the local authorities to move Vietnamese council tenants, as indicated by answers to the questionnaire. Racial harassment is a fairly common complaint as corroborated by a report on the housing conditions and needs of refugees in London (Bell and Clinton, 1992). In a good many authorities, however, housing associations have remained the principal providers of houses for refugees and one London authority has established close working links with housing associations nominating refugees on their lists and has promoted the creation of refugee-run housing associations. In the same borough free premises were lent to a Tamil group. As a conclusion, local authorities seem to concur that the dispersal policy was a failure and had adverse effects on settlement.

SOCIAL SERVICES

The social services department is often the one most sensitive to the special needs of particular client groups (Joly, 1988). Indeed the service they provide is heavily dependent upon good communication and sensitivity to the situation of the people concerned. Several social services departments (seven) have appointed a Vietnamese/Chinese social worker or employee and this helps them tackle the biggest immediate problem they face when dealing with refugees: communication. Social services remain 'hopeless' if they have nobody who speaks the language of their clients, as is stated by one of the local authorities. In terms of specific provisions, attention has been paid to the needs of older people: five authorities set up a luncheon club for elderly Chinese/Vietnamese. One authority opened a day centre for adults and youngsters; another employed three home-helps from Vietnam. Many serious problems have been brought to the attention of social services. The refugees need some advice on their entitlement and the functioning of welfare benefits. Many of them have serious psychological problems and concomitant sequels resulting from trauma; these problems do not always become apparent until months or years after their arrival. Many cases of depression among the elderly, women and even young people including children, were recorded by Social Services in this survey. Local authorities make it clear that these have met with inadequate provisions as health workers could not communicate with patients. Problems of gambling and wife battering and serious conflicts within the family were also mentioned. On some occasions, traditional medical practices from Vietnam had left traces which were mistakenly identified as child abuse and this caused further trauma to parents and children alike. In addition there were problems of homeless people who could not cope and the question of finding housing units for minors.

Altogether social services stressed the inadequacy in granting aid. Other refugees than the Vietnamese are not mentioned. For all refugees an important difficulty appears to be that they do not know their entitlements and do not understand the role of social workers; this is not helped by the attitude of some Social Services Departments which wait for clients to come forward 'as need arises' while a proactive approach is clearly desirable. The scarcity of information on the refugee situation also hampers adequate provisions and the need for special training for social workers dealing with refugees is stressed by the Strathclyde study (McFarland and Walsh, 1988) and by a UNHCR workshop (UNHCR, 1984).

MISCELLANEOUS ISSUES

In a few authorities, leisure and community services stated that they had some library provisions of books in the refugees' languages and library outreach programmes for Vietnamese, Latin Americans, Kurds, Iranians, Greek Cypriots and Africans. A few authorities have helped projects such as one

Saturday school, and camping space for a Vietnamese scout group. In one single authority, one Vietnamese association had made a successful bid to purchase in bulk 500 plots in one piece of land in a cemetery.

A limited number of grants have been awarded for the benefit of refugees. Eight local authorities obtained grants under the Urban Programme and two of them awarded mainstream grants to refugee projects from a variety of departments. Two more grants were given through the housing panel and mention was made of a grant obtained through the European Social Fund. A good many MSC community workers' posts were awarded to refugee agencies, refugee associations and even to support groups. Probably more grants exist which were not recorded but the data obtained from the questionnaire on their own demonstrate little use of grants for refugees through local authorities.

CONCLUSION

The first comment to be made on the results of this survey relates to the overall prominence of refugees from Vietnam in the vast majority of the responses. Indeed other refugees have been little considered or even noticed. This is probably a result of the successive Vietnamese programmes and the efforts made by refugee agencies to draw the attention of local authorities to the Vietnamese. Indeed, most achievements in this respect derived from the intervention of refugee agencies. However the lack of local authority awareness of the existence and needs of refugees remains remarkable. By way of a conclusion, it appears relevant to take up a few of the points made in one local authority report on refugees as it reflects widespread comments made in this survey. In the first place the absence of policies or funding from central government was deplored and a demand was made for 'strong and clear national policies on refugees' as well as central government funding to be made available to local authorities. The report pointed to the need for a provision of experts at national level who could be called upon for advice. It criticized the dispersal policy and described it as altogether detrimental to refugee settlement because it scattered refugees and resources, making the provision of services more difficult and hampering the creation of communities. A whole section of the report was devoted to the question of health, expressing concern for the lack of expertise and provisions concerning refugees' physical and mental health and making strong recommendations to health authorities to remedy this situation.

The only issue that was not broached throughout the responses, one which refugees themselves often tend to raise, was the question of preparation and assistance towards return to the homeland. This might be accounted for by the salience of refugees from Vietnam in this survey, few of whom seem to be interested in returning.

In the nineties some changes have taken place with regard to local authorities' involvement with refugees. Some authorities which did not have any stated policy on refugees adopted one, such as Birmingham's corporate strategy (1993) which defines as its purpose:

— to affirm Birmingham City Council's commitment to responding to the needs of refugees arriving or living in Birmingham;
— to establish a genuine role for refugees in the planning and development of services to address their needs;
— to establish the basic principles upon which the Council will provide its services to refugees;
— to set forth a programme of action for the implementation of these commitments;
— to ensure a coordinated response by the City Council to the needs of refugees.

The strategy adopted by refugee agencies to encourage community development has brought about the creation of regional refugee councils with the support of local authorities and central government. There are four of these in Britain: the Midlands Refugee Council, the Scottish Refugee Council, the Northern Refugee Council and the Welsh Refugee Council. They are supposed to enrol the refugees' own resources and fill a gap in statutory services (AMA, 1994). The 1993 amendment to Section 11 of the Local Government Act 1966 can now include all refugees, as the criterion 'substantial numbers of immigrants from the Commonwealth' was replaced by 'persons belonging to ethnic minorities' (Home

Office, Wright, 1993). Unfortunately this source of funding is
at present being phased out. Central government granted to
local authorities special financial assistance destined for the
provision of services to Bosnian refugees and unaccompanied
minors for 1992–93 and 1993–94 (Department of the
Environment, 1993). But none has been made available
towards the bulk of refugees which come from other home-
lands and this persists as the greatest obstacle to local authorities' interests in refugees. It is still the case that services to
refugees are inadequate and insufficient despite continued evidence that these are required long after arrival. The level of
provision often remains a matter of goodwill dependent on
the assiduity of agency workers, refugee associations and the
presence of a sensitive officer, enhanced by the media coverage over particular groups of refugees (AMA and Refugee
Council, 1994).

APPENDIX A

List of Authorities, England

Greater Manchester
Bolton
Bury
Manchester
Oldham
Rochdale
Salford
Stockport
Tameside
Trafford & Wigan

London
London Barnet
London Bexley
London Brent
London City
London Enfield
London Hackney
London Hammersmith & Fulham
London Haringey
London Harrow
London Havering
London Hounslow
London Islington
London Kingston upon Thames
London Lambeth
London Merton
London Redbridge
London Richmond
London Southwark
London Sutton
London Tower Hamlets
London Waltham Forest
London Wandsworth

Merseyside
Knowsley
Liverpool
St Helens
Sefton
Wirral

Tyne & Wear
Gateshead
Newcastle upon Tyne
North Tyneside
South Tyneside
Sunderland

South Yorkshire
Barnsley
Doncaster
Rotherham
Sheffield

West Midlands
Birmingham
Coventry
Dudley
Sandwell
Solihull
Walsall
Wolverhampton

West Yorkshire
Bradford
Calderdale
Kirklees
Leeds
Wakefield

APPENDIX B

Refugee Charter (undated; 1980s)

LONDON	REFUGEE CHARTER	ARHAG
AGAINST	FOR EUROPE	AFRICAN REFUGEE
RACISM		HOUSING ACTION
		GROUP (LTD)

ARHAG IS ONE OF A NUMBER OF GROUPS IN THE EEC WHO ARE
CAMPAIGNING FOR A CHARTER TO COVER THE NEEDS OF
REFUGEES

The six clauses are set out below

1 Every refugee granted asylum by a member country of the European Economic Community should enjoy the same rights of movement, work and political activity as a national within the EEC.
2 As soon as the application for asylum is submitted, the applicant should be entitled to all welfare rights and benefits.
3 There should be an independent appeals system with legal rights for all those facing deportation, detention or repatriation. The criteria for assessing whether asylum seekers are refugees should be CLEARLY interpreted, taking into account the conditions prevailing in the country of origin.
4 There should be an expeditious processing of applications for asylum. If the application is not disposed of within three months, the asylee should have the right to seek employment and/or study awaiting decision.
5 Refugees, and those with exceptional leave to remain, should be able to obtain permanent residence, and if refused, should have the right of appeal.
6 At all points of arrival, there must be a directory in English and all appropriate languages, with the names, addresses and telephone numbers (including emergency numbers) of advisors, advisory and advocacy services. Their assistance should be available to asylum seekers from any country. All asylum seekers must be offered such information and be given full opportunity, as of right, to contact such services or people.

MIGRANTS, IMMIGRANTS	COMING TOGETHER
& REFUGEES	FOR EQUAL RIGHTS

6 Towards a Study of Refugees in the Country of Exile

INTRODUCTION

The purpose of this chapter is to develop a framework for the study of refugees in Western Europe. It is a complex proposition as, despite the seemingly well-circumscribed character of the project, namely refugees in Western Europe, the nature of the social phenomenon under study requires that one draws from several broad domains of social and political science.

The main issues to be addressed concern the refugee's experience in the country of exile and do not focus on refugees at the point of flight. Therefore theories of settlement and social integration will have to be considered. But one key question must be asked: is there anything specific about refugees in the land of exile which distinguishes them from other migrant groups? To find out about this, one cannot ignore the particularities of the process of migration pertaining to refugees. This draws upon theories of international migration and wider theories of the State. This chapter does not attempt a comprehensive survey of theories on refugees but seeks out from the body of refugee literature and the main debates taking place, instruments towards an analysis of the refugee situation in Western Europe.

Firstly, one needs to define what is understood by the term 'refugee'. Lawyers have spent a long time examining this question and there are a number of international conventions providing precise but differing definitions of refugees. They can be useful as a starting point but more important is finding a sociological definition. This is not easily achieved, however, as there is no clear consensus among sociologists. In one sense refugees also pertain to migration theory within the framework of international migration. However, although migration theory literature is extensive it seldom concentrates on refugees and most often does not even mention them. One needs to search carefully among such literature to find a space occupied by refugees.

INTERNATIONAL MIGRATION: DETERMINING
SOCIETAL FACTORS

The debate on the definition of refugee is mostly developed in relation to the causes of their departure. In this respect differing views are expressed in relation to the societal factors leading to refugee movements. The main question to be asked is whether there are specific factors producing refugee flows which are different from those causing other types of migration and in particular economic migration.

One prevalent view has been that refugee movements are primarily engendered by political factors. As early as 1958 Petersen argued that the determining 'activating agent' (Petersen, 1958, p.261) of refugee movements is the state or some functionally equivalent social institution. This is a notion which recurs as a key feature posited to differentiate refugees from economic migrants and one which will be retained in this study. However, this explanation is not universally accepted without modification as other authors like Richmond (1988) reject the commonly accepted distinction between the economic and socio-political determinants of population movements. A wider range of phenomena can be included such as population movements arising from famine, floods, volcanic eruptions and other ecological disasters which produce 'environmental' or 'ecological' refugees (Richmond, 1994). Cohen (1988) evokes factors contributing to the exacerbation of refugee crises in the 1980s, namely the reduction of aid and social development programmes in the Third World resulting from protectionist measures in the industrialized countries. As a result the increasing importance of North–South tensions caused greater numbers of refugees to come from the South than from the East.

The question of North–South relations and of development must be considered but cannot be reduced to economic parameters and must bring into play a political dimension. In my opinion the most convincing analysis is that of Zolberg et al. (1989) who, while accepting that economic and political processes are interconnected, reassert the predominance of socio-political conflicts in the creation of refugee movements. They argue that under-development and structural violence on their own do not cause refugee movements but only do so if they coincide with political (physical) violence or when the margin of subsistence is so minimal that war entails a large-scale disaster. Such violence can be exercised by the state but also by sections of the population and can result from the breakdown of a society under civil war or foreign invasion. It can be directed at specific groups which are considered as opponents of the ruling group and regime, at ethnic or religious minorities (target groups) or at unselected victims of generalized violence. Zolberg et al. also challenge the assumption widespread among policy-makers that the causes of refugee movements are haphazard and unpredictable, and proceed to establish a typology of the kinds of conflicts likely to provoke refugee flows. In the twentieth century these include the formation of new states through the dismantling of empires and decolonization, ethnic conflicts in these new states, and social conflicts. This typology constitutes a useful tool of analysis for our framework (see below). Moreover, Zolberg and colleagues stress the international or rather transnational character of this phenomenon, as such conflicts result from interconnecting processes both internal and external to the states concerned. Internally displaced populations also have a claim to be called refugees on the basis of those criteria (while this is not possible in legal terms).

INTERNATIONAL MIGRATION: THE MOTIVATION OF REFUGEES

From the point of view of sociological analysis refugees can be defined as a social category determined by their motivation to migrate. What is important is not only the conflict within which populations are caught up and which leads them to become refugees but also their own consciousness of the pressure brought upon them through these conflicts and how this leads or compels them to consider flight as an option. Naturally, to become an option, the concrete feasibility of flight must also exist. The main debate here revolves round the voluntary or involuntary nature of the flight in parallel with the above discussion on 'political' versus 'economic' factors causing flight. For heuristic purposes this discussion is examined separately from the debate on societal factors considered above, but they are closely related and follow the same broad parameters.

The predominant characteristic which has been underlined by a variety of authors is the involuntary character of refugee movements. For Petersen (1958) refugees fall into the category of forced migration subdivided into forced and impelled migration; the former including displaced people physically forced off the land, the latter comprising people in flight. In an extreme situation, refugees could be persons physically expelled from a country like the Palestinians taken by force to Lebanon and prevented from returning to Israel by the Israeli army posted on the border in 1993. But in the vast majority of cases refugees at some point take a decision to leave, albeit under duress. Kunz's definition attempts to cover these points. Kunz (1973) situates refugees within the framework of a push-pull paradigm, migrants being primarily pulled but refugees being pushed. He identifies two broad types of refugee movements, anticipatory refugees who leave before the crisis breaks out (push-permit) and acute refugee movements (push-pressure-plunge) and subdivides his categories according to the form of displacement by flight, force or absence. Kunz argues that the refugee is a distinct social category because he or she moves against his or her will; what distinguishes him or her from the voluntary migrant is 'the reluctance to uproot oneself, and the absence of positive, original motivations to settle elsewhere' (p.130). For Hathaway (1984), disenfranchisement from one's home society in a way deemed fundamental is the common element to all refugee situations. Shacknove (1985) contends that persecution as stipulated in the Geneva Convention fails to capture what is essential about 'refugee-hood' and puts forward a broader criterion: 'the absence of state protection of the citizen's basic needs' (p.277), spelt out as physical security, vital subsistence and liberty of political participation and physical movement. Zucker and Zucker (1987) confirm Kunz's view (1973) contrasting migrants who are drawn to a country with refugees, who are driven. Immigrants are deemed to be propelled by hope to better their life whereas refugees are trying to rebuild some part of what they have lost. The actual self-perception of the move is crucial for an adequate definition of refugee and in no way can the objective circumstances deemed to cause flight be sufficient as a variable.

For other authors the difference between economic migrants and refugees is not clear. Richmond (1988) refutes the distinction between voluntary and involuntary movements and replaces it by two poles designated as proactive and reactive according to the degree of autonomy exhibited by the actors in their decisions regarding migration, with a large number of migrants falling somewhere in between. With regard to reactive migrants (which refugees are, in the main), Richmond (1988) argues that their number is a function of the degree to which 'societal institutions in place *a* [the place of origin] have disintegrated to the point that they are unable to provide a substantial section of the population with an adequate sense of group inclusion, trust and ontological security, qualified by the perception of place *b* [the place of arrival] as capable of reducing the anxiety thus created' (p.23).

Zolberg et al. (1989) reassert the intrinsically involuntary character of refugee movements, stressing the violence involved as the determining feature. However, he postulates the existence of different degrees of 'refugeeness' thus explained:

> For the purposes of sociological analysis the concept of refugee can be thought of as a variable on the basis of an index of danger, which might combine the magnitude of the threat with the probability of its occurrence.

The involuntary character of refugee movements is one main tenet of the approach developed in this chapter.

REFUGEES AND SOME THEORIES OF SETTLEMENT

Having traced the *lignes de force* relating to a refugee definition within the framework of departure, I will now turn to refugee characteristics in the situation of exile and the consequences of their flight.

Psychological approach

A number of psychological and psycho-social studies have considered refugees (Cohon, 1981) which are not systematically reviewed here. What are retained are those which examine in what way refugee settlement may be influenced by the psychological factors involved in the circumstances of flight and psychological studies can make a useful contribution in research on refugee settlement. Social psychology is one area where a large measure of consensus is arising. Social psychologists have examined the impact of the trauma of flight and exile on refugee adaptation, showing that it tends to hamper and delay settlement although, in a few cases, it may precipitate it.

Zwingmann and Pfister-Ammende (1958) present the refugee as obsessed with the past, finding it difficult to think of the future and racked by anxiety. Keller (1975) postulates that three residual psychological characteristics due to trauma and flight affect refugees for years to come, namely guilt, a feeling of invulnerability and aggressiveness; these can manifest themselves in a variety of attitudes including violence towards others or oneself, and boldness to innovate and take risks. Looking at Lithuanian refugees in the USA, Baskauskas (1981) finds that grief for what has been lost is the prevailing sentiment that pervades the refugee experience, causing conservatism. In a study of Chilean exiles in Britain, Munôz (1981) analyses the exile syndrome as *gestalt* and interprets it as a form of bereavement. Eitinger's (1981) study of refugees in Norway explains the combination of causes which lead refugees to be more prone to mental disturbances than natives. One of the most useful contributions is that of Vasquez (1983) who stresses the importance of time for refugees who perceive exile as a transitory phase in their lives. She delineates three main stages: a first stage characterized by trauma and bereavement evidenced through reactions of refusal, retreat, paranoiac behaviour and irritability; a second stage of disorientation *vis-à-vis* institutions and transculturation with an over-valuing of the culture of origin; and a third stage marking the beginning of integration with the lessened strength of myths. Reid and Strong (1987) underline psychological resistance to adaptation due to the traumatic circumstance of flight. Chan and Lam (1987) find that what is central to the refugee experience is a sense of loss and bereavement compounded with a sense of uprootedness from one's socio-cultural milieu and an awareness of forced dislocation from a social network comprising kin, neighbours, friends and acquaintances. They indicate that to an extent the primary preoccupation with the reunion of families delays the adjustment of Vietnamese refugees in Canada.

General theories

On the whole, is is difficult to find general theories on the settlement of refugees to distinguish them from other groups of
migrants and which could be used as a framework for research
on refugees in Europe. Sociological theories on the settlement
of refugees have generally been subsumed under theoretical
studies of immigrants and only recent research begins to treat
refugees as a group *per se*. The main aspect to be retained from
these works is the delineating of stages in refugees' adaptation,
the length and nature of these stages varying according to the
author concerned. Eisenstadt (1954), dealing with the Israeli
experience, conceptualizes four phases in the absorption of immigrants: first, the acquisition of language, norms and
customs; second, the acquisition of new roles; third, a new
identity and the internalization of new values; fourth, participation in institutions of the host society. He indicates that a stage
of desocialization is necessary before resocialization in the
society of reception. However the value of this study remains
limited where refugees are concerned as they are not clearly
differentiated from immigrants. One major drawback in
Eisenstadt's analysis is his assumption that immigrants and
refugees alike want to be 'absorbed' in the reception society
and that the latter also wants to absorb them. No other option
is envisaged. This needs to be challenged where refugees are
concerned. Nevertheless, it is worth noting that he attributes
crucial importance to the 'immigrant's motives for migration'
(p.4) for understanding his initial attitudes and behaviour in
the new setting. This is clearly relevant in a study of refugees.
Ex (1966), studying Indonesian refugees in the Netherlands,
looks at factors promoting or hindering adjustment which
include: the individual personality of the refugee – the basic
personality consisting of the deposit of culture in which he
lived – language in common or differing from the autochthon
– the necessity of continuing with life for himself and his family
– membership of a group of people with corresponding lean-
ings in religion – philosophy of life – politics – interests – possession or not of a family – the feeling of being somebody in
the opinion of others – having a job – the level at which he be-
lieves the autochthon judges him – the level at which the immigrant evaluates the autochthon – the dwelling together of

people suffering the same fate (which is supposed to retard adjustment) – the possession of children and the achievement of a higher standard of living than acquired in the land of origin. Here again, although a group of refugees is being considered Ex (1966) fails to take on board the refugee character of the population he studies and merely treats them as any other group of migrants, without addressing the issue of what is specific to their 'refugeeness'. Richmond (1988) includes refugees in his multivariate model of immigrant adaptation comprising pre-migration characteristics and conditions and situational determinants in the receiving society.

Paludan (1974) points out that one must take into account the different characteristics of the new refugees of the sixties and seventies who mostly come from outside Europe. Stein (1981) is one of the few who addresses refugees *per se* as he specifies the existence of a first stage, taking stock of what has been lost before going on, thus differentiating refugees from other migrants. He outlines a pattern of refugee adjustment over time, divided into four stages across a spectrum of occupational and economic adjustment: (1) the initial arrival period of the first few months during which the refugees are confronted with the reality of what has been lost (their occupational and social status, their culture, their identity, their habits), (2) the first and second years during which refugees display an impressive drive to recover what has been lost to rebuild their lives, (3) after four to five years the refugee has completed the major part of adjustment; if the goal is not near at hand now, the refugee is likely to abandon the effort, (4) a decade or more later he will have achieved a certain stability; the general effect of exodus is found to produce lower status, and has an impact on social adjustment, cultural adjustment and mental health. What Stein fails to point out is that the respective length of each stage is likely to vary as a result of a number of factors but also that different social types of refugees may not go through these particular stages. Montero (1979) develops what he calls a theory of spontaneous international migration which is a model of Vietnamese immigration and resettlement in the USA. He argues that these refugees, while being 'acute' according to Kunz's typology, behave as 'anticipatory' refugees (who leave before the crisis breaks out). He postulates three phases: (1) the homeland, temporary camps and private sponsorship, (2) ethnic enclaves in the land of resettlement, (3) assimilation. It is difficult, however, to generalize this analysis to make it valid for other categories of refugee groups.

AN ANALYSIS OF REFUGEES IN THE LAND OF EXILE

It is not easy to determine what differentiates refugees from other migrants and no definite agreement has been reached on this point. However, it appears that when all the variables have been examined, what remains is that refugees had to leave as a result of factors which in the last analysis were not primarily economic and they did not make a decision with primarily positive connotations. What all refugees have in common is that they left their country of origin because a dramatic change jeopardized the life they were leading, although this change need not always be sudden. If things had continued as before the change, they would have stayed. Their move also involved a collective character. In that, they differ from so-called economic migrants as the latter have an individual project to change their life circumstances to improve them. This brings us back to the involuntary character of refugee movements as expounded by Kunz (1973) and Zolberg et al. (1989).

As a consequence, economic migrants can prepare themselves psychologically and materially for the move because they were able to plan it. The vast majority of refugees did not have a chance to do so and this adds to the often precipitous and traumatic circumstances of their flight, sometimes also fraught with experiences of detention camps, severe persecution, prison, torture and fear of death. Following from this many, although not all, refugees are dispersed at the whim of fate so that the discrepancy between their society of origin and of reception is likely to be greater unless they are able to remain in the vicinity of their country of origin. This is particularly the case of many refugees coming from the Third World to Europe. As far as these refugees are concerned they have traditionally been selected by the distance and the expense of reaching Europe. This means that Third World refugee groups arriving in Europe will include a larger proportion of educated and middle-class persons because of their know-how and resources. This does not apply to current refugees from former Yugoslavia. But in any case it would be less valid for refugees resettled through international agencies and NGOs; moreover, the popularization of air transport is making Europe accessible to broader categories of people, from far-away lands. Refugees display differentiated patterns of settlement in the country of reception: sometimes there is a greater willingness to adapt to the new society as fast as possible, sometimes a long-drawn resistance to change and attachment to the past. Similarly refugees can display a very passive and resigned attitude alongside great daring.

Most of the research concerning refugees considers them either in their land of origin and in flight or in the land of reception. The twain do not meet and it appears that one is dealing with two completely discrete situations. I will argue that such an approach makes it impossible to progress in the understanding of the refugee situation. Although the past informs the present in any migration, the overriding importance of the past to determine and understand refugee settlement is unique. It is therefore imperative to establish the correlation between the circumstances preceding and following exile and what happens in between.

Kunz (1981) is the only one who clearly attempts to do so. He divides refugee populations into: majority identified refugees who identify with the nation but not with the government and are convinced that their opposition to events is shared by the majority of their compatriots; secondly, alienated refugees (usually from minority groups) who are ambivalent or embittered in their attitude towards their former compatriots either because of events immediately preceding the situation causing flight or because of past discrimination. Concerning the refugees' attitude towards displacement Kunz classifies them as 'reactive fate groups' or 'purpose groups' which include self-fulfilling groups and revolutionary activists. To identify a majority identified refugee, Kunz postulates three types of characteristics: home-related characteristics such as inexperience in handling minority or marginality situations and compensatory activities resulting from guilt or emotional attachment to the homeland, treating resettlement as a transient phase; transit-related characteristics including the effect of displacement and the effects of midway to nowhere; and host-related factors.

Parameters for the study of refugees

With Kunz' categorization in mind I attempt to determine the parameters which have to be considered in a study of refugees in the land of exile. I will first look at the position of refugees in their society of origin to understand their characteristics in the society of reception. Adopting the view expressed by Rose (1981, p.769) quoting Zolberg et al. (1989) that 'refugees, past and present, are a result of social conflict' I propose to analyse refugee populations within the structure of conflict which led them to flee and preceded the crisis prompting departure. However, what is important is not only the refugees' objective position but also their subjective relation to these conflicts, how neutral or committed they are towards them. Did they exist as a group prior to exile or is it the common experience of exile that created them as a group; did they have a collective consciousness and project prior to exile? Is there a collective project of return?

The *relationship to the country of origin* seems to colour attitudes towards settlement not only shortly after arrival but also many years later. For instance, Luciuk (1986) shows that the homeward orientation of displaced Ukrainians, which he attributes to the sojourning in camps where they were influenced by the nationalist movement for the liberation of Ukraine (irredentism) is retarding adjustment. Portes and Mozo (1985) demonstrate that Cuban refugees in the USA display the highest rate of naturalization (barring Asian non-refugees), which they explain by the decision perceived as of irreversible consequences when they left the country. Kunz (1971) finds that even years after settlement events 'at home' can have a decisive influence on naturalization. In Vasquez and Araujo's view (1990), the notion of return to the homeland looms as a persistent feature of refugees' settlement. The issue of return, whether desired or forsaken, figures prominently in a study of refugees and, related to it, the perceived temporariness or permanence of exile. Time is a factor which has its importance in so far as events and circumstances may confirm the situation of exile or make it appear less definitive as time goes past.

Moreover, one needs to examine how this equation fits within the structure of conflict in the *society of reception*. Responses of the society of reception towards refugees have been shown to influence their settlement. Although refugees' lives are characterized by a dramatic change requiring adaptation, it is worth looking at what can be deemed to constitute not only rupture but also continuity in the refugee situation and how this is perceived by refugees themselves. One must examine the factors related to the country of reception and in particular the impact of discrepancies between the society of origin and of reception. The role of imagined communities here can be significant and the imagined picture which refugees and the society of reception have of one another. This is illustrated by a number of studies on specific aspects of the relationship to the society of reception. Bach and Carroll-Seguin (1986) attribute the poor economic success of Haitian refugees in South Florida to a social context which was unprepared to receive them either as economic immigrants or as political refugees; this was compounded by the presence of previously established Cuban refugees which did not allow a space for economic opportunities for Haitians. Luciuk (1986) argues that the most important host factor in the adaptation of refugees is the compatibility between the refugee background and the receiving population, pointing out the discrepancy between an established Ukrainian community in Canada and newly arrived Ukrainian displaced persons, because of the disparity between their respective aspirations. Wong (1967) finds that mainland Chinese refugees in Hong Kong suffer from anomie as they miss the all-encompassing organizational control to which they are accustomed. Moreover, the divergence between the ideologies prevailing in the country of origin and in the country of settlement work against adaptation. In a comparison of Ugandan Asian refugees in Britain, Canada and India, Bristow et al. (1975) identify education, economic resources outside Uganda prior to expulsion and kin located in the country of settlement as the factors most related to adjustment (from six variables which also include age, religious community and occupation in Uganda). However, the involuntary character of the refugees' migration often exacerbates their 'strangeness' in the reception society as, unlike Schutz's stranger, the refugee might not positively seek admission to the reception society nor extend efforts to master the cultural instruments necessary to engage with it (Schutz, 1944).

The *existence or constitution of a community* and the *role of associations* is another important aspect to be looked at in a study of refugees as well as the issues which mobilize them. The role of kin, ethnic group and community appear as prominent in several ways. This makes sense in the context of what psychological studies outline and in circumstances of sudden and brutal rupture with the society of origin. Community and associations may provide a key resource for the reconstruction of some kind of social world to replace what has been shattered. Rogg (1971) concludes that although the presence of a strong ethnic community may slow down the acculturation of its members, it favourably influences their adjustment by providing a reference base where the values, attitudes and cultural patterns of the refugee are still considered worthwhile. Finnan (1981), in a study of Vietnamese refugees in the electronics industry (USA), examines the occupational assimilation of refugees and defines it as a social and cognitive process. She stresses the importance of the ethnic community which promotes a favourable outlook on this particular outlet. Desbarats (1986), in a study of Sino-Vietnamese refugees in the USA, concludes that ethnicity emerges as the most important factor ahead of understanding English in accounting for the low utilization by Chinese of vocational training programmes. One reason advanced to account for this is that their resistance to and avoidance of cultural assimilation is a disadvantage in a society which demands conformity to Anglo-Saxon norms and culture as prerequisite for economic success. Mougne (1985), reporting on the experience of unaccompanied Vietnamese refugees in Britain emphasizes the need for the retention of cultural identity and advocates a gradual adjustment to life in Britain. Ethnic/community associations are found to meet a variety of needs: maintenance of the group cohesion and formation of community, relating to the land and culture of origin, relating to the society of reception (Joly, 1995). Indra (1987) outlines the need fulfilled by Vietnamese associations to establish links with the refugees' roots and explain their culture to Canadians, altogether acting as brokers between the refugees and the society of reception. One characteristic of refugee communities can be their fragmentation and the multiplication of associations servicing them (Gold, 1992).

Finally, the *collective sense of loss* (for want of a better phrase) largely affects refugees' settlement. Refugees have experienced the most complete dislocation of their social world and are deprived of power as social actors both in the country of origin and the country of reception. They have often suffered a severe defeat. This is sometimes compounded by events taking place during the journey from the home country to the reception society: refugees are often depersonalized and organized by others. They are temporarily left in camps, detention or reception centres, they are housed, fed and taken care of, one could say taken over, by large bureaucratic agencies; they are examined by doctors, their claims are processed by officials. Among aspects of refugee settlement which are specific to them stand out the losses incurred and how to cope with those. Brown (1982) identifies the main issues in the resettlement of Indo-Chinese refugees as the following: the emotional responses to separation particularly from the family, guilt and sense of obligation, downward social mobility, frustration and violence, internal migration, intergenerational conflict, the myth of the group's fulfilment through children's achievements and the pitfalls of sponsorship. Kay (1987) shows that among Chilean exiles in Scotland deprivation experienced by all the categories of social actors took different forms. For the politically involved men and women it focused on the loss of a valued public role, for women on their removal from the extended family, the loss of their main outlet for sociability. This led to a power struggle to renegotiate the terms of the gender order and politicized male–female relations. Vasquez and Araujo (1990) also deal with the issue of loss particularly in defining the first stage of settlement in the initial period.

TWO BROAD CATEGORIES OF REFUGEES

Let us now turn to the diversity of refugees resulting from different conflicts. Zolberg's typology of conflicts causing refugee movements is a useful starting point. Colonial conflicts and national liberation movements give rise to three kinds of refugee groups. Prior to decolonization, there are national liberation militants and their followers. After the retreat of colonial powers, two groups may get out: former settlers if they were forced to leave, and natives having collaborated with the colonial power, but also a mixed race population. The settlers and their offspring are in a refugee-like situation but enjoy more emotional and ontological security as their destination is certain and assured. The disintegration of empires or federalized states and the formation of nation-states follow a similar pattern. But in many cases ethnic and religious conflicts have arisen in their wake; in such situations refugees may originate from three main groups. Ethnic or religious minorities with a defined territorial base; ethnic and religious minorities without a well-defined territorial base (this may include tribes and castes); and ethnic and religious groups whose close or far ancestry came from another land. Social movements followed by a counter-revolutionary dictatorship may entail the flight of militants and sympathizers involved in the movement which could be based on several classes and social strata. Social revolution gives rise to the exile of previous ruling groups in society. So-called communist regimes have provoked the exit of individual dissidents as from Eastern Europe and from larger masses of people as those running away from Pol Pot in Cambodia. Civil wars and generalized violence may entail the flight of a motley collection of victims. Finally, some wars may provoke the exile of specific groups such as conscientious objectors and war resisters.

If one looks at refugees' position in the society of origin as a determining factor towards different modes of settlement it is possible to find two large categories. One category of refugees are those who had a collective project of society in the land of origin and take it with them in their land of exile. This category could include some individuals from any of the groups presented above and none of the groups will fit this description a hundred per cent as there are differentiated degrees of commitment to the projects involved. However, as an ideal type, one can posit that on the whole this category includes the following: social movements against a dictatorship, national liberation militants against the colonial power, territorially based national and ethnic groups and some religious groups.

The second category includes those who did not have a collective project in the land of origin or those who have forsaken it. It includes settlers in independent colonies which have gained independence, those natives who collaborated with the colonial power, non-indigenous religious or ethnic groups, victims of genocide and victims of generalized violence. War resisters, draft-dodgers, opponents of social revolutions or communist regimes may come under the first or second category depending on whether they are committed individually or as a group to a collective project.

The two broad categories proposed represent two types that will display differentiated patterns of adaptation in the land of exile and settlement. However, even the two main categories are not static as particular groups and individuals from any group may change category because of a number of factors. Modes of settlement will also display subgroups determined by the additional parameters mentioned above.

A collective project in the land of origin

Let us now examine in more detail the first type identified above, that is those who are carriers of a collective project of society. Their relationship to the society of origin remains very close and intense; they perceive their exile as a continuation of the project they had for that society despite the traumatic rupture they experienced. One central goal is to return home in order to implement that project and exile is seen as temporary. This is the main factor which will affect settlement.

Relationship to the society of reception will be set within this framework and conditioned by its ability to help further the project. The most important host-related factors will be ideological ones although economic factors cannot be discarded as survival and everyday life depend on them. This type of refugee displays a high level of community/political organization which plays an instrumental role in reconstituting a community and keeping alive the project; they primarily mobilize over issues pertaining to the homeland. Another feature of these organizations is that they generally partake of international/transnational networks and have a clear group identity. Their main objective is certainly not to adapt, integrate or assimilate; this is what may add relevance to the

concept of diasporas as applied to refugees (Cohen, 1993).
Time passing can undermine this general outlook if the relations of forces (internationally, nationally or among the
refugees' own organizations and resources) seem to point
towards a lessened or even total lack of possibility to realize
the project. Adaptation in the society of reception will thus be
influenced by the refugees' motivation for exile. If they find
refuge in a close country with a government sympathetic to
their project they could reconstitute an almost complete
society of origin in exile with minimal integration into the
society of reception. As long as the project is perceived as
viable the existence of the refugee group with such characteristics can last more than one generation (such as the
Palestinians in some Middle-Eastern countries). If the country
of refuge lies far away from the country of origin, with a political structure that tolerates but does not strongly support the
project of the refugees, the reconstitution of communities is
less complete, the degree of continuity is curtailed and a
greater measure of integration into the host society is en-
forced. But a good number of nuances have to be introduced.
If political parties or religious/ethnic groups find counterparts in the society of reception, or if their project attracts
sympathy from some sectors of that society, the refugees are
more likely to participate willingly in that society at least to
promote their project. Some measure of continuity will thus
be provided which makes the rupture from the society of
origin less brutal. If one wishes to speak of successful settlement in exile for this category of refugees, one should be
careful not to use only socio-economic criteria, as success, at
least in the eyes of the group, might simply mean, in an
extreme case, the maintenance of the group and project and
the return to the country of origin. At any rate, the preservation of the collective project has to be taken into account
while evaluating the settlement of this type.

It has to be said that no group is completely homogeneous
and that there are differentiated degrees of commitment to
the project; what counts is the strength of the collective commitment, which varies according to the proportion of refugees
in the group ready to give active support to the project and
the ability of the more committed to keep it up, although this
is not independent of the relations of forces at play and the

perceived viability of the project. This is why for instance one particular national or religious group may belong to this type of refugees and change type after a while. One needs to add that this description of the pattern of settlement is valid whenever the project is territorially based; this is true of the vast majority of cases as even most socio-political or religious projects of society are enacted within a national/territorial arena. Only a tiny minority of people would be so internationalist that they would set out to carry out their task anywhere, within the structure of the society of reception.

Severing links with the society of origin

The second category of refugees share a number of characteristics although differences exist with regard to some of the parameters. Their relationship to the society of origin stands at the opposite pole to that of the first category of refugees. They have turned their back on it and do not retain a commitment towards it although they may be concerned with the fate of their kin and others from the same group left behind and still have an attachment to their culture of origin. Return is not envisaged within the framework of options for the future and exile is perceived as definitive. The attitude of this category of refugees is not predetermined by a continued involvement in the society of origin. This may mean a greater propensity to have a positive attitude towards the society of reception and perhaps a greater availability to make a fresh start and to innovate. However, the fact that no definite plan for the future was involved in the move, combined with the regret of what was lost, may hinder settlement and lead to a double marginalization: from the country of origin and from the country of reception. The outcome will be largely determined by host-related factors. For all this category of refugees the central question will be socio-economic opportunities; the existence of a similar group in the host-society also has some importance.

Where community and associations are concerned subgroups need to be established. For groups who existed as a minority prior to exile the level of community reconstitution, networks and associations will generally be developed and play an important role in the adaptation of the refugees. These will mostly be involved in cultural activities and in relating with the society of reception on issues connected with settlement: they also provide a positive emotional and material resource for this particular group of refugees. An advantage and a measure of continuity is awarded by the experience of a minority situation prior to exile (Bonacich, 1938). If the structure of the society of reception makes a space for minorities this refugee group will certainly benefit greatly. The combination of all these factors may lead to a successful adaptation of the group and individuals. With time the minority groups can continue to exist as an entity and may find an adequate place within the reception society. In fewer cases the existence of the community may hinder settlement because of factors linked to the host society. For the group of refugees within this category who did not exist as a minority prior to exile, the process of community formation and the creation of associations will be delayed and may never happen. It may eventually constitute some kind of group with its networks or associations. In some cases the outcome will be integration and even assimilation. But for all this category of refugees there is also a possibility of marginalization and exclusion.

Finally, the situation is not necessarily permanent between individuals and groups, as some ambivalence may exist which brings together the two situations in a fluctuating tension.

CONCLUSION

What needs to be stressed most in this area is that we are analysing a process under way. The refugees' position in the structure of conflict of their society of origin and its relationship to the motivation to flee is the departure point and initially constitutes the inner drive of the actors once they arrive in the country of settlement. However, a great many variables and events will modify the actors' perception of their situation and influence their settlement. It involves a process of construction of the refugee reality, i.e. a social process. Where a collective project is concerned, its construction, maintenance and reproduction or its loss are not a static feature but undergo changes under the influence of a variety of factors, including events in international relations, in the country and region of origin, among the group itself, depending on the numbers, generations, gender, etc. It can also be influenced by the process of flight and the 'transit' period. Altogether, the two broad categories of refugees posited above are neither watertight nor static but are to be used as tools of analysis. If there is no collective project several processes can develop such as assimilation, integration, community enclosure and a variety of others.

7 Refugee Associations: Between Society of Origin and Society of Exile

INTRODUCTION

The main purpose of this chapter is to examine the refugees themselves from their own vantage point. A good deal has been said with regard to policies both on asylum and settlement issues. It is more than appropriate for the people who provide the main concern of this book to be considered in their own right. A comparative study was deemed useful and two national groups have been selected in two European countries: refugees from Chile and Vietnam in France and Britain. Both groups exist in substantial numbers in the two countries and were the beneficiaries of relatively favourable asylum and reception policies, which helps to make them comparable. They differ in several ways, however, and in the first place in terms of the regime they were fleeing from, the Chileans escaping from an extreme right-wing military dictatorship which enjoyed US support and the Vietnamese from a communist regime which had just defeated the United States in a protracted war and had also been involved in a short war with China. Moreover these groups come from two different continents both far removed from Europe but entertaining historical links with the old continent.

The *coup d'état* which took place in Chile in 1973 scattered Chileans all over Latin America, Europe and beyond. They continued to arrive in Europe from Latin American countries where dictatorships were installed subsequently and from Chile itself as repression and persecution continued over the seventies and eighties. These arrivals encompass a spectrum of social classes and political parties. Generally the Chileans were urbanized and literate; they had also had some experience of organizations such as political parties, trade unions and neighbourhood associations. They came to France from 1973 until the nineties but they were only allowed into the UK between 1974 and 1979. In both countries they enjoyed a great deal of sympathy from the host population, particularly left, humanitarian and Christian circles. In France they found more direct affinities and counter-parts in the substantial Socialist and Communist parties, the Catholic church and also the Latin culture and language; even Chilean Radicals could find a fraternal Radical party in France.

People came out of Vietnam initially in 1975, with a peak in numbers shortly after the fall of Saigon and they have con-tinued to flee to the time of writing, with an enhanced outflow after the Sino-Vietnamese war in 1979. Many took to small boats and landed in neighbouring South-East Asian countries where they were generally granted temporary asylum and lived in camps until an opportunity for resettlement occurred. They have been going to France in large numbers since 1975 whereas in Britain a substantial population arrived only between 1979 and 1983. Because of France's selection criteria and its early intake, a greater proportion of its refugees from Vietnam were educated and spoke French. France's historic links with Vietnam not only meant that French was the lan-guage of the middle class, it also created a reciprocal positive *imaginaire* among the Vietnamese arriving in France and among the French. Another consequence was the existence of a settled community of Vietnamese prior to the arrival of the refugees in the seventies. In the UK a greater proportion of North and Chinese Vietnamese entered as they were selected later and from Hong Kong camps. This meant that a smaller number were educated or even literate; those who read Chinese were still at a disadvantage as they did not use Roman script as the Vietnamese language does. Moreover, many of the people who came to Britain had sojourned in camps for a long time and would have preferred to go to the USA. Because of this, refugees had a less positive outlook, and where the British were concerned, the Vietnamese were simply perceived as the 'boat people' whose plight they had seen on television.

THE FRAMEWORK OF THE STUDY

As refugees these populations share a number of features which do not pertain to a particular national origin or country of reception. In general they did not arrive with the same positive motivation as labour migrants who came individually to seek work with the purpose of improving their prospects. There is a collective character specific to the movement of refugees who flee into exile as a group having suffered a severe defeat. They experience the most complete dislocation of their social world and they have lost all their power as social and political actors. Exile in itself constitutes the absolute denial of their existence as social actors in the home society and they have not gained any status in the reception society. Family links, economic and political influence, status and all forms of network have been largely shattered. On account of asylum regulations they do not have the possibility of organizing a chain migration as labour migrants such as Portuguese in France and Turks in Germany, reconstituting entire villages in the host society (Hily and Poinard 1987, Gitmez and Wilpert 1987). This chapter looks at some of the ways through which refugees rebuild their social relations in the country of exile and regain some control over their lives.

Associations were chosen as a useful indicator of the refugees' viewpoint, of the networks and issues important to them. Altogether 36 associations were examined through in-depth interviews and for some of them, participant observation: 22 Chilean and 14 Vietnamese associations[1] over 1990 (in the UK) and 1991 (in France). A sample was selected to include the main categories of associations such as political, cultural, advice, sports, etc. This was done on the basis of prior knowledge of these populations acquired through research work carried out on refugee communities since 1987. In a situation where kin and primary community networks had been broken, associations appeared to be the medium which would play a central role in the reorganization of the refugees' social relations. This process is enhanced by the modes of functioning in the modern societies which received them (Joly, 1987a). Moreover, political refugees generally had the experience of working through associations in their homeland which equipped them for such ways of operating without delay. Finally, associations reflect the dynamics of conflicts in which refugees are involved.

The most important dimension which needed to be explored was reference to the homeland. As I have posited, that relationship to the society of origin was one key component of refugees' settlement in the society of exile, more so than for any other migrant. Inevitably, the relationship to the society of reception in which they live must also be taken into account. One main parameter will thus be the society of reference. Indeed, in previous research on immigrant associations these two dimensions already appear (Joly, 1987a).

Associations can be classified into two major groups according to the interests they further: like interests, and common interests. As a guideline for this study of associations I have used previous work carried out on immigrant associations by a variety of scholars. I retain John Rex's broad categorization of the main functions of associations: (1) overcoming social isolation, (2) helping individuals in the solution of personal and material problems, (3) combining to defend the group's interest in conflict and bargaining with the wider society, (4) maintaining and developing shared patterns of meanings (Rex 1973). The first two generally express like interests and the last two common interests. Other sociologists have arrived at a similar classification to Rex's which they create on the basis of the purpose (*finalité*) of the association: 1. *affective*, 2. *fonctionnelle*, 3. *d'influence*, 4. *culturelle* (Bardet-Blochet et al. 1988). Rex envisaged these functions mostly within the context of the society of settlement and this is why he finds it necessary to add another function in subsequent work, i.e. maintaining and strengthening links with the society of the homeland (Rex and Tomlinson, 1979). I prefer not to adopt the latter as a separate category as I shall explore all the functions with respect to the society of origin as well as the society of reception. For instance 'combining to defend the group's interest in conflict' applies very much to the political campaigning and support to the opposition against the regime which caused the refugees' exile as well as their situation in the reception society.

The interview guideline comprised seven broad areas:

— Basic data on the association, date of foundation, address, funding and history
— Character of the association, its functions and objectives
— Activities
— Human and other resources, members, clients and structures

— Relations with the country of origin
— Relations with the country of reception
— General comments on identity and settlement.

SOCIETY OF REFERENCE

Let us turn now to general considerations on the society of reference resulting from this survey. The two national groups differ markedly in this respect. Chile appears to be or to have been an important society of reference for 21 out of 22 Chilean associations (the odd one out is a nursery for Latin American children). Seven of the associations out of 22 function solely in relation to Chile; political parties organize on issues pertaining to Chile and Latin America and they actually constitute a section of Chilean national parties (working clandestinely in Chile). The Chileans in exile are thus considered as an extension, a continuation of the Chilean people outside Chile. For 14 of the associations out of 22 the UK or France represent a reference point alongside the homeland, out of which only three hold the reception society as their main reference point; these three are a women's group in the UK, an association of psychologists and a cultural/friendship association in France, the latter being formed at the time of the elections in Chile which marked the end of exile. When the two societies are taken on board by associations this may express a variety of processes. For instance for many of these associations interaction with the society of reception serves as a means to further a project directed at the society of origin such as political campaigning in the host society against the regime in the homeland, or collecting funds to send for social and political projects back home. For others the society of origin is an inspiration for cultural and ideological manifestations practised by and mostly addressed to the Chileans in the host society but they are rarely devoid of more concrete links with the homeland. The content of these cultural manifestations in music, painting and literature itself carries a clear ideological message which opposes the dictatorship directly or indirectly and makes part of the exiles' identity. Finally for most of the Chileans of the left (this is generally the case among the refugees) there exists a broader notion of the society of origin which extends from Chile to Latin America, sharing a common baggage of the culture of resistance recognized in Uruguay, Argentina, Nicaragua, El Salvador and throughout the continent. It expresses itself by cultural references to Latin American artists and the participation in campaigns supporting the movement in a variety of Latin American countries. Some of the associations actually include refugees from different Latin American countries. Finally, one association and a section of another are worth signalling as their specific purpose is to help people to prepare for their return; this demonstrates the actualization of the wish to return often stated by Chilean refugees.

Links with the society of origin illustrate the above as 17 Chilean associations out of 22 have direct concrete links with the homeland. These take the shape of an organic relationship for political parties and of organizational links for other groups and campaigns: ten of the associations state that they are part of or support a political group in Chile to which they contribute politically and financially. Some of these add that they also help socio-cultural projects and seven more are sending funds to sociocultural projects. When asked if any event in the homeland has influenced the development of the association, an overwhelming number, 19 out of 22, cite the elections and the democratization process; for most it is related to the return of exiles, as they mention that their ranks are becoming depleted, causing problems of continuation for the association. Several note that this changes their perception on the future of the association as it will probably entail the reformulation of its objectives, i.e. to insure the maintenance of culture for the younger generation and of social relations among the whole group. One interviewee actually explains these changes within the context of the transformation of the Chileans abroad from a group of exiles to an ethnic minority group. This does not mean the end of support for social projects which are still envisaged but those will lose their direct anti-dictatorship correlation. An additional consequence of the democratization in Chile is said to be the greater difficulty in attracting interest and support from the society of reception. Other events in the society of origin are mentioned by some of the associations: the division of political parties, the upturn of the repression (as for instance when an attempt was made to kill Pinochet), and the *protestas* (the demonstrations against the dictatorship in the early to mid-eighties).

Contacts with the society of reception take place at local level in the majority of cases: 13 out of 22 Chilean associations have some contact with the local authority which may lend them premises or other kind of support. Outside funding remains limited as only eight associations obtain any: in two cases funding is provided by the local authority, two more associations are helped by other public institutions (the Greater London Arts Council and the Service Social d'Aide aux Emigrants (SSAE)), and the remainder comes from a health NGO, charities, trade unions and the European Community. A variety of public spaces and buildings are used by 14 of the associations which rent or borrow them from churches, public institutions, trade unions, etc. They are in touch with MPs and councillors or other politicians of the host society in the case of 13 associations. This demonstrates that the Chileans do not constitute an enclosed group. But in the main the nature of these contacts does not imply an objective of rapprochement and engagement with the host society as a group; they tend to constitute means rather than ends, in order to further aims related to the homeland.

In addition it appears that Chilean associations have established links with a great variety of other organizations: trade unions and political parties (as could be expected) but also refugee agencies, churches, humanitarian NGOs, and other refugees and minority groups associations, with whom they may collaborate. Moreover, five of the associations are involved with European institutions. A good number (13) claim to be aware of the host country's policy on refugees but rarely take action about it. Finally, none of the associations in France found that 1981 made any difference to their ability to get organized as an association, while this is precisely what could have been expected since all restrictions were lifted then on foreigners' associations. This could be explained by the vast amount of support extended by French people so that they circumvented all the restrictions existing prior to 1981. When we asked whether contacts with the host society institutions were difficult, a few associations answered positively mainly for reasons of 'culture and language' (primarily in the UK) and a couple in France mentioned the 'bureaucracy', as language

and culture did not stand out as a major problem for most;
but none attributed much importance to such factors as 'we
never intended to do much work directed at this society'.
Altogether findings are pretty consistent across the two sides
of the Channel and the society of reception does not seem to
have caused major differences, most probably because of the
overriding influence of the relationship to the society of
origin and the specific exile character of this population.

The prevailing trend among refugees from Vietnam stands
in contrast with the Chileans. Their main orientation lies
towards the society of reception.

Out of 14 associations, none holds Vietnam as sole reference point and eight combine Vietnam and the society of reception in their references. These include a minority (two)
pursuing political endeavours and a majority engaged in cultural activities. But most do not have any direct link with
Vietnam barring family concerns. One single association provides help for a social project in South East Asia as a main objective but it is a Franco-Vietnamese association. One religious
association supports its counterpart in Vietnam financially,
possibly also contributing to a social project. When the associations interact with the Vietnamese beyond their society of reception it will more often be Vietnamese populations in other
European countries and in North America. All the Vietnamese
associations in France and Britain relate to the society of reception: they include professional associations, advice centres,
old people's help groups, religious associations, sports groups
and educational associations. They all contribute to some
aspect of life and settlement in the host society and several
have made it their aim to 'facilitate integration as rapidly as
possible'. Cultural manifestations are definitely addressed to
the Vietnamese in their host society and are quite often
'neutral' (Le Huu Khoa 1985) in so far as they do not carry a
clear political message *vis-à-vis* the regime back home.

Links between Vietnamese associations and the society of
origin mostly remain within the private sphere as the only ones
clearly stated are those involving the family (five out of the
14 associations) with the exception of one Catholic association
in France which entertains regular contacts with the church
in Vietnam to which it sends funds. Six associations out of
14 refer to events in the country of origin as having some

resonance, namely underdevelopment and more prominently repression, the latter being characteristic of a refugee situation.

Within the realm of the host society nine out of the 14 Vietnamese associations are in contact with the municipality. The majority of associations in Britain have close links with the local authority which grants them funding towards social projects and one organization receives funds from the church while in France a minority of associations are in receipt of funding from the local and national state, from a charity and from the church. Only six out of 14 associations state that they make use of public spaces but 11 entertain links with a broad span of organizations including churches, pagodas, schools, refugee agencies and humanitarian NGOs, and more rarely with political parties. However, eight of them are in contact with councillors and MPs, mostly on issues pertaining to settlement but also on the question of human rights in Vietnam. Three of them only are in touch with European institutions, one of which refers to the church in Europe. All the associations seem to be acutely aware of policies towards refugees which they differentiate into national and local, often to praise local authorities for their assistance (in France). The same cleavage appears as did for Chilean associations with regard to difficulties encountered in relating to institutions of the host society: in Britain all put forward the issue of language and culture as an impediment, while in France none seem to find such problems; only two of them mention some difficulty resulting from distrust or lack of interest on the part of the French.

ROLES AND FUNCTIONS OF ASSOCIATIONS

Social isolation

It is difficult to determine exactly the extent to which associations help to overcome social isolation; almost invariably all do so but this is rarely stated either as an objective or an achievement. It is clearer where women's groups are concerned, as well as old people's groups, youth groups and sports or recreational associations. Religious communities also fulfil this role but only *inter alia*. Altogether no more than eight out of the 36 associations make it apparent that this is

one of their functions, and for those that do, this takes place
entirely within the context of the society of reception.

Overcoming personal and material problems

This is perhaps the most tangible of the functions fulfilled by
associations (Salinas et al., 1987). Out of the 22 Chilean associations six help to overcome difficulties: one which works *inter
alia* as an advice centre, one nursery, one women's group, one
religious group, one counselling group, all meeting needs
which arise from the refugees' situation in the host society.
The last association of this type also gives advice but has the
peculiarity of advising on problems to be met in the society of
origin on return.

Vietnamese associations devote a good deal more of their
efforts to such tasks, as 10 out of 14 help with issues and problems related to living in the host society. As we have already
noted that a greater number of Vietnamese associations
focused on the society of reception it is understandable that
they would also address the type of questions considered in
this category. These are advice centres, religious associations,
old people, youth groups and an educational group. This
function assumes more prominence in the UK than in France,
which tallies with the more disadvantaged position of the
Vietnamese in Britain.

Combining to defend the group's interest in conflict

The approach we adopted in the study of refugees makes this
function particularly pertinent as we take into account their
position within the structure of conflict of the society of
origin. The notion of conflict here requires some explanation
in particular where Chilean associations are concerned. As the
military dictatorship overthrew a Popular Unity government
which was implementing a vast social programme it not only
violated human rights but also eliminated social rights for the
vast majority of the population. Apart from the upper middle
class and the military all became impoverished and deprived
of access to social welfare such as education and health, while
unemployment soared. Art and culture themselves were severely controlled. As a consequence all attempts to improve

this situation almost inevitably came up against the regime. Moreover all the parties opposed to the dictatorship were driven underground and organized through social projects. This is a situation which differs from some other countries where supporting a social project does not necessarily entail opposing the regime. It has meant that most of the exiles' associations which related to the society of origin were involved in some aspect of the conflict directly or indirectly. Political parties and campaigns clearly acted against the dictatorship with a view to bringing it down. But the other associations also indirectly participated in the same movement as they supported social and cultural projects in Chile. Through these activities they were rebuilding their position as social and political actors in Chilean society from a distance. Out of the 22 associations 19 are thus involved in supporting political or social projects against the dictatorship. None of them plays an important role in terms of negotiating with the society of reception, with the possible exception of the nursery and Chile Democratico.

With regard to the Vietnamese it was also conflict that drove them into exile but their position differed somewhat from the Chileans for two main reasons. In the first place many of the associations seem to have opted for integration rather than a return orientation towards the homeland and therefore do not get involved in the conflict back home. Only a small minority of associations thus clearly state a political commitment against the regime. Secondly, the nature of the Vietnamese situation signified that the opposition generally did not launch initiatives in support of social projects, so that involvement with the homeland had to be directly political or private, in the shape of correspondence and help to the family left behind. As a result only three out of 14 associations are involved in opposing the Vietnamese regime. But several more act in the way of a mediator between the Vietnamese and the society of reception. Their main thrust is to gain social power and participation in the host society.

Shared patterns of meaning

Chilean associations display a great deal of homogeneity towards the military regime: they all opposed the dictatorship, holding up Popular Unity and Salvador Allende as common symbols. None of the associations would ever state that they were not interested if this was mentioned. (This does not apply to associations formed after the elections of the nineties, that is, after the dictatorship had technically ended.) Those which were not political associations nonetheless shared in this attitude. Cultural groups are identified by the character and ideological content of the culture they promote, i.e. a Chilean and Latin American popular culture as had begun to develop before the *coup d'état* and a culture of resistance; this often includes indigenous aspects (Amerindian) generally underrated and repressed by the ruling classes which identify with the more European input. Within a global context, it also meant opposition to US imperialism and interference in Latin America. Several of the cultural associations stated as one of their objectives the reproduction and maintenance of Chilean culture for the young generation and all partook of the same interpretation. However, there were a great many diversifications and divisions on the basis of political parties. Very few of the associations, whether cultural or social, brought together people from a variety of parties, or from parties which had not formed alliances; this has become increasingly more feasible as the years of exile pass, however.

Among the Vietnamese there are to be found clearly differentiated patterns of meaning. Although there is a widespread pro-capitalist anti-Communist ideology taken up by many associations, this is by no means the prevalent identity message which is transmitted by the associations. The shared patterns of meaning expressed by Vietnamese associations are very diversified. Three out of 14 associations, i.e. the more political anti-Communist organizations, emphasize human rights and resistance to the Vietnamese regime, representing another Vietnam outside (Le Huu Khoa, 1985). Strong Catholic associations promote a religious identity with a clear message of integration in the host society while retaining aspects of the Vietnamese culture, the latter being more marked in the UK; they also extend their support services to non-Catholics. Despite their anti-Communist subjacent ideology they seem to have made a decision to underplay this dimension. Some associations are addressed to the youth and focus on developing their knowledge about Vietnam and Vietnamese culture, not necessarily associated with an ideological bias. Others emphasize traditional family and moral values. Professional associations of Vietnamese artists also have a clear cultural and ideological content which forms the basis of their existence.

HISTORY OF ASSOCIATIONS

The date of foundation of the Chilean associations reveals three main groups: (1) those founded within two years of the *coup d'état* which include political parties, campaigning organizations against the dictatorship, a political women's group (also with a campaigning emphasis) and a Christian community organization which existed in Chile prior to the coup; (2) associations founded between 1977 and the end of the eighties; they tend to be socio-cultural organizations, either emanating from political parties or distanced from the parties but still clearly identified with the struggle against the dictatorship; some are concerned with issues affecting the group in the host society; (3) associations assuming a distinct character when an end of the dictatorship is considered to be approaching; *inter alia* the return committee finds a place here.

This corresponds to a periodicization of the exiles' behaviour and perception. Initially the sole objective was the immediate or rapid overthrow of the dictatorship, with the perspective of returning home in the near future. As the period of exile lengthened, the dictatorship became consolidated and the opposition came under fiercer repression. The Chileans abroad became involved in more diverse social, cultural and sports activities and many loosened their direct connections with political parties while keeping their support for socio-political projects against the dictatorship. A few of the associations then began to address issues pertaining to life in the host society. The problems encountered by the parties back home continued to be reflected abroad through splits and alliances. Finally, as democracy approaches the whole character of the associations changes: from exiles they become ethnic minorities and create associations to maintain Chilean culture among the youth and to promote friendship links between the host society and Chile, without the same political edge. The history of the associations and their evolution seems to confirm such a periodicization. For instance a musical group composed of militants of a political party gave all its proceeds to the party barring a minimal salary for its artists throughout the seventies; in the eighties the group kept the income from its performances except for concerts that were played free of charge for the party which then received all the proceeds. In the nineties they are wondering what option to adopt. The Christian community also changed over the three periods indicated and now services Latin Americans in Paris without much political content. Alternatively the Lawyers Committee for Chile campaigning on human rights is preparing to disband or to change its purpose.

One cannot find such clear periodicization among Vietnamese associations. It seems that the first period has been skipped and the third period not yet attained or envisaged. To be more accurate and on the basis of larger research the majority of Vietnamese seem to have distanced themselves early on from political organizations which tended to inspire distrust (Guillon and Taboada-Leonetti, 1986). Nevertheless the evolution of Vietnamese associations displays a number of interesting features indicative of the situation in the society of reception. For instance the Catholic associations in France and the UK enjoyed a differentiated reception. In France it was immediately welcome and supported by host society institutions (as early as 1975) while in the UK the first Vietnamese priest who tried to set up an association in London was looked upon with suspicion and established his base in Birmingham, where an Irish Catholic group gave him a better welcome; the association thrived and he thereafter created a branch in London. This illustrates the impact of previous historical links between the society of reception and the society of origin. One association for the aged was founded in France in 1977 as a split from the pro-Communist association which existed among the Vietnamese community settled in previous years; this is not to be paralleled in Britain where no prior community existed. As for a writers' association founded in 1978, it found that its headquarters were moved from Paris to Canada in 1989 as a more substantial population of Vietnamese and greater logistical support exist in North America.

NATURE AND CHARACTER OF ASSOCIATIONS

To gain an accurate understanding of the nature and character of associations several areas must be examined, such as their stated aims and objectives, their roles and functions, the reason for their creation and also their activities and achievements. The refugee character of these organizations makes this all the more necessary as they may not wear all their agenda on their sleeve. For instance, in answer to questions on its role and objectives one association simply said that it was a cultural group for the purpose of maintaining and disseminating the cultural expression of Chileans in the UK. However, this is not the whole story: on closer look the cultural aspect appears to be only a secondary interest. The association's primary interest is revealed by the reason stated to explain its creation, i.e. 'the need to support Chileans in Chile', and by a detailed examination of its activities; these indeed involve artistic and social public functions as indicated earlier but those are organized mostly for the purpose of collecting funds for political and social projects in Chile. Now we are getting to the primary character of the association, which was mentioned in passing as though it belonged only to its history: 'the cultural expression of a political party' whose main interest was to support the struggle against the dictatorship. This is confirmed by the membership of the association, 'all members of the socialist party'. However, it is still the case that the association fulfils a cultural function, and it also helps to overcome social isolation, although this is not even mentioned.

Chilean associations

Several of the associations considered here are political parties and their stated aims all involve supporting the fight against the dictatorship, coupled with individualized programmes according to each particular ideological option (socialist, communist, Marxist-Christian etc.). Their activities include internal party meetings, political education seminars, public meetings, campaigns and mobilization on specific issues such as the announced visit of Pinochet in Europe. In addition they organize several fund-raising activities which range from *fiestas* to cultural events, selected according to the idiosyncracies of

Chileans when these are directed at their own community or to the cultural patterns of the reception society. For instance, sponsored walks are enormously successful in Britain while they remain practically unknown in France where musical groups and the sales of *empanadas* (pastry with a meat or cheese filling) certainly attract much interest. Some of these organizations concentrate on raising funds from the Chilean community while others aim at the majority society, but on the whole they are proficient in their interaction with the reception society to obtain its support for their struggle in Chile. Human rights campaigning organizations fall within the same broad category and describe their aims as in the short term, 'the investigation of human rights violation' and 'the liberation of political prisoners', and in the long term the removal of Pinochet and the restoration of 'genuine' democracy. These generally comprise many non-Chilean activists and have both internal and external activities: on one hand organizational meetings of the association and on the other hand public manifestations, conferences, meetings, demonstrations, the lobbying of host society political institutions, missions in Chile, appearances in the media, the defence of prisoners and human rights activists (including lawyers) in Chile, etc. These activities are mostly directed at the reception society to obtain support for Chileans back home.

Another category of associations are those which address issues pertaining to settlement and include aims such as 'maintaining the culture and improving the quality of life' of its members, 'looking after women's welfare', 'providing education for under fives' and 'helping towards integration'. They provide welfare and social work advice, organize cultural events and give counselling; one runs a nursery for Latin American children. In two out of the four associations involved the beneficiaries are members as well as clients while in the remaining case the members service a clientèle. Another broad category of associations can be called cultural and ideological, furthering the aim of 'developing Chilean culture in the UK and in Chile', 'furthering Chilean culture and political awareness', 'providing a space for thinking' and creating an arena for the 'spiritual and material support' of Chileans in exile and in Chile. Their activities are varied; for members they may include the practice and learning of musical instruments, dances and other artistic activities. Others bring their members together to reflect upon their situation as exiles, to pray collectively, and to study the Chilean situation. Public manifestations may include artistic performances, masses and readings of the gospels, and debates, most of which help to collect funds for projects in the homeland: a women's group organizing soup kitchens or supporting prisoners, a Christian group assisting community organizations, a human rights group investigating the disappeared, a health project in a neighbourhood, etc. One association which appeared to be purely recreational is a football association but it states that its aim is to 'prepare its people to gain a better physical and mental state to serve Chilean society'; in addition to training and matches it also organizes *fiestas* in order to gather funds to be sent to Chile. This link with Chile is often concretely expressed through the sending of funds and seems to represent an indispensable condition legitimating the existence of most associations and perhaps symbolizing the public *raison d'être* of the exiles.

Vietnamese associations

As noted above, the vast majority of the Vietnamese associations deal with issues pertaining to life in the reception society. One large group mostly concentrates on practical and personal problems; this is the case of most of the associations in the UK but several of them do similar work in France. They define their aims as 'helping people in every way and giving them advice', 'looking after the spiritual and material needs of people', 'giving social and administrative assistance', 'obtaining a space for the Vietnamese in cemeteries', 'fostering relations between young and old people', 'achieving the integration of the Vietnamese as fast as possible', and helping towards 'the physical, intellectual, moral and social education of the youth while helping them in their social promotion'. They have set up advice centres whose main activities consist of providing advice and counselling on a daily basis; they do welfare and social work, giving assistance on filling in forms, informing on social benefits and on pensions rights; they may organize social gatherings, outings and fêtes. One association set up intensive classes to support pupils and students, including French, English and computing lessons up to

A-level, as well as artistic and craft classes. These objectives are sometimes pursued through more comprehensive activities which mostly involve Catholic associations: religious meetings, cultural and social activities and language teaching. As a concomitant all these objectives may have to be served through negotiations with institutions of the reception society, for instance with a view to obtain a separate plot in cemeteries or to fund the advice work mentioned above.

The other broad category of associations are cultural-ideological ones which express two tendencies. On the one hand some emphasize a cultural 'neutral' approach and they claim to 'foster cultural exchanges', 'promote liberty, virtue and friendship between writers', 'help integration and the maintenance of Vietnamese culture': this involves activities such as meetings, debates, the publication of writings and studies, teaching Vietnamese and practising Vietnamese dance, music and arts. In other cases the associations clearly lend an anti-Communist bias to the culture they peddle; this is formulated as 'the cultural and pluralist democratization of Vietnam' and 'denouncing cultural censorship in Vietnam'. As a consequence some of these associations accompany their cultural activities with campaigning actions, i.e. the publication of writings on human rights, the participation in meetings and demonstrations on the same issue. One youth association which combines sports with cultural activities is the only one that could be considered as clearly political since it states its aim as 'the political struggle for the democratization of Vietnam' and 'help towards refugees in France'; in addition to organizing matches and holiday camps, it participates in protest meetings and political tasks such as providing stewards in demonstrations, distributing leaflets, etc. Finally, one Franco-Vietnamese association 'assists children in South-East Asia' through sponsoring, raising and sending funds, intervening in the media and so on.

MEMBERSHIP

On the whole the Chilean associations considered here are of medium or small size, barring two of them which comprise more than one thousand members; one is all-encompassing and counts on its list most of the Chileans in the UK while the second is a British Chilean campaigning organization. But in these two cases not all members are active. The rest of them comprise eight out of 22 associations with a membership between 25 and 100 while nine have less than 25 members, but for these two groups membership implies some active participation. Moreover, several of these associations have an audience or a clientèle over and above their membership, if for instance they provide services such as advice or organize public activities. The vast majority of members are Chilean nationals (including some Mapuches, Amerindian natives of Chile and Argentina), who almost all arrived as refugees in Europe; eight out of 22 associations comprise only Chileans while 16 include a minority of different nationalities: other Latin Americans such as Uruguayans, Argentinians, Guatemalans and Peruvians (often refugees) but also respectively French and British. In France this mixed nationality membership is predominant. All the members in France and the vast majority of them in the UK speak the language of the reception society; in both countries most of them (and in particular the leaders) had had experience of being involved in associations prior to exile. Only three of the associations enjoy the services of paid staff while all the others are run by volunteers. The age and gender profile reveals a majority of middle-aged men with a substantial minority of women and young people.

As discussed above, these associations have links with a variety of other groups in the societies of reception and in the homeland. But in addition to associational links their members partake of other kinds of networks which involve politics, religion, locality/region of origin, ethnic identity (for the Mapuches), family and sharing 'common experiences', such as being in prison together, transiting in the same first country of exile before arriving in Europe, or living in the same reception centre on arrival. These networks extend beyond the locality throughout Europe and Latin America lending Chilean communities a singular cosmopolitanism.

Where associations of Vietnamese are concerned a distinction needs be established between the situation in France and Britain with regard to the membership. In the UK they tend to claim a numerous membership (above 4000) which should often be called a clientèle as these persons are the beneficiaries of services provided by the associations (with the exception of the Catholic association). In France only one association claims a large number of members counted in thousands and this is the Franco-Vietnamese association of support for South Asian children. The remainder of the associations can be divided evenly into those which have between 100 and 650 members and those with less than 100 members. Like the Chilean ones, several of these associations also have an audience which attends functions and fêtes. Although all the members in France and Britain are of Vietnamese nationality, associations in Britain tend to have a more composite ethnic mix, as more than 50 per cent are Chinese ethnics while in France only one association claims a minority of Chinese ethnics. South and North Vietnamese appear to be present in a substantial number of associations on both sides of the Channel. In addition in France several associations include a small minority of Cambodian and Laotian nationals and also in one case Hungarians, Czechoslovakians and Maghrebins. Surprisingly, associations in Britain reveal that 90 per cent of their members do not speak English while all the associations in France but one (which expresses some reservations) state that their members speak French. Again, in the UK the majority declare that they had no experience of involvement in associations back home while in France all but one have had some. Finally, associations in Britain often have paid staff while only one does so in France. These enormous discrepancies reveal important factors which must influence the mode of settlement in the respective countries of reception.

The refugees from Vietnam enjoy dense international networks which draw from the nature of the associations involved but are also based on less formal links. Family and kinship are paramount, yet they are completed by religion, ethnicity and region or locality of origin. This results in frequent and intense communication across European borders and the oceans with the USA, Canada and Australia.

GENERAL

A number of general themes were also explored which pertain to more individual issues involving identity and settlement, and can help towards understanding the refugees' viewpoint.

Chileans

When questions related to identity were broached, most interviewees answered that they 'felt Chilean' and then proceeded to emphasize two major aspects: on the one hand, language and culture which included things like music, dance, family values, way of life, social relations, *alegria* (joy of life) and *imaginaire*; but also their political commitment expressed as 'political awareness and aspirations', 'history of exile' and 'striving for a more just society'. Moreover, they claimed that they differed from the British mostly because Chileans were characterized by their greater sense of community and human relations while individualism and materialism were perceived as important features of British society. Some added that the Chileans were also far less disciplined and more *machista* than the British. Differentiation from the French homed in on 'Chilean sensitivity' versus 'rationality', more conviviality and a different conception of time and space, but it was found that the French and Chileans shared a similar education system and food habits and that they were 'Latins'. Again the women's position was identified as different in France.

With regard to their specific situation as refugees one aspect stands out above all: the Chileans' political awareness and affiliation and the fact that they were forced to leave. Others express it as the 'will to struggle' and 'the need to organize'. This is reinforced by the overwhelming desire to return home quoted as the main aspiration of most or a large proportion of the associations' members (more overwhelmingly in Britain than in France) sometimes coupled with 'real democracy' and 'socialism' in Chile. In some cases return 'with a job' expressed realism among the refugees aware that some of their compatriots had faced enormous material difficulties on return. In this respect Chileans in France have a more cautious approach to return; several state that they would want to be in 'both places' and many are acutely aware of the dramatic problems confronting those who have already returned; 'In the French embassy there are queues of returnees wanting to come back to France' commented one refugee. One is left to wonder if this is not a justification by some who hesitate to make the move. According to other interviewees, in addition to material questions, there are also family break-up and

problems of adaptation back home, as the past had been ideal-
ized. But the fact of being refugees is also cited as a factor im-
peding settlement, expressed as: it was difficult to settle here
'because of the defeat', 'being forced to lead a new life led to
negative attitudes here', some people had 'a rejection of the
language, integration', and 'even of the food!'.

The vast majority of Chileans in Britain state that they encountered major problems of settlement: housing and language are quoted as the two most important areas, followed by
employment and then education. Moreover, the impression of
being unwelcome, the combination of trauma due to exile and
racial discrimination and the break-up of families are said to
contribute to these difficulties in the UK; this is where the two
reception countries differ markedly, as Chileans in France on
the whole felt that they have been welcome and never spoke of
racism and discrimination throughout the interviews. In
France housing is hardly included at all in the list of problems
while language appears as the single main difficulty, followed
by employment on a par with homesickness. Both in France
and Britain some mentioned that on the whole their material
situation was better in the reception society where lower socio-
economic groups are concerned while many professionals
found that they had lost status and position. However the
refugees claim that they continue to suffer emotionally from
their situation in exile and would be much better off in Chile,
particularly those who are resident in Britain. With regard to
those resident in France they note that a proportion of them
are very well integrated and that many have married French
partners. Moreover the advantages accrued to refugees as a
result of their status is a recurrent comment about the French
situation and never surfaces in Britain; Chileans in France
claimed that 'it opens the door to all the rights', 'we are much
better off than immigrants' and 'it facilitated our settlement'.

Vietnamese

One notable difference arising from the survey is that
Vietnamese in France already found a settled community on
whom they could draw for support and advice while this was
not the case in Britain. In both countries of reception they
stress similar features pertaining to their identity and the

aspects of it they would like to preserve: language and culture figure prominently together with family values including traditional morals such as 'the respect for elders'. Another feature which assumes great importance is their work ethics, expressed as 'the desire to work hard', 'pride and perseverance' and 'the will to succeed'. At no point do the interviewees emphasize differences between host populations and Vietnamese, perhaps out of politeness, merely stating that economics, politics and culture are different but they develop more what they can contribute to the host society: their work ethics, cultural pluralism and a certain sensitivity. While the majority of people interviewed argue that their characteristic as refugees did not influence their settlement, a substantial minority put forward a variety of features pertaining to the refugee situation: for one it is the feeling of being 'permanently temporary', for several it is 'the motivation to succeed', 'the fight for survival', 'the will to manage well with dignity' but they sometimes add a more negative aspect such as 'quarrels' and the 'lack of collective spirit' (see also similar aspects in Gold, 1992). Among the Vietnamese in Britain, one overriding aspiration is to get a job and occasionally to 'live in peace' while in France aspirations are more diversified and include professional success, good education and future for the children, to get together with other Vietnamese to 'live in a Vietnamese ambience', to help Vietnam to become more democratic, to 'create a Europe–Asia link' and to integrate into French society. Most of them do not envisage return as a real possibility and do not strive towards it, barring the elderly who deeply aspire to 'die in Vietnam'.

With regard to settlement issues the Vietnamese in Britain unanimously state that they encountered great difficulties while a proportion of those in France claim that they did not meet too many problems apart from 'nostalgia'. In the UK employment issues stand out as the main ones followed by language and family whereas in France housing, employment, family conflicts, language, health, isolation and homesickness are mentioned more or less equally, none seeming to be markedly more prominent. For old people homesickness and isolation definitely occupy the first place in both host countries. As with the Chileans there is a general feeling that professionals could have done better in their home society, *mutatis mutandis,* while others did better in the host society. However, it is noted that being without a job undermines status more considerably in France than in Vietnam as it is 'possible in Vietnam to live from one day to the next whilst in France it leads to *clochardisation*' (being a drop-out). One final item becomes apparent through discussions with the inter- viewees: the fact that the associations greatly assist the Vietnamese in their settlement process.

CONCLUSION

The purpose of this comparative study was to gain an insight into the refugee situation so that a number of conclusions could be reached which did not simply pertain to specific cul- tural or national characteristics either of the refugee popula- tion itself or the society of reception. Through this survey the refugees appear to fall into two distinct categories.

It is clear that for the Chileans a collective project identified with the society of origin is overriding; it influences their process of settlement and their relationship with the society of reception in both France and the UK. Their primary goal was to regain their power as social actors in the society of origin, albeit from a distance. Time and events in the home- land modify the expressions of this identification and a diversification takes place but the homeland orientation never disappears totally on a collective level. A core of political parties is later completed by socio-cultural projects combining a presence in the host society with a strong link with the society of origin. This is compounded by the ideological content of social and cultural expressions emanating from the associations. On an individual level, however, a larger measure of diversified orientations appears to develop over the pro- longed duration of exile. The cycle is completed and vindi- cated when the possibility of return occurs, to be taken up by a substantial proportion of this population. This is when a dramatic change occurs in the outlook of the group.

The position of the Vietnamese differs markedly from their Latin American counterparts. Their main orientation is that of the society of reception. Apart from a small minority of the associations all their efforts tend to address adaptation and

settlement in the host society. The associations do not entertain links with the homeland on an organized plane but concentrate on doing so with the reception society. Their aim is to
gain social power in the host society and they tackle a variety
of aspects pertaining to this task including the preservation of
culture and community. They seem to have burnt their
bridges and forsaken any project involving Vietnam. The concrete desire for return does not make part of their strategy. It
also means that the impact of the society of reception will
affect this group more than the Chileans and greater discrepancies are observed across the Channel. This readiness to
strive for integration distinguishes the Vietnamese from the
Chileans who display great reluctance to do so, but also from
most labour migrant populations who slowly come to the
awareness that 'they are here to stay' and proceed accordingly
only after a significant length of time.

However, both groups identify specific features associated
with the fact that they are refugees; for the Chileans it is the
reluctance to integrate coupled with their political commitment while for the Vietnamese it is the will to succeed and the
fight for survival. One feature is shared by these populations:
the importance of their associations and their role as brokers
with the society of origin and that of reception.

The impact of the society of reception is greater on an individual level and this is where the better facilities offered in
France and the very positive attitude towards these two populations are noticeable. Both Vietnamese and Chileans appreci-
ate the fact that they enjoy so many advantages as refugees in
France, which is confirmed concretely by the greater problems
of settlement both populations encountered in the UK. Other
particularities of the reception societies played their role such
as the presence of a Vietnamese community already established in France, the historic links between France and
Vietnam, possibly the greater cultural and political proximity
between Chile and France, while the absence of similar features in Britain definitely did not help the refugees. This
might be compounded by variations in the socio-economic
composition of the refugee population in the two countries of
reception, especially with regard to the Vietnamese.

A broad sketch has been drawn here which inevitably involves
oversimplifications. This has been done for heuristic purposes

but one needs to be reminded that reality is more complex, as the groups themselves are neither homogeneous nor static and subject to the influence of a multiplicity of variables.

NOTE

1.   Refugees from Vietnam include Vietnamese and Chinese settled in Vietnam centuries ago. The associations studied here mostly concern Vietnamese although a few may have a mixed Vietnamese/Chinese membership and clientèle.

Conclusions

Tensions and contradictions run within the three areas of refugee research considered in this book. One major issue is the discrepancy between on the one hand the social reality of refugees and on the other the legal instruments and policies relating to them. Such discrepancies are compounded by the lack of knowledge on the refugees themselves and by political and ideological trends which are adverse to the acceptance of refugees. The main instrument which has governed the treatment of refugees in Europe has been and is still the 1951 Geneva Convention. Its definition of a refugee corresponds to specific social and historical refugee movements but also reflects an international consensus carried by a relatively high level of concern with human rights and social justice in the wake of the defeat of fascism. Of course, this does not mean that political and ideological considerations were not taken into account all the more as the Cold War had already set in. Nor was the 1951 Convention designed to prevail for the next fifty years to come, but introduced geographical and historical limitations. However no major obstacle interfered with the removal of these limitations through the 1967 Protocol which made the dispositions of the Convention applicable to non-European refugees. In the nineties, it is clear that the Convention definition does not suffice to cover all the refugees who reach the shores of Europe and cross the borders of European states, and this mismatch is already to be found within the clauses of this very Convention. Today the populations defined in Article 1, that is the definition of refugee, are no longer one and the same as those benefiting from Article 33, the non-*refoulement* clause. In other words many individuals cannot be returned to their countries of origin because of the dangers awaiting them despite the fact that they do not come under the Convention definition of a refugee (Lobkovitcz, 1994). In France the situation of persons coming from '*régions troublées*' in former Yugoslavia perfectly illustrates this point. They benefited from measures guaranteeing that they would not be returned to their country of origin but this in itself did not entitle them to the granting of a residence permit or a legal status. This discrepancy has been pragmatically recognized by most European states which have granted protection under a motley collection of alternative statuses to those who came to be called *de facto* or humanitarian refugees. The logical and ethical step that could have been expected was a reformulation of the Convention definition or a supplementary legal instrument, as had been done in other continents, to reduce the discrepancy which had developed in Europe. On the contrary, this was ignored throughout the eighties; non-Convention refugees were not even alluded to in the instruments being drawn up to further European harmonization until the nineties.

In order to understand why this happened it was necessary to examine the factors underpinning asylum policies. This study ponders over yet another hiatus: a horde of varied considerations intertwine to influence asylum policies which have nothing to do with internationally agreed standards or with the merits of the case. For each national asylum policy at a particular point in time and even for particular refugee groups, decisions result from a complex combination of foreign policy, domestic policy and ethical factors within a context of broad parameters. Until the end of the eighties the Cold War contributed heavily to asylum policies in the Western World while it was not the sole factor to be taken into account. In the 1990s the one single common denominator is the economic recession and the crisis of society which has hit Europe and the rest of the industrial world. It is not only that unemployment hits hard, that the welfare state is receding and that the standard of living has gone down. This is exacerbated by the concomitant societal and ideological crisis whereby a vacuum of values and hopes was created: the myth of a buoyant and prosperous economy full of opportunity for all has been shattered and the pursuit of material rewards once capable of yielding satisfaction now often brings about mere disillusionment and frustration. Moreover, the collapse of communist states dealt a severe blow to most ideologies carrying messages of social justice and to the hopes or myths about building a better society. No alternative is offered but capitalism and its current critical problems. It has meant that domestic factors predominantly unfavourable to a generous policy on refugees prevail, leaving little space for ethical considerations.

As a consequence the refugees who did not exactly fit the Convention definition were treated less and less kindly, often being labelled 'bogus', 'fake' and subsumed by the authorities, the media and the public into what were perceived as illegal entrants attempting to circumvent immigration regulations. Their numbers increased while Europe became less and less open to receive any category of 'migrants', having closed its doors to labour immigrants in the seventies. The changing context of refugee movements in Europe in the late 1980s and early 1990s made the potential number of bona fide refugees extremely high, and this situation was compounded by possible shifts from the migration queue into the refugee queue. As a result European initiatives on asylum moved from human rights to intergovernmental fora. European Union states took the lead in developing conventions and agreements which are predominantly characterized by their restrictionist bias; they created a pole of attraction for neighbouring states including former EFTA states and more recently Central European ones. However, the magnitude of the crisis in former Yugoslavia and the horrendous persecutions associated with it have forced European states to formulate a response to the mass movement of refugees resulting from it. A package of measures was devised which combined assistance in the home country ('safe havens') in the region of origin (in former Yugoslavia) and the creation of a new status which recognized the existence and validity claim to protection of refugees who did not meet all the 1951 Convention criteria. This was enshrined in two EU resolutions awarding 'temporary protection' to certain persons from former Yugoslavia. One might detect here the harbingers and the bases for a new regional convention. If this is the case we remain far from an international or even regional instrument which would meet the social reality and the needs of contemporaneous refugees. One major shortcoming of this 'temporary protection' is its narrowness in scope and vision; only very selective groups are entitled to benefit, its interpretation and application vary enormously between one reception country and another, raising issues of parity, and, as nothing is foreseen short of a prompt return to the country of origin, no 'plan B' exists to cater for a long-term situation of 'temporariness', should the continuing conflict delay the feasibility of return for a long period. The social rights and conditions of reception associated with this status are another serious handicap as they appear to leave much to be desired. Questions of reception and settlement can therefore not be ignored while considering asylum issues.

It is almost self evident that asylum and reception policies are linked, although governments seldom acknowledge this publicly. The residence of substantial numbers of refugees which result from access to the asylum procedure necessitates rules and policies on their social rights and their place in the relevant society. The comparative study of reception programmes in France and Britain shows that it is necessary to acquire a fine appreciation of the populations involved in order to set up an appropriate reception programme. In the first place the structural character of refugee movements must be recognized and reception structures need to cater for present and future refugee groups. A sensitive programme cannot simply treat refugees like labour migrants and even needs to establish distinction between social (or rather sociological) categories of refugees. The debate on legal status, if it reflects social realities, is thus relevant for a discussion of reception facilities. The programmes studied in this book are those of better days when the general attitude to refugees was much more propitious, in particular towards the national groups examined above. None the less our study shows that the approach of the host society to this question is indicative of the underpinning philosophy and ideology of that society built through its history and traditions. This is in turn modified by the economic and political conjuncture and altogether by the same factors which underlay asylum policies. It will generally be easier to obtain well-funded reception programmes and broader social rights for refugees when asylum policies are more generous. Alternatively, restrictive asylum policies are often associated with 'deterrent' conditions of reception and settlement. In the case of reception policies, NGOs mustered a greater degree of influence as in the countries under study they carried out the bulk of the work. Nevertheless one important point is to be retained from this study: the fact that refugee reception and settlement have to be taken on by the nation collectively. The relationship between asylum and reception policies is not unilateral. Reception and settlement policies, or more exactly the modes of settlement which they condition, may have an influence on asylum policies. For instance, if appropriate measures enable the refugees to make an active contribution to their society of reception they are less likely to be perceived as a social burden and will bring about a more favourable attitude to other refugees. Alternatively it may occur that acceptances will be slowed down if it is felt that reception structures cannot cope. In any event, reception and settlement policies will have a determining impact on the refugees themselves and this research indicates that the absence of reception structures and *laissez faire* policies could lead to situation of grave distress and possibly to social tensions, particularly in the present conjuncture laden with economic recession and ideological uncertainties. A number of recommendations are also put forward based on the experiences examined in this comparative study, but there is no doubt that further research is necessary to establish the most positive policies and practices in this area.

The debate on the specificity of refugees opened in legal terms as soon as the awarding of protection and status were envisaged. Refugees have been carefully defined in international conventions but these reveal discrepancies and seem to indicate that different categories of refugees may exist. The question then had to be framed within a sociological debate; are refugees a social type distinct from other types of migrants such as labour migrants or are there perhaps different social types of refugees? An exploration of these questions might not only enlighten sociologists but also help policy-makers both in the area of asylum and settlement policies. Our view is that there are such social types as refugees with their own characteristics and their own modes of settlement in the host society. Of paramount importance for refugees is the impact of the past on the present, that is their positioning within the structure of conflict which led them to flee from their homeland and its influence on their mode of settlement in exile. Moreover refugees are not one single category and this study shows that there exist at least two social types: those who nurture a collective project oriented towards the society of origin and those who do not (they never did so or abandoned it). The legal status awarded does not necessarily reveal clearly the category to which particular groups of refugees belong. Here again sociological and legal categories often fail to co-incide. It is likely that refugees of the second type have considerably increased in the nineties. What is clear, however, is that both types differentiate themselves from labour migrants in their motivations, their aspirations and their mode of settlement. I have posited here ideal social types, extracted from a more nuanced reality. Indeed, refugee groups are neither homogeneous nor static and may shift from one type to another as a result of a variety of factors. At any rate, settlement policies must be sensitive and take on board such specificities as insecurity and trauma derived from exile and what caused it, together with a clear understanding of the need for refugees to preserve their specific identity. Policies cannot force the refugees to choose between stability and participation in the society of reception on the one hand and attachment to the society of origin on the other; both are necessary ingredients for the best possible outcome. Another important piece of data is that the refugees are not only at the receiving end of asylum and reception policies but that they interact dynamically with them. Policies undoubtedly affect the refugees and may determine their mode of interaction with the society of reception in so far as they modulate possibilities of access, integration and exclusion. In a certain way the refugees are socially constructed by policies. However, the refugees themselves do not remain passive but influence policy-makers and policies through their associations. They can participate actively in the making of a place for themselves in the land of exile even when they were not expected nor called upon to do so. It seems therefore that the most constructive approach would be to welcome and encourage their participation rather than preclude it, as is often stipulated by host societies.

From the refugees' point of view, interconnections between asylum policies, reception policies and refugee communities are self-evident and all three form parts of the same question. Policy-makers often compartmentalize and divide issues so that they may not be aware that all three areas must be considered together to gain a better grasp of each of the component parts. Perhaps this piece of integrated research can help them to broaden their horizons, thus contributing to more appropriate policies.

The themes of asylum and refugees are far from exhausted here. New issues appear on the agenda and point to further research. For instance, it will be necessary, in addition to EU policies, to look at the OSCE, the Intergovernmental Consultations and the Council of Europe in greater depth to understand the development of asylum regimes in Europe. Moreover, the prevailing trend of restrictionism is now supplemented by new formulas such as temporary protection, regionalization, return and internationally protected zones. Refugees groups themselves have today undergone changes in terms of their relationship to the structure of conflict in the country of origin, their legal status and conditions of reception in the asylum country. A study of these new groups can help deepen the theoretical framework attempted in this book.

Bibliography

Ad Hoc Group on Immigration (1991) Report from the Ministers responsible for immigration to the European Council meetings in Maastricht on immigration and asylum policy, Brussels, 3 December 1991 (WG1 9301 SN 4038/91)

Ad Hoc Group on Immigration (1992a) Brussels 21 May 1992, SN 2782/92 (WG1 1108). Conclusions regarding the implementation of controls on persons on the basis of the draft Convention between the Member States of the European Communities on the crossing of their external frontiers

Ad Hoc Group on Immigration (1992b) Brussels 21 May 1992, SN 2520/92 WG1 1102. Definition and harmonised application of the principle of first host country (draft conclusions)

Ad Hoc Group on Immigration (1992c) Brussels 21 May 1992, SN 2781/92 (WG1 1107). Establishment of a Centre for Information, Discussion and Exchange on asylum (clearing house) draft decision

Ad Hoc Group on Immigration (1992d) CIREA, Brussels 24 September 1992, SN 3917/92 WG1 1186 CIREA 2. Working document on mutual exchanges of information via the clearing house (Brussels 15 October 1992)

Ad Hoc Group on Immigration (1992e) Brussels 26 October 1992 SN 4282/92 WG1 1230. Countries in which there is generally no serious risk of persecution. Proposal from the asylum Sub-group to the Ad Hoc Immigration Group, incl. Annex A. Draft report to Ministers from the Ad Hoc Group on Immigration

Ad Hoc Group on Immigration (1992f) Draft resolution on manifestly unfounded applications for asylum, Progress report on discussions in the Asylum Sub-Group.Note by the Presidency 1/11/92. SN 3926/92 WG1 1195 AS 128

Ad Hoc Group on Immigration (1992g) Brussels 16 November 1992, SN 4678/92 WG1 1266. Draft recommendation regarding practices followed by Member States on expulsion

Ad Hoc Group on Immigration (1992h) Brussels, 16 November 1992, SN 4682/92 WG1 1270 CIREA 9. The clearing House (CIREA) Future work. Note by the Presidency

Ad Hoc Group on Immigration (1992i) Brussels 16 November 1992, SN 4681/92 WG1 1269 AS 142. Transfer of applicants for asylum under the provisions of Article 11 and 13 of the Dublin Convention

Ad Hoc Group on Immigration (1992j) Draft report to Immigration Ministers by the Ad Hoc Immigration Group SN 4630 92 1268 AG 141

Ad Hoc Group on Immigration (1993a) CIREA, Dissemination of information SN 2274/1/93 WG1 1433 CIREA 51

Ad Hoc Group on Immigration (1993b) Draft for discussion concerning harmonised use of the definition of a refugee, as defined in Article 1, Letter A of the Geneva Convention, Translation (WG1 1361, 10.2.93)

Ad Hoc Group on Immigraton (1993c) Brussels 14 May 1993, SN 2834/93 WG1 1503 CIREA 66. First activity report from CIREA to the Ministers responsible for Immigration

Ad Hoc Group on Immigration (1993d) Brussels 14 May 1993, SN 2836/93 WG1 1505. Compilation of texts on European practice with respect to asylum

Ad Hoc Group on Immigration (1993e) Brussels 25 May 1993. SN 3017/93 WG1 1516. Draft recommendation concerning checks on and expulsion of third country nationals residing or working without authorisation

ADRI, (1988) Le devenir des réfugiés et demandeurs d'asile ayant sejourné dans les centres provisoires d'hébergement, Note de synthèse Paris, ADRI

Ajchenbaum, Yves (1981) *Les populations originaires d'Asie du Sud-Est accueillies en France au sein des centres provisoires d'hébergement 1975–1979*, Paris, FTDA

Aleinikoff, T. Alexander, (1984) 'Political Asylum in the Federal Republic of Germany and the Republic of France, Lessons for the United States', University of Michigan, *Journal of Law Reform*, Vol. 17 No.2, Winter, pp.183–243

Ambrose, Stephen E., (1983) *Rise to globalism, American foreign policy since 1938*, Harmondsworth: Penguin Books

Amnesty International (1992) *Europe: harmonisation of asylum policy, Accelerated procedures for 'manifestly unfounded' asylum claims and the 'safe country' concept*, Brussels, Amnesty International, November 1992

Arbatov, Georgi, (1983) *Cold war or detente: The Soviet Viewpoint*, London: Zed Books

Assemblée nationale (1987) Question: 11 mai 1987, 24408, M. Gérard Fuchs à M. le Ministre des Affaires Sociales et de l'Emploi; Réponse, 23 novembre

Association of Metropolitan Authorities (AMA) and Refugee Council (1994) UK Seminar London: 8 March 1994

Bach, Robert and Rita Carroll-Seguin, (1986) 'Labor force participation, household composition and sponsorship among South East Asian refugees', *International Migration Review*, Vol. 20, No.2, pp.381–404

Bang, Susanne (1983) *We come as a friend: towards a Vietnamese model of social work*, Leeds: Refugee Action

Bang, Susanne and Rosalind Finlay (1982) *Working to support refugees*, London: Save the Children Fund and Leeds: Refugee Action

Bardet-Blochet, Anne et al. (1988). *Les associations d'immigrés: repli ou participation sociale? L'exemple de Genève*, Genève: Centre de Contact Suisses-Immigrés

Barrou, Jacques et al. (1988) *Le devenir des réfugiés et demandeurs d'asile ayant séjourné dans les centres provisoires d'hébergement en région Rhône-Alpes*, Rapport de recherche réalisé pour le compte de la Direction de la Population et des Migrations, Ministère des Affaires Sociales et de l'Emploi. And Note de Synthèse

Baskauskas, Liucija (1981) 'The Lithuanian refugee experience and grief', *International Migration Review*, Vol. 15, (1–2), pp.276–291

Bell, John and Lola Clinton (1992) *The unheard community: A report on the housing conditions and needs of refugees from Vietnam living in London*, London, Community Development Foundation, August

Bettati, M. (1985) *L'asile politique en question: Un statut pour les réfugiés*, Paris: Presses Universitaires de France

Blaschke, Jochen (1989) 'Refugees and Turkish migrants in West Berlin' in Danièle Joly and Robin Cohen (eds), *Reluctant hosts: Europe and its refugees*, Aldershot: Avebury

Bohm, (1985) Report on living and working conditions of refugees and asylum-seekers, Council of Europe Parliamentary Assembly, 26 March, DOC 5380 revised

Bolzman, Claudio (1993) *Les métamorphoses de la barque. Les politiques d'asile, d'insertion et de retour de la Suisse à l'égard des exiliés chiliens* Genève: Les Editions IES

Bonacich, Edna (1938) 'A theory of middleman minorities', *American Sociological Review*, 38, Oct. pp.583–594

Bourdillon, François (1986) 'La santé des demandeurs d'asile', *Hommes et Migrations* No.1096, 15 octobre, pp.32–35

Bristow, Mike (1976) 'Britain's response to the Uganda Asian crisis: government myths versus political and resettlement realities', *New Community*, Vol.V, No.3, Autumn, pp.265–279

Bristow, Mike, Bert N. Adams, and Cecil Pereira (1975) 'Ugandan Asians in Britain, Canada and India: some characteristics and resources', *New Community*, Vol. 4, No.2, pp.155–166

Brochman, Grete (1993) 'Immigration control, the welfare state and xenophobia towards an integrated Europe', *Migration* 18/93, pp.5–25

Brown, Charlotte (1991) *Strangers in a foreign land. Reception of asylum-seekers in Europe*, Brussels, Quaker Council for European Affairs, August 1991

Brown, Geoffrey (1982) 'Issues in the resettlement of Indochinese refugees', *Social Casework*, pp.155–159

Browne, Ann (1979) *Latin American Refugees: British government policy and practice*, An annual review of British Latin American relations, London, Latin American Relations

Candappa, Mano and Danièle Joly (1994) *Local Authorities, Ethnic Minorities and 'Pluralist Integration'*, Monograph No.7, Coventry: CRER, University of Warwick

Carens, Joseph H. (1988) 'Nationalism and the exclusion of immigrants: lessons from Australian immigration policy' in Mark Gibney, ed., *Open borders? Closed societies? The ethical and political issues*, New York: Greenwood Press, pp.41–60

Chan Kwok, B. and Doreen Marie Indra (eds) (1987) *Uprooting Loss and Adaptation: the Resettlement of Indochinese Refugees in Canada*, Ottawa: Canadian Public Health Association

Chan Kwok, B. and Laurence Lam (1987) 'Psychological problems of Chinese Vietnamese refugees resettling in Quebec', in Chan and Indra (eds), *Uprooting Loss and Adaptation: the Resettlement of Indochinese Refugees in Canada*, pp.27–42

Chant, John (1983) Letter from John Chant, Honorary Secretary of the Association of Directors of Social Services (ADSS) to T.E. Noder, Deputy Secretary of the DHSS

Chile Democratico (1985) Provisional report on the survey carried out among the Chilean community in Britain in March–April 1984, London

Chomsky, Noam, Steele, Jonathan and Gittings, John (1984) *Superpowers in collision: The new Cold War of the 1980s*, Harmondsworth: Penguin

Chomsky, Noam (1984) 'The United States: from Greece to El Salvador' in Chomsky, Noam, Steele, Jonathan and Gittings, John, *Superpowers in collision: The New Cold War of the 1980s*, Harmondsworth: Penguin, pp.24–58

Christensen Arne Piel and Morten Kjaerum (1990) 'Refugees and our role in the European House' *International Journal of Refugee Law*, Vol. 2, 1990, pp.323–333

Cimade (1975) *Du Chili à la France exil et accueil des réfugiés*, Paris: Cimade Information, février

Circulaire (1974) A l'attention des directeurs de centres accueillant des réfugiés, 25.1.1974

Circulaire (1974) Annexe 1, Note sur l'utilisation des HLM pendant la période de prise en charge, 25.1.1974

Circulaire (1974) Annexe IV, La recherche d'emploi, 21.1.1974

Cohen, Robin (1988) 'Citizens, denizens and helots: the politics of international migration flows in the post-war world'. Paper for the International Symposium on Cultural Changes in the period of Transformation in the Capitalist World System, Faculty of Social Studies, Hitotsubashi University Tokyo, 19–20 September, pp.1–18

Cohon, Donald (1981) 'Psychological adaptation and dysfunction among refugees', *International Migration Review*, Vol. 15 (1–2), pp.255–275

Commission of the European Communities (1992) Background report *Immigration and asylum*, 10 March 1992, ISEC B6 92

Commission of the European Communities (1994) Communication from the Commission to the Council and the European Parliament on Immigration and Asylum Policies Com (94) Brussels 23 February 1994

Common Security, (1982) *A programme for disarmament, The report of the Independent Commission on Disarmament and Security Issues*, London: Pan Books

Conseil (1995a) Note de la Présidence Française au Groupe Directeur I. Programme de travail prioritaire pour la Présidence française au sein du Groupe Directeur I (Asile/Immigration) 12394/94

Conseil (1995b) 'Communication à la presse' 09/10.3.95. Garanties minimales en matières de demandes d'asile

Conseil (1995c) Conseil de l'Union Européenne. Communication à la presse. Luxembourg les 20/21 juin 1995. 8133/95 (Presse 194)

Costa-Lascoux, Jacqueline, (1987) Réfugiés et demandeurs d'asile en Europe, REMI, Vol.3, No.1 and 2. 1e–3e, Trimestre, pp.239–263

Council of Europe (1993) Contribution to the CSCE Human Dimension seminar on migration, including refugees and displaced persons, (Warsaw 20–23 April 1993) 14 April 1993

Council of Europe (1994) Parliamentary Assembly Recommendation 1236 (1994) on the right of asylum

Council of Europe Parliamentary Assembly (1975) *Report on the situation of de facto Refugees*, 5/8/75, Doc. 3642

Cox, David (1979) 'Australia's immigration policy and refugees' in Robert Birrell et al., (eds), *Refugees, resources, reunion: Australia's immigration dilemmas*, Australia: VCTA, pp.7–20

CSCE (1990) *Charter for a new Europe*, Paris 1990

CSCE (1991) Document of the Moscow meeting of the Conference on the *Human Dimension of the CSCE*, Moscow 3 October 1991

CSCE (1992a) CSCE Helsinki Document 1992, *The Challenges of Change*, 8 July 1992

CSCE (1992b) Summary of conclusions of the Stockholm Council Meeting, CSCE, Stockholm 15 December 1992

CSCE (1993) *Vienna Declaration and Programme of Action*, 25 June 1993

Dahya, Badr (1974) 'The nature of ethnicity in industrial cities in Britain', in *Urban Ethnicity*, Abner Cohen (ed.) London: Tavistock, 1974, pp.77–118

de Wangen, Gérold (1977) Lettre circulaire. Objet, Insertion Médicale des réfugiés du Sud-Est Asiatique, 24 juin

de Wangen, Gerold (1980) *Historique de l'accueil et de la formation initiale des réfugiés en France*, Paris: FTDA, Mars

Declaración de Cartagena, Bajo los Auspicios del Gobierno de la Republica de Colombia, Cartagena, 19–22 de noviembre de 1984

Delegations of Germany, Italy, Spain and the United Kingdom (1992) Proposal submitted by the delegations of Germany, Italy, Spain and the United Kingdom. The enhanced involvement of non-governmental organizations to the CSCE process. CSCE, Helsinki follow-up meeting 1992, CSCE/HM/WG3/23, Helsinki 15 June 1992

Department of the Environment (1993), *Local Government Finance (England) Special Grant Report* (No.8) London: HMSO, 14 June

Desbarats, Jacqueline (1986) 'Ethnic differences in adaptation: Sino-Vietnamese refugees in the United States', *IMR*, Vol. 20, No.2, 1986, pp.405–427

Dienesch, Marie Madeleine (1973) Secrétaire d'Etat auprès du Ministre de la Santé Publique et de la Sécurité Sociale à Monsieur le Préfet du Cabinet, signé Marie Madeleine Dienesch R.D. 1, R.V.3, R.V.4

Drücke Luise (1992) *Asylum policies in a European community without internal borders*, Churches Committee for Migrants in Europe, Briefing paper No.9, October 1992

Dutch Refugee Council and Netherlands Institute of Human Rights (1989) Report of the International Conference Refugees in the World: the European Community Response. The Hague, 7–8 December 1989, SIM Special No.10

ECRE (1990) *Asile en Europe*, Paris, France Terre d'Asile

ECRE (1993) Working paper on the need for a supplementary refugee definition, April

ECRE (1993a) Temporary protection note. Ad Hoc Meeting of ECRE agencies, Schiphol, 12 February 1993

ECRE (1993b) Survey on the status of persons arriving from former Yugoslavia. ECRE-Conference on the status and treatment of refugees from former Yugoslavia, 12 February 1993

ECRE (1993c) Report of ECRE bi-annual general meeting, Berlin, April 23, 24, 25 1993

ECRE (1993d) *Asylum in Europe: An introduction, Volume I*, London April 1993

ECRE (1995) Note from the European Council on Refugees and Exiles on the harmonisation of the interpretation of Article 1 of the 1951 Geneva Convention

ECRE and Amnesty International (1995) Press Release, 10 March, 'ECRE and Amnesty International believe new EU minimum guarantees for asylum procedures are insufficient'

Edholm, Felicity et al. (1983) *Vietnamese refugees in Britain*, London: CRE

Eisenstadt (1954) *The Absorption of Immigrants*, Routledge & Kegan Paul

Eitinger, Leo and David Schwarz, (eds) (1981) *Strangers in the World*, Bern: Hans Huber Publishers

European Consultation on Refugees and Exiles (1992) Report of ECRE bi-annual general meeting. Geneva October 3–4 1992

European Council (1992a) General Secretariat of the Council, Lisbon 12 June 1992, SN 2886 11/92. Press release. Meeting of Ministers with responsibility for Immigration (Lisbon 11 June 1992)

European Council (1992b) London 30 November 1992, Press release. Subject, Conclusions of the meeting of the Ministers responsible for Immigration (London, 30 November–1 December 1992)

European Council (1992c) Conclusions of the Presidency, European Council in Edinburgh 1992

European Council (1993) General Secretariat of the Council, Brussels 2 June 1993. Press release subject, Meeting of Ministers with responsibility for immigration (Copenhagen, 1 and 2 June 1993)

Ex, J. (1966) *Adjustment after migration*, The Hague: Martinus Nijhoff

Fabre, Daniel (1984) Premier Ministre Délégation interministérielle aux réfugiés à Mr. Michel Rouah, Directeur, France Terre d'Asile, Paris, le 27 juin

Field, Simon (1985) *Resettling refugees: the lessons of research*, Home Office Research Study No.87, London: HMSO

Finlay, Ros and Gill Reynolds (1985) *Better Social Services for Refugees*, Leeds: Refugee Action

Finnan, Christine Robinson (1981) 'Occupational assimilation of refugees', *IMR*, Vol. 15 (1–2), pp.292–309

Fle, Catherine (1988) Rapport final de l'étude sur le devenir des réfugiés et demandeurs d'asile ayant séjourné dans les centres provisoires d'héberge-ment (Région Ouest) demandé par la Direction de la Population et des Migrations Ministère de la Solidarité, de l'Emploi et de la Protection Sociale, 30 décembre. And Note de Synthèse

France Terre d'Asile (1984) FTDA *Rapport d'activité 1984*, Paris: FTDA

Gallagher, Dennis (1989a) *The Era of Refugees: The Evolution of the International Refugee System*, Refugee Policy Group, Washington

Gallagher, Dennis (1989b) 'The evolution of the international refugee system', *IMR*, Vol.23, pp.578–598

Gamrasni-Ahlen, Nina (1992) 'Recent European developments regarding refugees: the Dublin Convention and the French perspective' in Jacqueline Bhabha and Geoffrey Coll (eds) *Asylum law and practice in Europe and North America*, Washington, Federal Publications Inc., pp.109–123

Gibney, Mark, and Stohl, Michael (1988) 'Human rights and US refugee policy' in Gibney, Mark (ed.) *Open borders? Closed societies? The ethical and political issues*, New York: Greenwood Press, pp.151–184

Gibney, Mark (1988) (ed.) *Open borders? Closed societies? The ethical and political issues*, New York: Greenwood Press

Gibson, Urban and Jan Niessen (1993) *The CSCE and the protection of the rights of migrants, refugees and minorities.* Churches Committee for Migrants in Europe, Briefing paper 11, Brussels, March 1993

Gitmez, Ali and Czarina Wilpert (1987) 'A micro-society or an ethnic community? Social organisation and ethnicity amongst Turkish migrants' in John Rex, Danièle Joly and Czarina Wilpert, *Immigrant Associations in Europe*, Aldershot: Gower

Gittings, John (1984) 'What the Superpowers say' in Chomsky, Noam, Steele, Jonathan, and Gittings John, *Superpowers in Collision: The New Cold War of the 1980s*, Harmondsworth: Penguin, pp.9–23

Glezer, Leon (1979) 'Immigration and the environmentalists: a comment', in Robert Birrell et. al. (eds), *Refugees Resources Reunion: Australia's Immigration Dilemmas*, Australia: VCTA, pp.93–108

Gold, Steven J. (1992) *Refugee Communities*, Newbury Park: Sage

Gomane, Jean-Pierre (1992) *Permanence du réflexe colonial; l'accueil des réfugiés-indochinois*, Actes du Colloque, Les réfugiés en France et en Europe: Quarante ans d'application de la Convention de Genève 1952–1992, 11–13 juin 1992, Paris, OFPRA, pp.236–247

Goodwin-Gill, Guy (1983) *The Refugee in International Law*, Oxford, Clarendon Press

Goodwin-Gill, Guy (1986) 'Non-refoulement and the new asylum-seeker', *Virginia Journal of International Law*, Vol.26:4, pp.897–918

Goodwin-Gill, Guy (1989) *International law and human rights; trends concerning international migrants and refugees* IMR, Vol XXIII, No 2, pp.526–546

Goodwin-Gill, Guy S. (1992) 'Safe country? Says Who?' in *Refugees*, No.89, May 1992

Goodwin-Gill, Guy S. (1993) 'Towards a comprehensive regional policy approach: the case for closer inter-agency cooperation', UNHCR, Conference on *Security and Cooperation in Europe. Human dimension seminar on migration, including refugees and displaced persons*, Warsaw 20–23 April 1993

Grahl-Madsen (1989) Atle, *Archiv des Völkerrechts*, International Refugee Law Today and Tomorrow, pp.411–467

Gramsci, Antonio (1971) selections from the Prison Notebooks, ed. Q. Hoare and G. N. Smith, New York: International Publishers

Granet, Paul and Paul Dijoud (1975) Secrétariat d'Etat auprès du Premier Ministre Secrétariat d'Etat auprès du Ministre du Travail Direction de la Population et des Migrations, No.25–75, Paris, le 17 décembre

Groupe Ad Hoc Immigration (1991) Bruxelles, le 8 octobre 1991. SN 2881/1/91 WG1 837 REV 1. Description et planifaction des travaux préparatoires nécessaires en vue de l'harmonisation du droit d'asile matériel. Contribution du sous-groupe 'Asile' du Groupe ad hoc 'Immigration' au rapport destine à être présenté au Conseil Europeén des 9 et 10 décembre 1991

Groupe Ad Hoc Immigration (1992a) Bruxelles le 9 avril 1992, SN 2084/92 WG1 1059. Création d'un Centre d'information, de réflexion et d'échanges en matière d'asile (C.I.R.E.A), Project de décision

Groupe Ad Hoc Immigration (1992b) Bruxelles, le 8 mai 1992, SN 1729/2/92 WG1 1008 REV2. Avant-projet de Convention parallèle à la Convention de Dublin du 15 juin 1990

Groupe Ad Hoc Immigration (1993) Rapport sur l'activité du Centre d'Information, de réflexion et d'échange en matière d'asile à l'intention des Ministres chargés de l'immigration, SN 2834/93 WG1 1503, CIREA 66

Guillon, Claude (1992) Evolution des dispositifs d'aide aux demandeurs d'asile et aux réfugiés, Actes du Colloque. Les réfugiés en France et en Europe: Quarante ans d'application de la Convention de Genève 1952–1992, 11–13 juin 1992, Paris, OFPRA, pp.279–292

Guillon, Michelle and Isabelle Taboada-Leonetti (1986), *Le triangle de Choisy, un quartier chinois à Paris*, Paris: L'Harmattan

Hall, Dorothea (1981) 'Adult education among Vietnamese refugees', *Adult Education*, Vol. 54, part 2, pp.146–151

Hammar, Tomas and Anders Lange (1989) in Danièle Joly and Robin Cohen (eds) *Reluctant Hosts: Europe and its Refugees*, Aldershot: Avebury, pp.195–204

Hansard Parliamentary Debates, Lords. Vol. 347, Col.442

Hansard Parliamentary Debates, Commons, Vol. 863, Written Answers, Col.21

Hansard Parliamentary Debates, Commons, Vol. 902, Oral Answers, Col.424

Hathaway, James C., (1984) The evolution of refugee status in international law : 1920–1950, :33, ICLQ, pp.348–380

HCR (1992) Position du HCR sur la question de l'application de la Convention de Genève aux demandeurs d'asile en provenance de l'ex Yougoslavie, Paris, 2 décembre 1992

Hily, Marie-Antionette and Michel Poinard (1987) 'Portuguese associations in France' in John Rex, Danièle Joly and Czarina Wilpert, *Immigrant associations in Europe*, Aldershot: Gower

Hitchcox, Linda (1987) *The Vietnamese refugees in Britain*, Conference on government and voluntary agencies in the resettlement of refugees in Europe, 24–25 October, University of Warwick

Holborn, Louise W. (1975) *Refugees: a problem of our time. The work of the United Nations High Commissioner for Refugees, 1951–1972*, Vol. 1, Metuchen, NJ, Scarecrow Press

Home Affairs Committee (1985) Refugees and asylum, with special reference to the Vietnamese, Third Report from the Home Affairs Committee, Session 1984–85, London: HMSO

Home Office (1988) *A scrutiny of grants under section 11 of the Local Government Act 1966*, final report, (mimeo)

Home Office (1993) Payment for grant under Section 11 of the Local Government Act 1966 – ethnic minorities. Implications of the Local Government (Amendment) Act 1993. London, 10 August

Hope-Simpson, J. (1939) *The Refugee Problem: Report of a Survey*, London, OUP

Howorth, Jolyon and Patricia Chilton (eds) (1984) *Defence and Dissent in Contemporary France*, London: Croom Helm

Hutchinson, Gordon (1985) Interview, London

Indra, Doreen Marie (1987) 'Bureaucratic constraints, middlemen and community organisation: aspects of the political incorporation of South East Asians in Canada', in Chan and Indra (eds), pp.147–170

Jaeger, Gilbert (1981) 'Refugee, asylum: policy and legislative developments', *IMR*, Vol. 15, Spring, 1981 to Winter, pp.52–67

Jaeger, Gilbert (1991) 'Are refugees migrants? The recent approach to refugee flows as a particular aspect of migration', Refugees and asylum-seekers in a common European house, *Oikoumene – Refugees* special issue, August, pp.18–24

Jaeger, Gilbert (1991) 'Refugees in and from Central and Eastern Europe', *Oikoumene – Refugees* special issue, August. Refugees and asylum seekers in a common European house, pp.33–37

Jaeger, Gilbert (1992) 'Comparative asylum and refugee jurisprudence and practice in Europe and North America', in Jacqueline Bhabha and Geoffrey Coll (eds), *Asylum Law and Practice in Europe and North America*, Washington, Federal Publications Inc, pp.1–8

Joint Committee for Refugees from Vietnam (1982) JCVN *Report of the Joint Committee for Refugees from Vietnam*, London: Home Office

Joint Working Group for Refugees from Chile in Britain (1975) JWGCh. Refugees from Chile, An interim report, London, JWGCh. December

Joly, Danièle (1987a) 'Associations amongst the Pakistani population in Britain' in John Rex, Danièle Joly and Czarina Wilpert, *Immigrant Associations in Europe*, Aldershot: Gower

Joly, D. (1987b) 'Britain and its refugees: The case of Chileans', *Migration* I(1) July pp.91–108

Joly, Danièle (1988a) *Refugees in the UK: an annotated bibliography*, Bibliography in Ethnic Relations No.9, Coventry: CRER, University of Warwick

Joly, Danièle (1988b) *Refugees from Vietnam in Birmingham: community, voluntary agency and the role of local authorities*, Research Paper in Ethnic Relations No.9, CRER, Coventry

Joly, D. (1989) 'Le droit d'asile dans la communauté Européenne', *International Journal of Refugee Law*, Vol. 1, No.3, Oxford

Joly, Danièle (1991) *The French Communist Party and the Algerian war*, London: Macmillan

Joly, D. and R. Cohen, (eds) (1989) *Reluctant Host: Europe and its Refugees*, Aldershot: Gower Press

Joly, D. with C. Nettleton (1990) *Refugees in Europe*, London: Minority Rights Group

Joly, D. with Clive Nettleton and Hugh Poulton (1992) *Refugees: Asylum in Europe?* London: MRG

Joly Danièle (1995) *Britannia's Crescent: Making a Place for Muslims in British Society*, Aldershot: Avebury

Jones, Peter R. (1982) *Vietnamese refugees: A study of their reception and resettlement in the United Kingdom*, Research and Planning Unit, Paper 13, London: Home Office

Jones, Peter R. (1983) 'Vietnamese refugees in the UK: the reception programme', in *New Community* Vol. X, No.3, Spring, pp.444–463

Kay, Diana (1987) *Chileans in Exile: Private Struggles, Public Lives*, London: Macmillan

Kay, Diana and Miles Robert (1992) *Refugees or Migrant Workers? European Volunteer Workers in Britain 1946–1951*, London: Routledge

Kaye, Ronald and Charlton Roger (1990) *United Kingdom refugee admission policy and the politically active refugee*, Research Paper in Ethnic Relations No. 13, CRER, University of Warwick

Keller, S.L. (1975), *Uprooting and social change: the role of refugees in development*, Delhi: Manohar Book Service

Kiejman, Georges (1992) Discours de Monsieur Georges Kiejman prononcé à l'occasion de la scéance inaugurale du collogue organisé par l' OFPRA, 11–13 juin, Paris, Les réfugiés en France et en Europe quarante ans d'application de la Convention de Genève 1952–1992

King, Mike (1993) 'The dynamics of inclusion and exclusion of refugees between Eastern, Central and Western Europe', paper presented to the ECPR Joint Sessions Workshop on *Inclusion and exclusion: migration and the uniting of Europe*, Leiden, 2–8 April 1993

Kjaerum, Morten (1993) Note on temporary protection in Europe in the '90s for the CSCE Expert seminar on Migration including refugees and displaced persons, 20–24 April 1993, Warsaw

Komoroczki, Dr Istvan (1993) Opening statement, Head of the Hungarian delegation, MFA, CSCE Department, Warsaw 20 April, 1993, CSCE Human dimension seminar on migration including refugees and displaced persons, Warsaw 20–23 April 1993

Kormendi, Eszter (1989) 'Refugees in Denmark', in Danièle Joly and Robin Cohen (eds) *Reluctant Hosts: Europe and its Refugees*, Aldershot: Avebury, pp.195–204

Kunz, E.F. (1971) 'Political events "at home" and the concept of catharsis naturalization among refugees', *International Migration Review*, Vol. 9, Pt 1/2, pp.55–67

Kunz, E.F. (1971) 'Some basic determinants of post-war refugee naturalisations in Australia', *Australian and New Zealand Journal of Sociology*, Vol. 7 (2) October, pp.38–57

Kunz, E.F. (1973) 'The refugee in flight: kinetic models and forms of displacement', *International Migration Review*, Volume 7, No.2, pp.125–146

Kunz, Egon (1981) 'Exile and resettlement: refugee theory', *International Migration Review*, Vol. 15 (1–2), pp.42–51

La Cour Bodtcher, Anne et al (1993) *Legal and social conditions for asylum seekers and refugees in selected European countries*, Copenhagen, Danish Refugee Council, February 1993

Lapeyronnie, Didier (1993) L'individu et les minorités, Paris: PUF

Lapping, Brian (1970) *The Labour Government 1964–1970*, Harmondsworth: Penguin Books

Lawyers Committee for Human Rights Europe (1991) Report on US Foreign Policy and Human Rights, Topic II: Conference on Security and Cooperation in Europe, September 1, 1991, Washington DC: Patlon, Boggs and Blow

Lawyers Committee for Human Rights (1992) *Refugee Project, Refugees, displaced persons and non-nationals in the CSCE countries*, Report on the February 19, 1992 Conference Summary and outlook

Le Huu Khoa (1985) *Les Vietnamiens en France: insertion et identité*, Paris: L'Harmattan

Leibowitz, Arnold H. (1983) 'The Refugee Act of 1980: Problems and congressional concerns', *ANNALS-AAPSS*, 467, May, pp.163–171

Leite, Jose (1991) 'The CSCE, the European House and priorities for the churches' in *Oikoumene*, – *Refugees* special issue – August 1991. Refugees and asylum seekers in a common European house, pp.9–13

Levin, Michael (1981) *What welcome? Reception and resettlement of refugees in Britain*, London: Action Society Trust

Lobkovitcz (1994) Interview, Brussels 8 December

Loescher, Gilbert (1987) 'Humanitarianism in crisis in Central America' in Gauhar R. (ed.) *Third World Affairs*, pp.330–336

Loescher, Gilbert, and John Scanlan (1985) *Human rights, power politics and the international refugee regime: the case of US treatment of Caribbean basin refugees*, World Order Studies Program, Occasional Paper No. 14, Princeton University, June

Luciuk, Lubomyr (1986) 'Unintended consequences in refugee resettlement: post-war Ukrainian refugee immigration to Canada', *IMR*, Vol. 20, No.2, pp.467–482

Maciver, R.M. and Charles H. Page (1952), *Society*, London: Macmillan

Majka, Lorraine (1991) 'Assessing refugee assistance organisations in the United States and the United Kingdom' *Journal of Refugees Studies*, Vol. 4, No.3, pp.267–283

Marrus, M.R. (1985) *The Unwanted: European Refugees in the Twentieth Century*, New York, OUP

Masse, Jean-Pierre (1992) L'institutionnalisation de l'accueil, in Actes du Colloque, Les réfugiés en France et en Europe: Quarante ans d'application de la Convention de Genève 1952–1992, 11–13 juin 1992, Paris, OFPRA, pp.366–379

McFarland, Elaine and Dave Walsh (1988) *Refugees in Strathclyde*, Glasgow: Scottish Ethnic Minorities Research Unit, Glasgow College

Melander, G. (1987) *The two refugee definitions*, Report No.4, Raoul Wallenberg Institute, Lund, pp.9–22

Melander, Goran (1992) 'Country of first asylum' issues: a European perspective in Jacqueline Bhabha and Geoffrey Coll (eds) *Asylum law and practice in Europe and North America*, Washington, Federal Publications Inc., pp.101–107

Mignot, Michel (1983) L'influence de l'accueil des réfugiés en provenance du Cambodge, du Laos, du Vietnam sur le paysage communal français, *AWR Bulletin*, Nos 2–3, pp.96–99

Ministère de la solidarité nationale (1981) Circulaire No.81–3, Paris, 29 juillet

Ministère du Travail (1975) Circulaire du 18 septembre

Ministers responsible for immigration (1991) Report to the European Council in Maastricht on immigration and asylum policy, Brussels, 3 December 1991, Annex 2

Montero, Darrel (1979) Vietnamese Americans, Patterns of Resettlement and Socioeconomic adaptation in the United States, Boulder, Colorado: Westview Press

Mougne, Chris (1985) *Vietnamese children's home: a special case for care?* London: Save the Children Fund

Munôz Liliana (1981) 'Exile as bereavement: socio-psychological manifestations of Chilean exiles in Great Britain', Mental health and exile: papers arising from a seminar on mental health and Latin American exiles, London: WUS, pp.6–9

Muus, Philip et al. (1993) *Reception policies for persons in need of international protection in Western European states*, Geneva, UNHCR, September

Naess, Ragnar (1989) 'Refugees and national policies: the Norwegian case', in Danièle Joly and Robin Cohen, *Reluctant hosts: Europe and its refugees*, Aldershot: Avebury, pp.67–75

NGOs (1993) NGOs statement to closing plenary CSCE Human Dimension seminar on migration, including refugees and displaced persons, Warsaw 20–23 April 1993

Nichols, Bruce (1988) *The uneasy alliance: Religion, refugee work and US foreign policy*, Oxford: OUP

Olcese, Miguel (1986) 'Avec les exilés et les torturés', *Hommes et Migrations* No.1096, 15 octobre, pp.36–38

Paludan, Anne (1974) 'The new refugees in Europe', in *Summary of the Report on problems of refugees and exiles in Europe*, Geneva: International University Exchange Fund on behalf of the Working Group on Refugees and Exiles in Europe, pp.3–47

Petersen, William (1958) 'A general typology of migration', *American Sociological Review*, 23(3) pp.256–266

Portes, Alejandro and Rafael Mozo (1985) 'The political adaptation process of Cuban and other ethnic minorities in the United States: a preliminary analysis', *IMR*, Vol. 19, IV 1, pp.36–63

Price, Charles A. (1979) 'Family reunion and refugees, development and outcomes of official policy', in Robert Birrell et al. (eds) *Refugees, resources, reunion: Australia's immigration dilemmas*, Australia: VCTA, pp.147–156

Proudfoot, M.J. (1957) *European Refugees: 1939–52*, London, Faber and Faber

Refugee Council (1989, estimated date) *Vietnamese refugee reception and resettlement 1979–88*, London, Refugee Council

Reid, Jeanice and Timothy Strong (1987) *Torture and Trauma*, Sydney: Cumberland College of Health Sciences

Rex, John (1973) *Race, colonialism and the city*, London: Routledge and Kegan Paul

Rex, John and Sally Tomlinson (1979), *Colonial immigrants in a British city*, London: Routledge and Kegan Paul

Richmond, Anthony H. (1988) 'Sociological theories of international migration: the case of refugees', *Current Sociology*, 36: 2, pp.7–25

Richmond, Anthony H. (1994) *Global Apartheid*, Toronto: Oxford University Press

Risdale, Sean (1994) Interview. London, 7 February

Robinson, Vaughan and Samantha Hale (1989) *The geography of Vietnamese secondary migration in the UK,* Research Papers in Ethnic Relations No. 10, Coventry: CRER, University of Warwick

Rogg, Eleanor (1971) 'The influence of a strong refugee community on the economic adjustment of its members', *International Migration Review,* Vol. 5, 4, pp.474–481

Rose, Peter, I. (1981) 'Conference report: Towards a sociology of exile: a report on an academic symposium', *IMR,* Vol. 15 (1–2), pp. 769–256

Rouah, Michel (1988) *Le devenir des réfugiés trente deux cas de réfugiés et demandeurs d'asile sortis de centres provisoires d'hébergement,* Paris, PASSION, December. And Synthèse de l'Etude

Rudge, P. (1987) *Fortress Europe in World Refugee Survey (1986 in Review),* US Committee for Refugees, Washington, Virginia Hamilton

Rudge, P. (1989) 'The spirit: historical and social perspectives, The failure of the spirit', *The Refugee Crisis, British and Canadian Responses,* International Symposium, 4–7 January, London

Rudge, Philip (1991) Letter from Philip Rudge, dated 24 September 1991 to Mr Pankin, His Excellency the Foreign Minister, Union of Soviet Socialist Republics, Moscow

Rystad, Goran (1990) 'Victims of oppression or ideological weapons? Aspects of US refugee policy in the post-war era', in Goran Rystad (ed.), *The Uprooted: Forced migration as an international problem in the post-war era,* Lund: Lund University Press, pp.195–226

Salinas, Maria, Diana Pritchard and Apophia Kibedi (1987), *Refugee Issues,* BRC/QEH Working Papers on Refugees, Vol. 3, No.4, July

Salomon, Kim (1991) Refugees in the Cold War, Lund: Lund University Press

Sayers, Robert (1989) 'Resettling refugees: the Dutch model' in Danièle Joly and Robin Cohen, *Reluctant Hosts: Europe and its refugees,* Aldershot: Avebury, pp.19–40

Sayfullah Khan, Verity (1977) 'The Pakistanis: Mirpuri villagers at home and in Bradford' in *Between two cultures,* James Watson (ed.) Oxford: Basil Blackwell, pp.57–89

Scanlan, John and Kent, O.T. (1988) 'The force of moral arguments for a just immigration policy in a Hobbesian universe. The contemporary American example' Gibney, Mark (ed.) *Open borders? Closed societies? The ethical and political issues,* New York: Greenwood Press, pp.61–107

Scanlan, John, and Loescher, Gilbert (1983) 'US foreign policy, 1959–60: Impact on refugee flow from Cuba', *Annals,* AAPSS, 467, May, pp.116–137

Schierup, Carl-Ulrik (1990) '"The duty to work" the theory and practice of refugee policy in Sweden' in *New Community* 16 (4): pp.561–574, July

Schutz, Alfred (1944) 'The stranger: an essay in social psychology', *American Journal of Sociology,* Vol. 49, No.6, pp.499–507

Scott-Nance, David (1982) 'The individual right to asylum under Article 3 of the European Convention on Human Rights'. Transnational legal problems of refugees, *Michigan Yearbook of International Legal Studies,* New York, pp.477–492

Secretariat of the Inter-governmental Consultations on Asylum, Refugee and Migration Policies in Europe, North America and Australia (1994). Working paper on reception in the region of origin September 1994

Shackman, Jane (1982) *Speaking through others, A study of the use and training of interpreters in Bristol*, Derby: Refugee Action

Shacknove, Andrew E. (1985) 'Who is a refugee?' *Ethics*, 95 (January), pp.274–284

Shacknove, Andrew E. (1988) 'American duties to refugees, their scopes and limits', in Gibney, Mark (ed.) *Open Borders? Closed societies? The ethical and political issues*, New York: Greenwood Press, pp.131–150

Shengen Agreement (1990)

Simon-Barouh, Ida (1992) L'intégration des réfugiés dans une ville moyenne, l'exemple des cambodgiens, laos, vietnamiens à Rennes. Actes du Colloque, Les réfugiés en France et en Europe Quarante ans d'application de la Convention de Genève 1952–92, 11–13 juin 1992, Paris, OFPRA, pp.506–524

Singer, Peter and Renata (1988) 'The ethics of refugee policy', in Gibney, Mark (ed.), *Open borders? Closed societies? The ethical and political issues*, New York: Greenwood Press, pp.111–130

Srinivasan, Shaila (1994) *An overview of research into refugee groups in Britain during the 1900s*, Oxford. 4th International Research and Advisory Panel Conference, 5–9 January

Standing Committee of experts in international immigration, refugee and criminal law (1994) *Who is a 'refugee'?* Utrecht, June 1994

Standing Conference of Local and Regional Authorities of Europe (SCLRAE) (1984) 19th Session Strasbourg 16–18/10/84 Opinion No.25 (1984) (1) on reception of refugees and asylum-seekers by local authorities. Council of Europe

Stein, Barry N. (1981) 'The refugee experience: defining the parameters of a field of study', *International Migration Review*, Vol. 15, No.1, pp.5–7

Stepick, Alex and Alejandro Portes (1986) 'Flight into despair, a profile of recent Haitian refugees in South Florida', *International Migration Review*, Vol. 20, No.2, pp.329–350

Suhrke, Astri (1983) 'Indochinese refugees: the law and politics of first asylum', *Annals*, AAPSS, 467, May, pp.102–115

Suhrke, Astri (1993) *Safeguarding the right to asylum*. International conference on population and development 1994, Expert Group Meeting on Population Distribution and Migration, Santa Cruz, Bolivia, 18–22 January

Tapinos, G.R. (1992) Migratory pressure: an expression of concern or an analytical concept? in World Employment Programme Working Paper, Migration and Population, Two views on international migration, Geneva, ILO, May 1992

Teitelbaum, Michael T.S. (1980a) 'Right versus right: immigration and refugee policy in the United States' *Foreign Affairs* 59 (1) Fall, pp.21–60

Teitelbaum, Michael T.S. (1980b) 'Immigration, refugees and foreign policy' *International Organisation*, 38, 3, Summer, pp.429–450

Training and Employment for Refugees in France (1987 presumed date), translated by British Refugee Council

UNHCR (1979) *Collection of International Instruments Concerning Refugees*, Geneva, UNHCR

UNHCR (1979) *Handbook on procedures and criteria for determining refugee status under the 1951 Convention and the 1967 Protocol relating to the Status of Refugees*, Geneva, UNHCR, September

UNHCR EXCOM (1981) No.22 (XXXII) Protection of asylum-seekers in situation of large scale influx 1981 (Executive Committee 32nd session)

UNHCR (1984) Social Services Workshop Europe, Geneva, 18–21 June

UNHCR (1985) ExCom. 36th session note on the consultations on the arrivals of asylum-seekers and refugees in Europe, A/ac96/inf, 174, 4 July

UNHCR (1985b) Note sur l'intégration des réfugiés. Séminaire de 1983 sur l'intégration des réfugiés en Europe, Genève 12–15 septembre

UNHCR (1988) Comments on the Preliminary Draft Proposal for a Council Directive to Approximate National Rules on the Grant of Asylum and Refugee Status, pp.1–7

UNHCR (1991a) Intergovernmental consultations on asylum, refugee and migration policies in Europe, North America and Australia, Strategy Platform, Geneva, September 1991, in Report of ECRE Bi-annual General Meeting, Geneva, 5–6/10/91, Appendix 14

UNHCR (1991b) Troika Meeting of Coordinators of Free Circulation of Persons and UNHCR on 19 December 1991, Brussels, 18032

UNHCR (1993a) Comprehensive response to the humanitarian crises in former Yugoslavia. Informal meeting on temporary protection, Geneva 21 January 1993, Background note

UNHCR (1993b) Comprehensive response to the humanitarian crisis in former Yugoslavia. Informal meeting on temporary protection, Geneva 25 March 1993, Background note, Addendum

UNHCR (1993c) Comprehensive response to the humanitarian crisis in former Yugoslavia. Survey of the implementation of temporary protection, 30 April 1993

UNHCR (1995a) 'Update: UNHCR concerned by EU agreement on asylum procedures', 10 March

UNHCR (1995b) 'Agents of persecution', Note of March 1995

UNHCR (1995c) Information note on Article 1 of the 1951 Convention

Van Boven, Theo (1991) 'The significance of the 'human dimension' for refugees and asylum-seekers' in *Refugees*, Special issue August, Refugees and asylum-seekers in a common European house, Oikoumene, Geneva, pp.25–28

Vasquez, Ana (1983) 'L'exil, une analyse psycho-sociologique', *L'information psychiatrique*, Vol. 59, No.1, janvier pp.44–58

Vasquez, Ana and Araujo, A.M. (1990) *Exils latino-américains: La malédiction d'Ulysse*, Paris: L'Harmattan

Vetter, H.O. (1987) Report on the Right of Asylum, European Parliament, 23/2, p.9

Vluchtelingen Werk (1993) Report. Fact finding mission. Croatia 22–27 January 1993. Why the flow of prisoners from concentration camps in Bosnia to 'third countries of temporary reception' stagnates. Amsterdam

Ward, Robin (1973) 'What future for Uganda Asians?' *New Community*, Vol. II, No.4, Autumn, pp.372–388

Weiner, Myron (1985) 'On international migration and international relations', *Population and Development Review*, 11 (3), pp.441–456

Weis, Paul (1970) 'The Convention of the Organisation of African Unity Governing the Specific Aspects of Refugee Problems in Africa', *Human Rights Journal International and Corporative Law*, Vol. 3, pp.449–464

Weis, Paul (1982) 'The development of refugee law, Transnational legal problems of refugees', *Michigan Yearbook of International Legal Studies*, pp.27–43

Whelan, Frederick C. (1988) 'Citizenship and freedom of movement: an open admission policy?' in Gibney, Mark (ed.), *Open borders? Closed societies? The ethical and political issues*, New York: Greenwood Press, pp.3–30

Wong, P. (1967) 'The social psychology of refugees in an alien milieu', *International Migration*, Vol. 5 (3/4), pp.195–212

World University Service (1986) WUS, 'A study in exile'. A report on the WUS (UK) Chilean refugee scholarship programme, London: WUS

Young, Stephen, B. (1982) 'Between sovereigns: a re-examination of the refugee's status', Transnational Legal Problems of Refugees, *Michigan Yearbook of International Legal Studies*, pp.339–373

Zarjevski, M. (1988) *A future preserved: international assistance to refugees*, Oxford, Pergamon Press/UNHCR

Zolberg, A. (1987) Keeping them out; ethical dilemmas of immigration policy in Robert J. Myers (ed.), *International ethics in the nuclear age*, University Press of America, pp.261–297.

Zolberg, Aristide R., Suhrke (Astri), Aguayo (Sergio) (1989) *Escape from violence, conflict and the refugee crisis in the developing world*, Oxford: Oxford University Press, p.380

Zucker, Naomi Flink (1983) 'The Haitians versus the United States: The courts as last resort' *Annals*, AAPSS, 467, May, pp.151–162

Zucker, Norman (1983) 'Refugee resettlement in the United States, policy and problems', *Annals*, AAPSS, 467, May, pp.172–186

Zucker, N.L. and Zucker, N.F. (1987), *The Guarded Gate: the Reality of American Refugee Policy*, San Diego, Harcourt Brace Jovanovich

Zwingmann, C. and M. Pfister-Ammende (eds) (1973), *Uprooting and After*, New York: Springer-Verlag

Index

Ad Hoc Group on Immigration 49, 52–66, 82, 84
Afghanistan 36, 63
Afghans 10, 29, 125
Africa 13–14, 15, 34, 36, 46, 65, 125, 131, 135
African Refugee Housing Action Group (Ltd) 140
aid 41, 65, 79, 142
Algeria 29, 71
Allende, Salvador 31, 87, 172
Amnesty International 29, 70
Angola 29
Argentina 30, 31, 46, 166, 179
Armenia 3, 73
Asia 14, 36, 40, 102–3, 109, 162, 168, 178, 180
    see also specific countries
Assyrians 3
Assyro-Chaldeans 3
Australia 17–18, 22, 23, 24, 31, 37, 40, 180
Austria 4, 6, 12–13, 22, 63
Azerbaijan 73

Belarus 73
Belgium 13, 26, 48, 50
Bolivia 125
Bosnia Herzegovina 73, 74–5
Bosnians 138
Britain 10, 17–18, 21–2, 24, 39, 60, 67, 73, 88, 152
    and Chilean refugees xi–xii, 23, 25, 30, 90–119, 146, 154, 181–6, 190–201
    refugee associations 161–180
    and Vietnamese refugees xi–xii, 81, 84–139, 154, 181–6, 190–1
    refugee associations 161–80
    Commonwealth 26, 28, 30, 96, 117, 121–2, 137
    local authorities xii, 91, 98, 102, 104, 105–6, 108, 120–39
    relationship with USA 17, 27, 30, 31
British Council for Aid to Refugees (BCAR) 93, 94, 99–100

British Refugee Council 94, 111, 124, 128

Cambodia 88, 89, 155, 180
Canada 64, 146, 152, 153, 174, 180
Caracas Convention on Territorial Asylum and Diplomatic Asylum (1954) 14
Cartagena Declaration (1984) 14, 81
Carter, President Jimmy 31
Castro, Fidel 28
Centre d'Information de Réflexion et d'Echange en Matière d'Asile (CIREA) 61–3
Centre for information, discussion and exchange on the crossing of frontiers and immigration (CIREFI) 53, 63, 69
Centres provisoires d'hébergement (CPH) 100–1, 103, 104, 107, 109–10
Chile 39, 46, 125, 133
    USA and 31–2, 118, 161, 172
    see also Chilean refugees
Chilean refugees
    in Britain xi–xii, 23, 25, 30, 85–119, 146, 154, 181–6, 190–1
    refugee associations 161–80
    in France xi–xii, 31, 86–120, 181–6, 190–1
    refugee associations 161–80
    see also Chile
China 28, 31, 152, 161
Christian Aid 93
Christianity 36, 173, 174, 175, 176
CIA 25, 30
Code de la Famille et de l'Aide Sociale 100
Cold War 20, 26, 27, 28, 32, 34, 39–40, 41, 42, 45, 46, 72, 79, 183, 184
Comité Juif d'Aide Sociale et de Réconstruction (COJASOR) 92
Comité Médical pour les Exilés 98
Communism 6, 20, 24–5, 28–9, 37, 41, 45, 72, 155, 156, 161, 172, 174, 175, 188

Conference on Security and
Cooperation in Europe (CSCE)
78–82
Convention against Torture and other
Cruel Inhuman or Degrading
Treatment or Punishment (1984)
10, 35
Convention for the Protection of
Human Rights and Fundamental
Freedoms (1950) 60, 79, 83
Convention on the Crossing of External
Frontiers 50–2
Council of Europe 16, 35, 39, 47, 69,
79, 83, 86
Croatia 73
Cuba
refugees in USA 28–9, 36, 151–2
Cypriots 135
Cyprus 125
Czechoslovakia 4, 6, 10, 74, 125, 180

de Gaulle, Charles 27–8, 31
Declaration on Territorial Asylum
(1967) 8
Denmark 50, 57, 66, 77
domestic policies 18, 20–6, 40–1, 188–9
drugs 26, 48, 49
Duarte, José Napoleon 29
Dublin Convention (1990) 50–2, 57,
64–5, 69, 83, 85n
Duvalier, Jean Claude 29

Eastern Europe 2, 6, 28, 32, 41–2, 45,
46, 65, 78–9, 125, 155
and the EU 72–82
see also specific countries
ecological refugees 15, 142
economic migrants 1, 5, 12, 29–30,
142, 145, 149, 191
economic recession 11, 21, 40, 41, 108,
118, 188
education and training xii, 23, 77, 86,
103–5, 108–12, 113–14, 116, 123,
124, 131–2, 170, 176, 182
EFTA 44–5, 69, 72, 78, 81, 82, 83, 189
El Salvador 14, 29, 166
employment xii, 61, 65–6, 77, 84, 86,
97–8, 101, 102, 108–12, 114, 118,
119, 131–2, 182, 183
English as a Second Language (ESL)
131
Eritrea 63, 125
ethical factors 21, 32–9, 42, 188–9
Ethiopia 63

ethnic minorites (UK) 121–3, 125–6,
128, 131, 137
Euro-Mediterranean Conference 65
European Automated Fingerprint
Recognition System (EURODAC)
69
European Commission 16, 48, 49, 66,
67, 83
European Commission for Human
Rights 11
European Community (EC) xi, 48, 49,
51, 52, 73, 167
see also European Union
European Convention on Human Rights
and Fundamental Freedoms
10–11, 35, 56, 66–7
European Court of Human Rights
(Strasbourg) 62
European Court of Justice 50
European Council on Refugees and
Exiles (ECRE) 67, 70, 71, 72
European Economic Community 27,
140
see also European Union
European harmonization
Ad Hoc Group on Immigration 49,
52–67, 82, 84
and Eastern Europe 72–84
long-term strategy 64–72
restrictions on asylum xii, 44–52, 69,
82–4, 189
European Parliament 16, 49, 67, 69,
82, 86
European Social Fund 136
European Union
Ad Hoc Group on Immigration 49,
52–66, 82, 84
and Eastern Europe 72–84
and Yugoslavia 16, 72–3, 75–8,
189–90
harmonization xii, 44–52, 81–2
Justice and Home Affairs Council 63,
72
long-term strategy 64–72
Resolution on the admission of third
country nationals 68
Resolution on burden-sharing, admission and temporary residence
70
Resolution on minimum guarantees
for asylum procedures 70
restrictions on asylum xi, 44–52, 69,
82–4, 189
see also specific countries

European Volunteer Workers (EVW)
21–2, 39

Falklands War 30
Fascism 5, 34, 187
Finland 50, 63
Fonds d'Action Sociale (FAS) 92, 103
Fonds d'Installation Locale des Réfugiés
(FILOR) 107
foreign policy 18, 20–1, 26–32, 39–40,
188–9
France 18, 20, 23, 24, 25, 37, 48
and Chilean refugees xi–xii, 31,
86–119, 181–6, 190–1
refugee associations 161–80
and Vietnamese refugees xi–xii, 29,
81, 84–119, 181–6, 190–1
refugee associations 161–80
and Yugoslavian refugees 187–8
colonies 26, 30
relationship with USA 27–8, 31
France Terre d'Asile (FTDA) xiii, 48,
92, 97, 100–1, 113

Geneva Convention (1951) 46, 54, 56,
57, 58, 60, 67, 69, 86, 95
definition of refugees 7–15, 30,
34–5, 40, 46–7, 77–8, 80–1, 82,
187–9
origins of 1–7
Protocol (1967) 7, 35, 46, 60, 187
Georgia 73
Germany 4, 5–6, 10, 12–13, 22, 24, 37,
48, 73, 163
Ghana 63
Gibraltar 50
Greece 20, 48, 49, 73
Groupe de Recherche sur l'Immigration
de Sud–Est Asiatique (GRISEA)
xiii
Guatemala 14, 29, 179

Haiti
refugees in USA 29–30, 36, 41, 152
Hart, Judith 103
Havana Convention on Asylum (1928)
14
health xii, 9, 23, 86, 92, 97–8, 99, 100,
101, 102–3, 104, 111, 112, 114, 116,
119, 135, 137, 148, 170, 183
Helsinki Document (1992 — *The
Challenges of Change*) 80
Holocaust, the 37
Home, Alec Douglas 88

Hong Kong 94, 152, 162
housing xii, 23, 86, 96–7, 99, 104–7,
108, 111, 113, 118, 121, 127, 128,
129, 132–4, 182, 183
Human Dimension Seminar on
Migration, Including Refugees and
Displaced Persons (1993) 81, 82
human rights 18–19, 29, 34–5, 37, 38,
39, 43, 44, 55, 65, 75, 77, 84, 86,
169, 172, 176, 189
refugees 4, 11, 33–6, 187
violations 10, 14, 15, 29, 30, 32, 41,
42, 80
humanitarian issues 4–5, 15, 37, 41, 56,
65, 70, 75, 78, 82, 93, 115–16, 188
Hungary 10, 74, 81–2, 125, 180

Iceland 50
Idi Amin 46
illegal immigrants 12, 22, 26, 61, 65,
69
Immigration and Nationality Act
(USA–1965) 24
India 17, 125, 153
Indo–China 28, 88, 90, 98, 100–1, 109,
118, 154
see also specific countries
Indonesia 147–8
Inter–American Commission on Human
Rights 29
Inter–Governmental Committee on
Refugees 5–6
International Committee of the Red
Cross 2
International Court of Justice 9
International Covenant on Civil and
Political Rights (1966) 35
International Covenant on Economic,
Social and Cultural Rights (1966)
35
International Labour Organisation
39
International Refugee Organisation 6
Iran 48, 63, 125, 129, 135
Iraq 63, 125
Iraq–Iran war 47
Ireland 50, 73
Israel 44, 147
Italy 13, 22, 48, 73

Jefferson, Thomas 24
Jews 36, 38–9
Joint Committee for Refugees from
Vietnam (JCVN) 104, 106

Joint Council for the Welfare of
Immigrants (JCWI)   128
Joint Working Group for Refugees from
Chile (JWGCh)   93, 94, 97
Joint Working Group for Refugees from
Latin America   93
Joint Working Group for Refugees from
Vietnam (JCRV)   94

Kazakhstan   73
Kennedy, Senator Edward   31, 37
Kurds   3, 125, 135
Kyrgyzstan   73

labour migrants   1, 10, 12, 47, 95–6,
115, 116, 121–2, 163, 185, 189, 190,
191, 192
Laos   88, 89, 180
Latin America   14, 20, 27, 31, 46, 108,
110, 129, 135, 162, 164–7, 172, 174,
176, 179
see also specific countries
League of Nations   2–3
Lebanese   10, 25, 48, 144
Lithuanians   146
Local Government Act (UK–1966)
121–2, 123, 130, 137–8
Luxembourg   48, 73

Maastricht Summit   49, 52, 65, 66, 83,
84
Macedonia   73
Malaysia   31

Manila Declaration on the Internal
Protection of Refugees and
Displaced Persons in Asia   14
Moldavia   69
Montenegro   69
Montevideo Convention on Political
Asylum (1933)   14
migration, international   141–5, 148–9
Moscow mechanism (1991)   79
Mozambique   29

Nansen, Fridtjof   2–3
NATO   26, 27, 31, 79
natural disasters   15, 142
Nazism   4, 5, 6, 20, 34
Netherlands   13, 26, 48, 50, 73, 91, 122,
147–8
Nicaragua   14, 29, 166
Nigeria   63
North America   20, 24, 79, 170, 174

North America *cont.*
see also Canada; USA
Norway   13, 50, 107, 146

Ockenden Venture   94, 98, 99–100,
128
Office for Democratic Institutions and
Human Rights (ODIHR)   80
Office Français de Protection pour les
Apatrides (OFPRA)   87, 92
OPEC   27
Organization for Security and
Cooperation in Europe (OSCE)
79, 83, 193
Organisation of African Unity   13–14,
34
Organization of American States   14

Pakistan   17, 29, 125
Palestinians   144, 157
Palma Document   49
Paris Charter (1990)   80
Peru   179
Pinochet, General   25, 30, 167, 175, 176
Pius XI, Pope   43n
Poland   60, 73, 125
Portugal   20, 26, 29, 48, 67, 73
Portugese   163

Race Relations Acts (UK)   122, 125, 133
Raison, Timothy   90
Reagan, President   36–7
reception policies
and Chilean and Vietnamese refugees
86–105, 111–13, 114–19, 190–101
refoulement   5, 8, 11, 13, 14, 35, 47, 56,
57, 187
Refugee Act (USA–1980)   30, 37
Refugee Action   93, 99, 106, 130
refugee associations
Chilean and Vietnamese   xii–xiii, 94,
161–80
Refugee Council   xiii, 90, 94, 137
refugee, definition   71–2, 81, 83
Refugee–Escapee Act (USA–1957)
24–5
refugees
and theories of settlement   141–56
categories of   xii, 154–60, 191–2
factors determining   141–5
in the land of exile   149–54, 191
Rhodes Group   49
Romania   74
Russia   2–3, 73, 79

Save the Children Fund (SCF) 94, 99, 100, 107, 128
Scandinavia 10
  see also specific countries
Schengen Agreement, Schengen Convention 44–5, 48–52, 60, 65–6, 73, 83
Serbia 73
Service Social d'Aide aux Emigrants (SSAE) 93, 101, 119, 167
settlement policies
  and Chilean and Vietnamese refugees 86–119, 181–6, 190–1
  local authorities 120–39
  theories of settlement and refugees 141, 145–59
Single European Act 44, 48
Slovenia 73
social security 86, 96, 99, 100, 111, 112
social services 23, 134–5, 170
  see also specific aspects
Somalia 63, 125
sovereignty 17–20, 33, 38
Soviet Union 2–3, 26, 28, 29
Spain 20, 48, 50, 69, 73
Sri Lanka 30, 48, 63, 125, 129
Standing Conference of Local and Regional Authorities of Europe (SCLRAE) 127–8, 129, 130–1
Standing Conference on Refugees (SCOR) 94
Sweden 13, 50, 63, 64, 81, 91, 121
Switzerland 12–13, 38, 57
Syrians 3

Tajikistan 73
Tamils 129, 134
Tempus Programme 74
terrorism 26, 49
Thatcher, Margaret 89, 94
Third World 26–7, 47, 121, 142, 149–50
torture 10, 35, 56, 87, 103, 149
Treaty of Rome 48
Treaty on European Union 45, 67–72
Trevi Group 49
Truman, President 28, 37
Turkey 125
Turkmenistan 73
Turks 3, 10, 163

Uganda 22, 46, 116, 120, 121, 123, 125, 152
Ukraine 69, 151, 152

unemployment 11, 22, 40, 41, 96, 105, 108, 113, 117, 124, 132, 170, 188
United Kingdom Immigrants Advisory Council (UKIAS) 128
United Nations 5, 7, 8, 10, 14–15, 35, 39, 75, 89, 94
United Nations Office of the High Commissioner for Refugees (UNHCR) 5, 7, 14–16, 22–3, 35, 39, 54, 55, 56, 57, 58, 62, 66, 67, 70, 71, 72, 74, 75, 76, 77, 80, 81, 86, 92, 135
  and Yugoslavia 42, 45, 74–8, 84
United States of America
  and Chile 31–2, 119, 161, 172
  and Vietnam war 28, 31, 87, 161
  Cuban refugees in 28–9, 36, 151–2
  foreign policies 26–32, 37, 41
  Haitian refugees in 29–30, 36, 41, 152
  immigration laws 7, 18, 24–5, 37, 38, 64, 90, 96, 146
  relationship with Britain 17, 27, 30, 31
  Vietnamese refugees in 28, 30, 148–9, 153, 162, 180
Universal Declaration on Human Rights 18–19, 34–5, 86
Universal Declaration on the Eradication of Hunger and Malnutrition (1974) 35
Uruguay 31, 46, 166, 179
Uzbekistan 73

Vietnam War 28, 31, 88, 161
Vietnamese refugees 31, 46, 146
  boat people 25, 28, 30, 40, 122, 162
  ethnic Chinese 31, 89, 124, 162, 180, 186
  in Britain xi–xii, 86, 89–139, 153, 181–6, 190–1
    refugee asociations 161–80
  in France xi–xii, 29, 86, 88–119, 181–6, 190–1
    refugee associations 161–80
  in USA 28, 39, 153, 160–1, 162, 180

war refugees 9–10, 20, 77–8, 143
war resisters 10, 156
Warsaw Pact nations 10, 26, 79
  see also specific countries
West Indies 125
Whitelaw, William 93
women 10, 110, 173, 176, 177, 179

World University Service (WUS) 93, 94, 108

Yugoslavia x, 1, 12–13, 20, 32, 41, 78, 150
  and the EU 16, 68–9, 73–8, 81, 83, 189–90

Yugoslavia *cont.*
  and UNHCR 42, 45, 73–7, 84
  refugees in France 187–8

Zaire 63